Eric CK Chan

YEWCASA

69, Westlea Avenue

Watford, Hertfordshire

WD25 9DH, United Kingdom

email: ericck8@yahoo.com

The Future of Leadership Development

The Palgrave Macmillan IESE Business Collection is designed to provide authoritative insights and comprehensive advice on specific management topics. The books are based on rigorous research produced by IESE Business School professors, covering new concepts within traditional management areas (Strategy, Leadership, Managerial Economics) as well as emerging areas of enquiry. The collection seeks to broaden the knowledge of the business field through the ongoing release of titles, with a humanistic focus in mind.

The Future of Leadership Development

Corporate Needs and the Role of Business Schools

Edited by

JORDI CANALS
Dean, IESE Business School, Spain

First published 2011 by
PALGRAVE MACMILLAN

Palgrave Macmillan in the UK is an imprint of Macmillan Publishers Limited,
registered in England, company number 785998, of Houndmills, Basingstoke,
Hampshire RG21 6XS.

Palgrave Macmillan in the US is a division of St Martin's Press LLC,
175 Fifth Avenue, New York, NY 10010.

Palgrave Macmillan is the global academic imprint of the above companies and has
companies and representatives throughout the world.

Palgrave® and Macmillan® are registered trademarks in the United States, the United
Kingdom, Europe and other countries.

ISBN 978–0–230–27928–5

This book is printed on paper suitable for recycling and made from fully managed and
sustained forest sources. Logging, pulping and manufacturing processes are expected
to conform to the environmental regulations of the country of origin.

A catalogue record for this book is available from the British Library.

A catalog record for this book is available from the Library of Congress.

10   9   8   7   6   5   4   3   2   1
20   19   18   17   16   15   14   13   12   11

Printed and bound in Great Britain by
CPI Antony Rowe, Chippenham and Eastbourne

Contents

About the Authors

Remei Agulles
Research Assistant, IESE Business School, University of Navarra

Antonio Argandoña
La Caixa Professor of Corporate Social Responsibility, IESE Business School, University of Navarra

J. Frank Brown
Dean, INSEAD

Jordi Canals
Dean, IESE Business School, University of Navarra

Nuria Chinchilla
Professor, IESE Business School, University of Navarra

Arnoud de Meyer
President of Singapore Management University

Pankaj Ghemawat
Anselmo Rubiralta Professor of Globalization and Strategy, IESE Business School, University of Navarra

Matt Golosinski
Executive Editor, Kellogg School of Management, Northwestern University

Dipak C. Jain
Professor and Dean Emeritus , Kellogg School of Management, Northwestern University and Dean Elect, INSEAD

Mireia Las Heras
Assistant Professor, IESE Business School, University of Navarra

Jay O. Light
Former Dean, Harvard Business School, Boston, MA, USA

Pedro Nueno
Bertran Foundation Professor of Entrepreneurship, IESE Business School, University of Navarra and President of China Europe International Business School (CEIBS)

Jeffrey Pfeffer
Professor, Graduate School of Business, Stanford University

M. Julia Prats
Assistant Professor, IESE Business School, University of Navarra

Josep M. Rosanas
Credit Andorra Professor of Markets, Organizations and Management, IESE Business School, University of Navarra

Introduction

JORDI CANALS, Dean, IESE Business School

The recent financial crisis highlights several significant weaknesses of market capitalism in an integrated global economy, and the dangers of permanent international financial imbalances. It also stresses some forgotten dimensions in corporate finance and corporate strategy, such as the impact of financial leverage on firms' valuations and the relevance of adequate risk management and control systems.

Nevertheless, this crisis also sheds light on a deeper challenge for the corporate world: the quality of leadership. What we are witnessing today in many companies is a combination of reckless strategic decisions, excessive short-term focus and poor governance mechanisms. It is true that the sheer force of external shocks – the housing bust and its impact on banks' profitability and firms' valuation, for example – is impressive. However, the financial crisis raises some fair questions that senior business leaders and business schools have to ponder about: What could companies have done differently? Was there another perspective to assess risks and evaluate investment decisions? Were the goals and objectives set up by boards of directors realistic? What types of business leaders have companies asked for, and universities helped develop?

These are some of the pressing questions that senior managers, board members and business schools, among others, have to think about. The challenge here is not so much to find the culprit, but to learn what could have been done differently, what the responsibilities of CEOs and board members are – and, more important, where the focus of leadership development should be.

In this context, leadership development was considered an appropriate subject for discussion in one of the academic conferences celebrated on the occasion of IESE's fiftieth anniversary. The conference was organized under the title of "The Future of Leadership Development: The Role of Business Schools", and was held at IESE in Barcelona on 17–18 April 2008. The speakers included deans of leading international business schools, management scholars, CEOs and heads of human resources management of international firms. The conference was attended by 500 senior executives and MBA students.

Since its foundation in 1958, IESE has shown a strong commitment to improving the practice of management and leadership in the corporate world. While other business schools in the United States and Europe were created and developed with the purpose of developing management as a social science, IESE was oriented more toward leadership development and research with a specific focus: their impact on the practice of management. IESE was lucky to be able to count on Harvard Business School's support when launching in 1964 what became the first two-year MBA program in Europe. A joint committee was set up by the deans of Harvard and IESE, its purpose being to design the objectives and curriculum for that program and to plan other educational projects. This committee has been active since then, working on new projects and being influential in helping to develop business schools in Africa, Asia, Eastern Europe and Latin America.

Structure of the Book

This book aims to offer an interdisciplinary, multiperspective approach to the topic of leadership development in the corporate world, in the light of new managerial challenges, such as globalization and the 2008 financial crisis. It brings together the ideas of a group of experts who are critical agents in this process: business school deans, leading faculty members, CEOs, and heads of human resource management in international firms. Most of the papers were presented in the 2008 IESE conference.

The book is organized in three parts. The first part is structured around the topic "The Deans' Perspective on Leadership Development and Business Schools". In my Chapter 1.1, entitled "In Search of a Greater Impact: New Corporate and Societal Challenges for Business Schools", I deal with some relevant topics for leadership development, such as the purpose of the firm, the role of senior managers in a company, and the challenges of integration and globalization, among others. INSEAD's Dean, J. Frank Brown, discusses in Chapter 1.2, "Millennials and the Changing Landscape of Business Education", the behavior patterns of a new generation of high potentials and their impact on issues such as employer–employee relations, lifelong learning and program design.

Arnoud de Meyer, President of Singapore Management University, presents a new model of leadership in Chapter 1.3, "Collaborative Leadership: New Perspectives in Leadership Development". De Meyer discusses how some major changes in the business world, such as alliances and innovation, should be introduced into new leadership development models. Former Kellogg's Dean, Dipak Jain, and Editor, Matt Golosinski, reassess in Chapter 1.4, entitled "The Enduring Value of the MBA Degree", the unique contribution that good MBA programs make to graduates, companies and societies. In Chapter 1.5, headed "Business Schools and the Demands of Business Leadership", the former Dean of Harvard Business School, Jay O. Light, considers the main issues around management education and leadership development in the USA and how schools will have to change to face new realities. In Chapter 1.6, on "The Contribution of Business Schools to the Twenty-first Century", Pedro Nueno, Bertran Foundation Professor of Entrepreneurship at IESE and President of the China Europe International Business School (CEIBS), China, offers his views on the main contribution of business schools in recent decades, and how they need to reinvent themselves for continued success.

Part 2 of the book is organized around some horizontal issues of special relevance in business education and leadership development. Chapter 2.1, by La Caixa Professor at IESE, Antonio Argandoña, and entitled "From Action Theory to the Theory of the Firm", discusses the main limits of the traditional view of the firm and presents guidelines for a more useful model. This topic is picked up by Josep M. Rosanas, Credit Andorra Professor of Markets, Organizations and Management at IESE, in Chapter 2.2 – "A Humanistic Approach to Organizations and Organizational Decision-making". While Argandoña deals with the theory of the firm, Rosanas discusses the limits of modern decision-making and how to consider a more realistic hypothesis of human behavior. In Chapter 2.3, entitled "Bridging the Globalization Gap at Business Schools: Curricular Challenges and a Response", Pankaj Ghemawat, Anselmo Rubiralta Professor of Globalization and Strategy at IESE, discusses the progress business schools have made in integrating globalization in their programs, and some steps they can take to improve it. In Chapter 2.4, "Leadership Development in Business Schools: An Agenda for Change", Stanford Professor Jeffrey Pfeffer argues that leadership development is an important challenge for business schools, and that more evidence on its impact has to be found if they want to have a deeper impact.

Part 3 is organized around two papers prepared by faculty members who introduced and moderated business leaders' panels at the 2008 Conference. Those papers introduce some practical ideas for leadership development and organize and present some of the speakers' main experiences. Chapter 3.1,

"How to Develop and Promote Leadership from the Top", by IESE Professors
Mireia Las Heras and Nuria Chinchilla, deals with some specific guidelines
and actions that CEOs can provide to help develop leadership in organizations. In Chapter 3.2, "Managing Managers as Professionals: Leadership
Development and Talent Transfer in a Global World", by IESE Professor
M. Julia Prats and Research Assistant Remei Agulles, reflect on how to help
the flow of ideas and talent development in companies with an international
scope.

Both papers benefited from the ideas and experiences of a unique array
of very distinguished speakers: Alejandro Beltrán (McKinsey, Partner and
Head of the Iberian Office), Rolf Breuer (Deutsche Bank, former Chairman),
Angel Cano (BBVA, CEO), Luis Cantarell (Nestlé, board member and CEO
America), Andrea Christenson (Käthe Kruse, CEO), Carlos Costa (The Boston
Consulting Group, Managing Partner), Julie Fuller (Avon Products, Executive
Director, HR, formerly PepsiCo, Global Head Leadership Development),
Franklin Johnson (Asset Management Inc., Chairman), Hans Ulrich Maerki
(ABB, board member, and former Chairman of IBM Europe, Middle East
& Africa), Ellen Miller (LBS, Executive in Residence, and former European
Head of Leadership Development at Lehman Brothers), David Moon (Merck,
Executive Director, Leadership Development), Rafael del Pino (Ferrovial,
Chairman), Marc Puig (The Puig Group, CEO), Anna Ruewell (British
Petroleum, Head of Talent Development), Alfredo Sáenz (Banco Santander,
CEO), Nicholas Schreiber (Tetra Pak, former CEO) and Gildo Zegna
(Ermenegildo Zegna, CEO).

I am very grateful to the authors of the different chapters for their excellent
contributions and suggestions on how to make the book more relevant
and interesting. I want to thank Stephen Rutt, Palgrave Macmillan Global
Publishing Director, and Eleanor Davey Corrigan, Palgrave Macmillan
Assistant Editor, for their interest in this project and the excellent guidance
they offered me during the preparation of this work. Keith Povey did an outstanding job in editing the book. Professors Luis Palencia, Juan Roure and Eric
Weber, and Henri-Christian Hartloff and Alex Herrera provided great help in
organizing the conference. Assumpció Cabré, Miriam Freixa and Ana Vericat
provided very efficient support. Many participants in the 2008 Conference
shared with the authors their knowledge, experience and expertise on this
subject and offered terrific inputs for the book. I am very grateful to them all.

PART 1

The Deans' Perspective on Leadership Development and Business Schools

CHAPTER 1.1

In Search of a Greater Impact: New Corporate and Societal Challenges for Business Schools

JORDI CANALS, Dean, IESE Business School, University of Navarra*

Introduction

Management was one of the greatest human innovations in the twentieth century. Scientific discovery had already been very important in previous centuries in Europe and Asia. Nevertheless, its application and impact on the lives of many people had been limited. With very few exceptions, such as the printing press or the steam engine, that paved the way to the first and the second industrial revolutions in the eighteenth and nineteenth centuries, most innovations and discoveries had a limited impact on the lives of individuals and society.

In the early twentieth century, a true revolution was happening in the organization of industrial production: the emergence of the modern corporation, which shaped manufacturing, sales and distribution. These new organizations made possible mass manufacturing and the application of new discoveries to solve basic human needs in modern societies – for example, automobiles, electricity or communications.

Professional managers at the helm of these organizations contributed to their growth. Chief executives and senior managers gradually replaced the investors or entrepreneurs who had started the companies. Management became an important profession in the twentieth century. Its principles were applied to the essential functions of organization, marketing, finance, operations and people development in a more rigorous and systematic way.

Business schools became the academic domains where the foundations of the profession of management could be learned and developed in a systematic way, and research on management problems and challenges could be carried out. Wharton, set up in 1881 within the University of Pennsylvania, was the first business school founded in the United States. Before the First World War, there were other graduate schools founded in the USA – Dartmouth, Harvard and Kellogg, among others. A flourishing of such institutions also took place before and after the Second World War in the United States. In Europe, most of the leading schools were founded in the late 1950s and the 1960s.

Business schools are still young institutions. But both the MBA programs and open, executive education programs have enrolled thousands of people around the world. Some failures and mistakes – including those related to the 2008 financial crisis – both of individuals educated at business schools and firms that trusted them, cannot hide the basic fact that the effects of business schools in developing good professionals and fostering through them job creation, investment, innovation and new firms have been very positive.

Moreover, in a relatively short time frame, leading business schools have become important paradigms of excellence in graduate education, and many of them have globalized education in a way that universities had not previously done. The many challenges of organizations and society in the twenty-first century will keep the demand for professional managers and entrepreneurs very strong, and business schools will continue to have a decisive role in educating them and providing society with the managerial talent needed to face some of its most compelling challenges.

In this chapter, we shall briefly review the main drivers of business schools' success over the recent decades (section 2), along with some of the major problems that they face today and what policies need to be changed (section 3). In section 4, we explore and discuss new challenges that business schools will have to tackle if they want to remain relevant institutions. Among other areas, those challenges include the reframing of the notion of the firm and the rediscovery of the role of senior managers.

The essential model of successful business schools in the twentieth century

It can be argued that business schools became prosperous institutions because economic growth in the second half of the twentieth century was higher than in the past, which is partially true. But one cannot forget that economic and business growth in that period was driven by the new professional manage-ment adopted by so many companies. Some of those professional managers were educated at business schools, and the knowledge and ideas developed there had an impact on a wider circle of professional managers. So, while it can be argued that economic growth over the period was fostered by technology and demographics, there was also a new factor at work, namely management, that gave life to a more efficient way of organizing the production and distribution of goods and services. Business schools contributed to this process by helping to educate some of those managers.

It is clear that there were different models of business school emerging in the United States and, later, in Europe in the twentieth century. In the United States, the Harvard Business School emphasized since its foundation its willingness to have an impact on the practice of management and its focus on an integrated, general management approach to this profession. Other institutions, such as Chicago, Stanford or Wharton did not put so much emphasis on its impact on management practice but rather on the development of a rigorous body of knowledge around the different managerial functions that could be applied successfully to the relevant problems.

In Europe, INSEAD and the London Business School, among others, initially focused their efforts on educating young students at the MBA level, while others, like IESE, put more effort into helping develop more senior managers.

Irrespective of the different models embodied by such schools, those institutions and others based their model on some key factors. The first was the creation and development of a full-time faculty made up of professionals with an academic qualification – most of them with a doctoral degree – and some knowledge or experience in the real business world. Faculty quality was key, both in designing good, solid graduate programs and having a great impact on students, so important in both the MBA program and in programs for more senior executives.

Faculty members also undertook research, creating or disseminating new knowledge around traditional disciplines such as marketing or operations, or new areas such as innovation or leadership. The quality of faculty and new, attractive programs were the essential drivers of good students, in particular, before and after the Second World War, times when those business schools were not yet well known and the programs they offered had no tradition in higher education.

The quality of students, the impact those programs had and the widespread use of some ideas, concepts and models developed by business school faculty members created a corporate demand for MBAs and executive programs, stronger in the USA than in Europe. Most alumni were pleased with the experiences and many of them became a great sales force for the schools.

Eventually, the positive experience of both alumni and companies was key to funding an endowment at those business schools, particularly in the USA, which was so important to build financially solid educational institutions.

The increasing number of students enrolled in those programs, the impact of them and their faculty on many companies, the new initiatives the schools introduced and the reputation they developed made possible the emergence of very strong brands, not only in management education, but also in the wider field of education.

This model – see Figure 1– has been the linchpin of the success of many business schools, in both the USA and Europe, in recent decades. Nevertheless, this successful model has created its own problems. Moreover, the business context in which the graduates have to work has also changed significantly. These circumstances have given rise to strong criticisms against business schools and their role.[1] Even if the empirical evidence for such criticisms is not strong, business schools will have to adjust and change if they want to retain a positive impact on people, firms and societies.

Figure 1: Business schools: a successful model

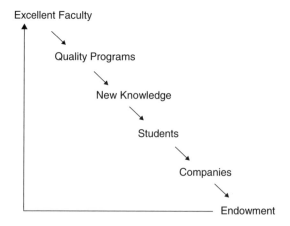

A model in crisis?

We can distinguish two categories of criticism against business schools. The first is related to external factors; and the second is related to some internal gaps or deficits in the business schools themselves.

External factors

The role of business schools and the financial crisis

As happened with the dotcom crisis at the end of the twentieth century, some observers have raised similar criticisms against business schools in the unfolding of the 2008 financial crisis. They have a point, though for reasons different than those they mention, such as the collapse of the banking system in the USA. It is true that many MBA graduates went to work on Wall Street, but even in the schools for which investment banking was the most important recruiting industry, the total number of MBA graduates in significant managerial positions in those financial companies was relatively small, and their responsibilities were probably similar to those of other professionals who had not attended business schools. There were other professionals who also had relevant responsibilities in those firms – for example, accountants, lawyers or financial analysts – as well as regulators who supervised them. Moreover, in most investment banks, graduate business schools were not the most important suppliers of talent, since the total number of students was small in comparison with the large volume of recruits offered by undergraduate schools in a variety of disciplines – including mathematics and physics.

On the other hand, for many schools, investment banking was not the most important recruiter. All in all, the claim that business schools were the main feeders of investment banks is not accurate. A different question is whether schools could have provided in their programs better frameworks on leadership, strategic decisions and ethics; or whether senior managers with a good education from a good graduate school could have done more to avoid such a disaster in the banking industry; and, more important, whether those graduates, with a better education, could have provided a better example of professionalism and integrity. As we shall see later, some business schools and their graduates may bear a heavier responsibility.

Globalization

Many Western companies have failed in their efforts to become more international or global. Some of them have made important mistakes in penetrating foreign markets, and many more have encountered cultural problems when working in a foreign environment. The development and transfer of talent in global companies has become a nightmare. Business schools have to do a better job of understanding, teaching and more important, practicing being more global in their different programs and activities. It is true that business schools have still a long way to go in terms of taking globalization seriously.

Corporate crisis

The third relevant factor is the serious damage to the firms' reputation that has been unfolding since the end of the 1990s. In many countries, companies used to be admired institutions that created jobs, generated investment and were drivers of progress. Business leaders – board members, CEOs or senior managers – were admired as professionals who deployed their skills and capabilities in the management of companies, that became important institutions in society.

Unfortunately, these perceptions have changed since the 1980s. Corporate crises have erupted, companies have suffered severe blows to their reputations, and many firms are seen as pure profit maximizers, so that their role in society seems to be in question. This perception goes beyond the role and crisis of investment banks and other financial institutions. At the same time, business leaders are seen today as the villains in those developments, either driving them or allowing them to happen. Public opinion sees them as opportunists, with a short-term focus on their own benefits and privileges, and responsible for many of today's corporate disasters.

As institutions educating managers and business leaders, business schools have to rethink the role of companies in society, the job of business leaders and how to include these dimensions in their programs.

Internal factors

We identify several areas with major deficits at many business schools: mission, governance, faculty development, relevance, humanistic approach, and the financial deficit.[2]

The mission deficit

Research has shown that organizations with a strong sense of mission can develop informal mechanisms that may lead to higher performance and increased work satisfaction. More important, a clear mission sends a signal to the whole organization in terms of why a firm exists, what values it stands for and its purpose (Barnard, 1938; Selznick, 1957; Drucker, 1974).

Even if a good deal of this research has been developed by business schools' faculties, some business schools do not have a clear sense of mission and what role they want to adopt in society. It is clear that all of them have a goal of helping to educate people and develop new knowledge. The question is whether this is still valid enough today and if it is, why do this and what is the balance between both activities that business schools want to have. In principle, there is not a superior model, but it is nevertheless important to understand why a business school exists and what it wants to do. Each school has its own views, but it is good to make them explicit and connect them with its strategy, faculty development, program design and research initiatives.[3]

The governance deficit

Academic institutions, in general, have a poor track record in terms of governance. Many explanations can be given, but the lack of professionalism in its management – very often academics with no particular leadership skills are in charge– and the powerful voice and influence of senior faculty members are important factors.

Business schools are influential institutions. As such, their governance matters a lot. There are several levels of governance in business schools to examine. The first is the relationship between the parent university and the business school, a link that can lead to situations where there is a lack of autonomy, both strategically and financially.

The second is the accountability and powers of the dean and senior faculty members. There is no single best model here, but it is certainly an issue not always well defined in business schools.

The third is the role of faculty members in designing programs, shaping research initiatives, promoting faculty to tenured positions and shaping the strategy of the school. Good governance needs to give faculty members an appropriate role in business schools, one that neither blocks change nor makes them completely alienated from the management of the school.

The faculty development deficit

It is well known that a faculty crunch is coming for many business schools (see, for example, special report on this topic by AACSB (The Association to Advance Collegiate Schools of Business) (AACSB, 2003). In informal discussions among business school deans and administrators there is a view that in the near future there might not be enough Ph.D. graduates to replace senior faculty in top business schools who will retire over the next two decades. This is particularly important because of the explosive growth of business education in Asia. Faculty growth for new projects is a major challenge. Moreover, the deficit looks even larger when one considers how to develop the kind of faculty needed to best achieve a business school's mission.

In many business schools, faculty development seems to be a task that evolves in a spontaneous ways. For some faculty members this may work well, but for others it does not and the worst effect is that it leads to a waste of time, resources and human aspirations, which might be devastating for students, scholars and schools. Leaving faculty development to the entrepreneurial initiative of each faculty member would be the equivalent of neglecting the role of coaches in any major team sport or in an orchestra, or the role of residence in medical schools.

The relevance deficit

The relevance challenge has an impact on both educational programs and on research. After the Second World War, business schools became relevant institutions because they helped to tackle a very important need: the education of professional managers and the development of a body of knowledge about the main management disciplines. In the 1970s and 1980s, many business schools became more interested in promoting a type of research similar to that of other social sciences schools (Khurana, 2007). Increasingly, research became more irrelevant for management practice, even if it was adorned with an allegedly superior academic rigor.

The relevance deficit also became very clear in the schools' programs. Many top US business schools did not offer executive programs until very recently. It was, in part, a matter of choice, but it was also attributable to the lack of faculty members' interest in working with senior executives on real business problems.

My assumption is that the risk of irrelevance in research, which is the most-mentioned problem when people speak about relevance, is smaller when faculty members work in the classroom with senior executives. Working with experienced managers stretches the capabilities and expertise of faculty members, and makes them more aware of real corporate problems. Not every school has to do it in the same way or with the same intensity, but it is a clear signal of how relevant for the real world a school is going to be.

The humanistic deficit

The aspiration to make management a more solid, science-based profession has had another unintended effect: the adoption of a model of the firm, based on economics, as an abstract organization whose social purpose is to coordinate, make a very efficient use of resources and maximize profits for shareholders (Roberts, 2004). Senior managers are agents whose functions have been delegated by the principals (shareholders).

It is true that, in the early stages of capitalism, the world was not as rosy as some optimists pretend. Nevertheless, at the beginning of the twentieth century, prominent business people perceived that companies had a social purpose beyond that of making money. In fact, the creation of schools to help them, such as Harvard, Dartmouth or IESE, and the willingness of the major donors, was related to the conviction that the education of general managers in a rigorous and ethical way was important for the good of society.

Unfortunately, some management and financial theories and the stronger role of capital markets as drivers of modern capitalism have displaced some of those early ideals in the business world. The force of pragmatism in getting results, irrespective of what happens to individuals working in the organization, has become the dominant paradigm in the practice of management (Ghoshal, 2005).

The outcome has been the growth of more impersonal organizations, where individuals are often treated as just one more resource. The outcome is that people's loyalty towards firms is vanishing. Companies are organizations based on people and made up of people. The claim that people are important is stronger than ever; but, in practice, many decisions are taken without considering their impact on either people or companies. We have management models completely devoid of the human presence, where decision-making happens in a mechanical way, and financial incentives shape people's motivations. Nevertheless, this approach is weak, because human freedom is irrepressible and economic incentives do not always work.

Business schools have contributed to the spread of this view by underplaying the role of individuals in organizations and business decisions. Moreover, new research paradigms have been build around models where human beings with their qualities and boundaries are either absent or manipulated with assumptions that do not fit with how people behave in the real world.

The financial deficit

In the race to build the best possible schools and develop the most gifted faculty members, business schools have been paying higher salaries. Higher faculty compensation, more scholarships, and greater investment in technology and other physical assets, have created a financial pressure on schools.

In the USA, business schools used to rely on endowments to pay higher salaries or attract students, and thus be less dependent on academic fees. In Europe, schools had to be closer to the real world and do more executive education. In both cases, there is a problem. For US business schools, the endowment model is good when stock prices rise, but it becomes a nightmare during deep share price falls. For European business schools, executive education is a great activity for many reasons, but in some cases business schools do it mainly for financial reasons, which is not the best motivator in the long term.

The challenge for business schools is how they can develop an economic model that will make them sustainable in the long term. There is no single method. Each school has to design its own model. The development of new models for business schools will be one more test of how well these institutions are led.

New challenges for business schools

The current financial crisis and its impact on corporate reputation seems to demand a more solid and comprehensive notion of the firm, and a positive perspective of the role of business leaders. Promoting such notions and ideas will help business schools to remake their role in society.

There are also some other areas where business schools need additional work. Companies, recruiters and executives expect this.

Reframing the notion of the firm

A fundamental challenge that business schools have to tackle is how they can contribute to a reframing of the notion and role of the firm in society, and what the role of business leaders should be in this context. This is a priority because business schools need healthy companies with a clear purpose if they hope to have a positive impact on them. If companies do not enjoy a high reputation in society, the role of business schools may become more irrelevant and they will have serious trouble in attracting outstanding faculty members and excellent students.

Let us start with what a firm is and what its role in society should be. We understand a firm as an organization, made up of people who work together with the purpose of producing and delivering goods and services for clients, creating economic and social value as a result of this process, and opportunities for professional and personal learning and improvement for the people involved in it. In this section, we shall discuss briefly some key areas around this notion of the firm.

Profit maximization

In recent decades, the dominant view of the firm in the theory of business has been a purely economic one. Borrowing from a tradition developed in economics, firms were considered to be profit maximizers. There is a confusion here. Most prominent economists have never said that this was the only goal a firm should pursue.[4] In their effort to build a theory, they merely chose a working hypothesis that firms are profit maximizers, in the same way as consumers are utility maximizers. It is not difficult to see that, even if conscious consumers try to be utility maximizers, there are many other dimensions in their lives that make them behave sometimes in ways where maximization is not the only driver and economic goals are not the only outcomes.

In the same way, companies try to create as much economic value as possible. Nevertheless, this is neither the only goal that a company has, nor an objective that could be achieved with purely economic means, for several reasons. The first is that companies are groups of people – communities of people – working together, and learning together how to serve clients' real needs in an efficient way. Profits are one of the indicators of how well the company is doing, but it is not the only one. At a more personal level, individuals want to get things done in the best possible way, which means they will have to work with others and cooperate with others to make things happen. In such personal relationships, trust is essential. People want to work with others with whom they feel at ease, or can learn from, or can communicate with, confident that opportunism is absent (Andreu, 2009). Corporate cultures and values that enhance this work environment should be a priority for top managers (Rosanas, 2008). Incentives that may destroy trust and these basic attitudes should be removed from the firm's policies, even if this may have a short-term impact on profits.

Too often, and as a result of using simple hypotheses that make things easier, economic models of the firm consider profits as the difference between revenues and expenses. This is true from an economic viewpoint.

Nevertheless, from an action viewpoint, profits are the outcome of thousands of decisions, on both the revenue and expenses sides. Such decisions are taken by diverse people in an organization whose main goal may not be maximizing profits, but merely doing good things. Nobody knows in the real world what maximizing profits actually means, or what the firm's maximum profit might be. Good professionals at all levels in any organization strive to work well, and effectively, thus making a good contribution to the firm. So let us look at profits as the outcome of a complex process to which the commitment and behavior of many individuals have contributed. In order to gain a good outcome, both the process and people's motivations have to be good. This means that people have to be excellent professionals, to work hard, to interact reasonably well with one another, to take care of the needs of the people they work for, to have a good level of motivation, to listen to others, to serve clients and employees as they wish to be served, to keep their pledges and commitments, to be accountable and to invest in their continuous learning, among other dimensions. In a nutshell, good leadership is about results, but also about the process of achieving those results.

Serving customers

Another dimension to be considered is how a firm and its senior managers understand their basic function in society: to serve customers. In this respect, making money comes second. If there is no real value-added for customers, the economic and commercial success of the firm will be doubtful, even if it generates profits in the short term. Making money is different from creating and developing a firm.

Again, in theory building and management learning there is not enough emphasis on how well companies have to behave when they serve their customers. This is something that faculty members tend to leave to Marketing courses. This is a huge mistake, since it is the first reason why a company has social legitimacy, the first outcome to be achieved and the driver of future profits.

People in organizations: a humanistic view of the firm

The dominant economic and sociological paradigms in management have elaborated a simplified and warped notion of individuals in organizations. In both approaches, the notion of individual freedom is replaced by determinism. Given the right incentives or the right environment, people will always behave in a certain way.

This assumption is at odds with one the basic tenets of many companies and management scholars with more humanistic roots: people do matter. Some companies talk about people as their most important asset. Innovation and creativity, so much needed today, depend on the talent, commitment and willingness of people.

A humanistic perspective of management also has some fundamental principles:

1. each person is unique and can make a unique contribution.
2. each person has an intrinsic dignity and the basic right to be respected both in the workplace and in society.

3. each person is born free, has the freedom to make decisions and the right not to be coerced to use this freedom against his or her own will.

4. each person is responsible for the use of his or her capabilities and rights, and he or she is accountable to others for external actions and the fulfillment of his or her duties.

5. each person has basic material needs, but also has aspirations and motivations that go beyond material or economic incentives, which cannot be bought.

6. each person has values that have to be respected as far as they do not harm other people.

Organizations that aspire to be respectful toward each person must take these qualities into account. In a similar way, senior managers in their decision-making should also consider some basic principles. The first is to try to do as much good as possible for people working in a firm, and avoid doing harm to them. The second is to recognize in all relevant ways each person's contribution to the firm. Third, respect people's ideas, values and beliefs. Fourth, give them challenges and opportunities to develop their capabilities and skills; good leaders also have to be demanding, but in a gentle way. Fifth, invest in their education and development. Sixth, help to create a context where the human aspirations that people have could be at least partially developed. And seventh, foster a climate of trust.

Over the past decades, many theories assume that management was neutral. Management is not neutral. It involves people making decisions and sharing values, and people receiving the influence of decisions (including the decision-maker herself). And decisions are based on choices and values held by each person. The isolation of the decision-making process as a purely rational process is not a real experience. Managers bring values to the work. There is a condition to make this process work in a sustainable way and avoid clashes with people with different values: that each person respects the other as a unique human being, with an intrinsic dignity and rights that deserve respect; one's values have to recognize this very simple idea.

Learning

The fourth dimension is that people working in a company, when designing, producing and delivering goods and services for their customers, must be provided with opportunities for learning, for several reasons. The first is that in any profession, learning and improvement happen when things get done. Doctors learn by seeing and advising patients, and engineers by designing and testing new mechanisms to solve physical problems. At every level in an organization, people learn by doing, and by working with others. The modern organization is essentially a team effort. Individuals learn from the skills, knowledge and attitudes of others. A good company that wants to serve customers better day in and day out has to foster a positive spirit of learning and improvement. But learning can also be negative. The second attribute around learning is that this becomes an important quality for professionals who look for challenging professional opportunities. For them, money is also important. But given that basic needs are covered, the best people look for opportunities to learn, to improve their capabilities and eventually to make a real difference. In this era, where talent is scarce, this dimension is more vital than ever. Economic compensation is important, but companies have to make sure that employees find great professional learning opportunities in their jobs.

Companies and society: the search for the common good

Companies are important institutions in society. They create jobs, invest, innovate, train people, help use scarce resources in an effective way and, from a variety of perspectives, they play an important role in modern society. It is true that the first and differential mission of a firm is to do what it has to do: serve customers well and generate economic value in the process. Nevertheless, companies can neither forget the internal mission of the firm – developing its own people – nor the society they live in. Our societies are increasingly complex, with new emerging needs in terms of problems to be tackled – such as education, globalization, immigration – or the challenges they face – public infrastructure, innovation, research, sustainability, for example. It is true that none of these challenges relate to any company in particular. But it is also true that all of them help to create what the classical philosophers used to describe as the common good, the good that is needed in any society to enable individual goods to be achieved.

Some of these areas are the responsibility of governments, but neither primarily nor exclusively. Moreover, the principle of subsidiarity requires that governments should not interfere in areas where the private sector could do a better job. In this respect, civil society and companies also have a share in the responsibility for improving the common good of the society to which they belong. Societies need educated people, virtuous citizens, professional opportunities, and a good deal of innovation and dynamism. Firms can do a great job in all these areas and make a very important contribution to the common good. From this description, it is clear that we are not speaking here about philanthropy, which is good for society, but not an individual duty for a single company. Companies may make philanthropic donations; it is up to them. What companies have to make is a positive contribution to the general common good of society, not ignoring issues and leaving them to the domain of governments or other people. Companies should avoid being free-riders, If companies want to be respected institutions in society, they also have to consider those dimensions.

These simple reflections remind us that companies are not only profit maximizers, and that economic or decision-making models that overemphasize this dimension, at the expense of forgetting others, may end up creating a view of the firm among business leaders that is far away from the healthy notion of the firm that a vibrant and dynamic society needs.[5] Since the 1980s we have seen an undisputed preeminence of capital markets, investment banks, financial goals and an almost exclusive view of firms as profit-makers. Many of the excesses and crises that have appeared over the years have been in part a natural output of a warped view of the firm. A positive notion of the firm goes well beyond the effort to avoid scandals, though it can certainly help to diminish their likelihood. It also helps to redefine the role of the public sector in the economy.

Reframing the role of senior managers
A new frame of the notion of the firm has implications for the functions and role of senior business leaders. In a close parallel with the notion of the

firm as profit maximizer, the role of senior business leaders, starting with the CEO, board members and members of the top management team, was seen as making commitments to shareholders and sticking to them. Some of them went even further, by emphasizing that they were doing their job by making shareholders wealthier. Nevertheless, a firm's wealth creation is the outcome of a process. If this process is not designed and managed well, the outcome cannot be good, even if some financial indicators say that there are profits to be made in the short term. The role of senior managers is to make sure that the company they serve fulfills its basic role in society, as described above.

This means that they take care of the context and process, as much as the final results. Business leaders must focus on people and managerial processes; and the results will follow. In contrast, when they are only results-driven, without concern for process or context, then crisis may follow. The processes senior managers have to look for are those that attract people to the organization and engages them in the firm's projects; those that design, produce and deliver efficiently goods and services that clients want to buy, creating economic value in this process; those that foster learning among its people; and those that get the firm involved in helping to solve some of society's problems.

This perspective does not ignore results, but understands that good performance is the outcome of many small decisions regarding people, clients, products, services, operations, marketing, and many other dimensions. The chief executive's role is to make sure that people work in a process that is both efficient and effective, that makes them feel proud about what they do, that generates pleased customers with what the firm offers them (that is, willing to pay for it above opportunity costs) and, as a result, shareholders are satisfied with the financial performance of their investment.

This basic notion of the role of senior business leaders has several implications. The first is that business leaders are professionals whose main function is to serve (Khurana and Nohria, 2008). Service is the key attribute in any profession worthy of its name, but also in the business world. A business leader who does not serve his/her people, clients, shareholders, and society, is not a good professional. He or she may help the company to make money in the short term but may create an unsustainable organization over the longer term.

The relevant time frame for senior business leaders in organizations is the long term, not the short term. A senior manager, while striving for the long term, may fail in the short term and perhaps be dismissed. A great company is built over a number of years. The fact that the CEO's tenure is getting shorter by the day, or that companies always have to bring in outsiders to fill the top jobs are neither the most coherent way to foster customer loyalty to the firm by customers and employees when they see so much change at the top of the firm, nor the most effective way of building a great organization in the long-term.

A final word about leaders as servants. There are many good theories about leadership, at least as many as bad ones. One of the good ones is that business leaders have to lead by example. This is an important feature of many successful organizations that have passed the test of time. The leaders' good examples consist of a mix of professionalism, fairness, virtue, courage, strength and generosity in thinking about and dealing with others.

With the notion of the firm described above, this idea of the role of business leaders clashes with the dominant view in many business theories and many programs and courses taught at business schools. In some of them, the notion of individual success, finding one's opportunities, discovering the mechanisms of power and influence, and thinking about the next professional move come first. These may be legitimate aspirations, but they look selfish if considered as the only aims of a good business leader. In the same way as a good surgeon is not supposed to think only about how much money he or she will make from a certain operation, the surgeon has to consider, first, how to help the patient recover his/her health, a good business leader cannot think first or exclusively of the personal material rewards derived from his/her job. This is legitimate, but it may become obscene when this aspiration overrides any other consideration regarding his/her responsibilities towards his/her people, clients, shareholders and wider society.

This perspective of the role of senior management can help managers to become a force for change in society and make management a profession that benefits not only other people, but also other people's good and that of organizations and society at large.

Integration

The firm as a modern institution developed in the twentieth century was built around business functions: purchasing, manufacturing, logistics, finance, marketing, sales and so on. The specific advantages of some firms were related to achieving the critical scale in some of its divisions so that functions that used to be very complex and inefficient could become easier and cheaper by aggregating them and coordinating them through managers. From an economic standpoint, this allowed firms to produce cheaper goods so that many more people could afford to buy them; it also made possible the commercialization of new discoveries and technologies that could reach the mass market more quickly.

The sheer power of specialized business functions – marketing, operations or finance, for example – is clear. Nevertheless, the problems that overspecialization can generate are also clear. The role of senior managers is not only to supervise those functions but to coordinate them, and to make the individual objectives of the different functions and units within a single firm compatible, so that the company's overall goal could be achieved.

Over the past few decades, many companies have grown in complexity. Some basic processes still can be managed with a specialized organizational form, but many others require a more complex organizational design. Among the latter, one can mention those firms working around projects or networks rather than traditional manufacturing processes, firms that have to go through an important organizational change or whose sources of innovation are interrelated with customers' behavior or jointly developed with other companies. At the same time, there are many other challenges firms have to face, from building a more efficient product design-to-market model, or to develop a more globally integrated organization, where the role of basic business functions is important but clearly insufficient.[6]

Unfortunately, business schools in general have not been very quick to react to some of those changes. Business programs and scholarship are still based around business functions. What is dangerous is what happens with courses where the reflection, diagnosis and decisions around business problems are considered exclusively from the perspective of the function, and not the perspective of the whole company.

This is an increasingly important perspective for senior managers. In the past, many business managers who were successful at running a unit, function or division were put in charge of larger or more complex units within the same firm. Some of them tackled the challenge successfully, but others, unfortunately, failed, in part because they tried to project their function perspective – that is, operations, marketing or finance – and run the whole firm based on this perspective.

General management requires integration. Yet business schools are not, in general, greatly concerned about it. Faculty members find it complex and not very useful for their research agenda. There are essentially three models to consider. The first is a market-based approach which says that each professor should teach students about the basic functions and the tools they will need and, if they are clever, they will learn how to integrate these. This approach has clear limitations.

Two other, more positive, approaches emerge. One is to change the curriculum and instead of talking about functions like marketing or operations, the focus of the discussion is shifted towards clients, capital markets or people. Schools such as Yale or IMD have made important efforts in terms of curriculum redesign, course development and faculty development. The second integrative approach, followed by schools such as Harvard or IESE and others using the case method, is to try to learn how to analyze, tackle and make specific decisions about business problems, not only from the perspective of the functional manager in charge, but also taking into account the whole company's perspective, the effects of that decision on people and other parts of the company, and the impact on its performance, in both the short and the long term. In this context, cases are not descriptive illustrations or structured situations where stylized models can be applied. The effort here consists of helping business leaders to think holistically about problems, solutions and decisions, and their impact on people, their units and the whole company, both short- and long-term. Teaching integrated courses is an important step, but helping people to think in an integrated way is a transformational experience towards which business schools should aim.

At the time of writing, the world is facing new and increasingly complex problems. Some of these are related to technical dimensions, but most are connected with leadership. Business schools can and should make a contribution to the whole society by helping it to tackle some of these problems where the knowledge and capabilities of business schools are proven. This is a unique contribution that schools can make to society: to encourage faculty members to work across disciplines and problems.

A framework for leadership development

An indirect effect of the lack of integration of some areas in business education is that there are not many coherent and comprehensive models of leadership development or management (Nohria and Khurana 2010). In other words, schools put together packages of knowledge and skills, and split them up among academic areas that teach them with rigor and professionalism in the best of cases, but often there is no a clear frame on how to integrate those concepts or skills, and how they serve in the process of educating for leadership responsibilities.

With the challenge of integration and cross-disciplinary, cross-functional learning, leadership development is not only a complex process, but also one that many schools leave to market forces and the spontaneity of students and faculty members alike.

Moreover, many schools have neither a shared view of what a senior manager or a business leader is and should do, nor how to train to develop those capabilities.[7] Again, the reference of another professional school – medicine – provides a sharp contrast. In medicine, there is a range of knowledge that medical doctors have to acquire and a set of practices they should command and know how to use. In business leadership, the knowledge is reasonably well defined, but the process of using this knowledge or developing skills and capabilities to manage effectively or to lead an organization or its people is far from explicit.

The problem here is that when there is not a frame describing what a business leader should do, it is very complex to design and deliver programs that may have a very deep impact on the individuals who study them. It is true that management is more complex than any other profession, because it involves not only knowledge, but also capabilities and attitudes that are related to working with and interacting with other people, who are also free and have their own interests, values, duties and motivations. Nevertheless, the sheer complexity of defining and sharing a model of leadership development should not stop business schools from working hard to make headway in this extremely important area for companies and societies alike.

Globalization

Globalization is one of the major forces in the world that has a deep impact on the way that companies are managed and operate. It is not a new phenomenon, as, at the beginning of the twentieth century the world also experienced a significant process of globalization (James, 2001). Nevertheless, we are seeing today the emergence of new countries in the world economy that are not only great markets for existing multinational companies, but are also the countries of origin of newly emerging multinationals.

Companies of all sizes and in all industries have been attempting to cope with this important challenge, by increasing their international operations, setting up plants or commercial offices in new countries, establishing joint ventures with foreign partners and offshoring operations and research centers in newly emerging economies. It is certainly a new landscape for many companies, and, in addition, this change has happened in a very short time frame.

Business schools have reacted to these changes in a variety of ways: introducing more courses on international business into their curricula and executive programs, establishing alliances for students and faculty exchanges, organizing international trips, or installing more international faculty members or students on campus.

The strategies that business schools are following to adjust and react to globalization are different. Nevertheless, in speaking with business leaders from different industries and countries, there is a widespread feeling that schools, even if they are launching some new initiatives, are not doing enough to help business leaders, managers and firms to cope with this new phenomenon (Ghemawat, 2008). The complexity of managing and leading international companies has greatly increased in recent years, so business leaders feel a strong pressure to deliver in a more uncertain environment. What business leaders observe is that some faculty members do not easily move from their own area of knowledge and expertise, and are not very active in dealing with international issues in their courses and programs; that schools are not innovative enough in the area of international executive education in developing leading-edge concepts and models helpful in understanding and managing the new realities; that there is a lack of basic knowledge on international business to be shared by companies and schools; that in custom programs, schools are still embedded in their national culture and systems, while companies have to move as smoothly as possible across cultures and countries.

It is obvious that there is no simple reaction to this challenge. On the one hand, business schools are higher education institutions where faculty members are the most important pillar in their development. Without excellent faculty members, it is very difficult to provide outstanding teaching and learning, or carry out research with impact. Faculty development is very expensive and takes up a lot of time. Within this constraint, schools can pursue more aggressively some strategies oriented toward internationalizing the faculty, staff and student body; increase the number and impact of exchange students and faculty exchange programs; organize executive programs in cooperation with schools in other continents; work with international firms, not only in student recruitment, but also in executive education; develop teaching materials and courses with a very strong international accent and content; make sure that the international content is present in all the required courses; and, finally, implement mechanisms so that class discussions or professional discussions on international business really take into account not a dominant view on how to do things, but different possible alternatives of actions depending on national environments.

Today, companies have to overcome a unique obstacle in making their companies operate more effectively in our global world: how senior managers understand differences across countries and can use those differences to make the firm better. This goal requires not only knowledge, but also a set of skills that have to be and can be trained, and an understanding of human values and attitudes. It is the role of business schools not only to make sure that there is solid international content in the curriculum, but also to help managers understand differences across countries and cultures, and know how to act professionally in their own context.

Relevance

As Khurana (2007) points out, since the 1970s most business schools have been attempting to catch up with other university departments in terms of knowledge generation, methodological rigor and research impact. The dominance of publications in top academic journals has become the paradigm of excellence and scholarship. This effort has been very impressive in management and its different sub-areas. Nevertheless, it has had an unexpected side effect: a significant part of this research output is considered to have very little relevance for management practice. This is not particularly coherent with the goal behind the foundation of business schools at the beginning of the twentieth century: to help improve the profession of management.

Leadership development requires knowledge and research, but research on important issues for the business world – research that could be relevant in terms of the challenges it aims to address and the answers it wants to provide. A particular answer to this question is that researchers have to take a wider perspective in studying their special research questions, and must produce more specific knowledge about some problems and solutions for practicing managers. Otherwise, business schools will become more like other university departments, such as those teaching economics or sociology. The identity and purpose of business schools may be in jeopardy.

The other dimension is that leadership development and business education requires research and knowledge, but it also requires good learning methodologies, and an excellent faculty that helps students to develop the necessary skills, capabilities and attitudes. It is very unfortunate that some faculty members in some business schools consider teaching as a necessary evil that has to be tolerated in order to survive professionally in a business school. This is very poor motivation for scholars who have to serve not only a scholarship in research, but also in teaching, and in particular in management and business leadership, where the process of teaching and learning is more complex than in most other academic areas.

An intriguing phenomenon around the relevance of business schools is how they have been responsible for some of the most useful management ideas generated in recent decades. Let us consider what has driven financial innovation and the growth of financial institutions in the West and the many deals around mergers, acquisitions, initial public offerings (IPOs) and other forms of financial advisory services. It is true that modern corporate finance was instrumental in developing valuation methods for some financial instruments. Nevertheless, growth in this industry has come from innovations driven by financial analysts rather than scholars. The recent financial crisis is a great opportunity for business schools to make a stronger contribution.

There are several schools doing an outstanding job of being relevant and having a positive impact on students, firms and society. The students and alumni of these are extremely pleased with the educational experience they received in their programs. Nevertheless, the social function of business schools and their reputation also depends on doing a great job in being both rigorous and relevant.

Lifelong learning and education

The explosion of diversity and complexity in all areas of knowledge makes a significant part of the educational process obsolete more quickly than in the past. This is a fact of life in scientific disciplines such as physics, biology or chemistry as well as in some social sciences – economics, for example. And it is now becoming evident in business leadership and management. It is true that there are basic frames and concepts of universal validity. But since the nature of leadership challenges change and new realities to be managed emerge, the specific capabilities for a given context may not be the right ones for another.

The speed of change in the business world and the accelerated rhythm of innovation creates new opportunities for leadership development. Nevertheless, schools seem to be too intent on just refining the current

undergraduate or graduate education model. The Bologna reform across the
European Union (EU) is a case in point. This agreement will have a profound
impact on the way students across Europe learn, get their degrees, acquire
a different cultural perception of individuals and countries, and develop
their education in a more standardized way across Europe. Nevertheless, the
Bologna agreement does not address the fundamental problem in a modern
society: how do educated adults keep learning? How can universities help
them to keep their jobs, get new jobs or to develop new professional projects?
And in the case of business schools, what do they offer for the continuous
learning of their graduates? Is continuous learning as well designed and
structured as other programs and courses within the school?

Continuous education is obviously a big challenge in present-day society,
but it is also a great opportunity for business schools: many graduates are
eager to keep learning or developing new capabilities, or to think about a
second or a third professional life. And companies and society at large need
business schools to keep contributing to the development of managers'
knowledge and capabilities.

This challenge requires that schools adopt a new strategy, more open to
considering classic undergraduate and graduate programs as initial steps in a
professional development process; and they also need to think about executive
education programs not as a portfolio of disparate areas and topics, but one
that may help to cover new educational needs of individuals and companies.

Continuous education has always been important, and it is a basic educational need that remains unfulfilled. The knowledge society we live in and the
demographics and longer life expectancy make this need more urgent than
ever and business schools must take it seriously.

Organizational structure

Business schools are relatively young institutions. Some of them have
developed a worldwide reputation in a very short period of time, with a
strong faculty, excellent students and alumni, great programs and a formidable brand name. This combination of success factors has not emerged by
chance; there has been excellent leadership behind those developments. Most
business schools have developed a professional approach to managing the
institutions that in many ways is among the best in professional schools, and
as such it is recognized across universities.

Some factors have helped here: the vision of the founders in many of those business schools; the focus on helping to educate business leaders and, in this way, to learn more about management and real firms; the need to survive in a very competitive market for both faculty members and students; and the need to pay close attention to students' development and to corporate clients, or to the influence of alumni.

Nevertheless, there is still room for improvement in business schools. Here we list some areas where business school leaders and faculty members need to consider:

- the impact schools have on students and corporate clients;

- the ability of faculty to develop and try new approaches and to improve current ones;

- professionalism in the management of internal operations, alumni offices, technology, staffing needs or customer service;

- the development of new courses for alumni; and

- the agility and speed of introducing changes or offering responses to new market challenges.

For some leading US business schools, growing endowments have meant an increasing source of revenue for the school. But this may not continue in the future, and it is today a source of deep financial pain. For other schools, a lack of endowments meant the need to set up new programs to obtain the funding required to be financially viable. We all need to think about models that may make our institutions more viable in the long term. Gifts and endowments will help, but learning how to manage a business school in a downturn and, more important, helping the whole faculty and staff adapt to the new realities, is a new fact our schools have to face.

Some final reflections

Management has become a very relevant and decisive profession in Western society, and is one of the factors that drove economic growth in the twentieth century. Business schools have been very successful institutions in recent decades, and most of them have had a very positive impact on many individuals, firms and society at large.

The challenge is how business schools face the new realities and demands in the world of the twenty-first century. These are different from the world of the early twentieth century, when the first business schools in the USA were founded, or the world of the 1950s and 1960s, when many other business schools in Europe, the United States and other parts of the world came to life.

The current crisis of the capitalist system goes beyond a crisis of management and leadership, but it certainly has some roots in the crisis of the banking system and the mediocre leadership in many banks and other nonfinancial firms. The problem in many of these firms was not lack of knowledge or technical skills, but lack of good leadership. Business schools alone cannot solve those problems. Nevertheless, business schools and their faculties have the potential to help address many of them. Even if the challenges are huge, the need for leadership development round the world and excellent business schools is even deeper today than it was about a century ago, when the first schools were founded. The opportunities for great educational programs and relevant research are bigger than ever.

NOTES

*R. Andreu, A. Argandoña, R. Bruner, D. Jain, C. Kester, A. Liekerman, C. Meyer, J. Pfeffer, J. M. Rosanas, J. C. Vázquez-Dodero and R. Vietor offered excellent comments and suggestions to improve this chapter. I am very grateful for their help.

1 Among others, see Pfeffer and Fong (2002), Mintzberg (2004), and Collins and O'Toole (2005).

2 Lorange (2008) and Thomas (2007) have described other challenges that business schools face today.

3 For example, since its foundation in 1958, IESE's mission has been to help develop leaders with the aspiration to have a deep, positive and lasting impact on colleagues, firms and society at large, through professionalism, integrity and spirit of service.

4 Nevertheless, the influence of the language of economics has been very strong in shaping this dominant view of companies. See Ferraro *et al.* (2005).

5 Ghoshal and Bartlett (1997) and Hamel (2007) made serious attempts at rethinking the role of management.

6 Martin (2007) has developed an important model of ways to help business leaders think in an integrated way.

7 The Center for Creative Leadership has developed a very robust model of leadership development and learning that helps senior managers to grow along several dimensions. In IESE's programs, many faculty members share a model developed by the late Professor Juan A. Perez-Lopez, in which he distinguishes between executive capabilities, strategic capabilities and leadership capabilities. There is no single answer to this challenge, but more experiments have to be run to make headway in this important area for firms and business schools.

REFERENCES

AACSB.2003. "Sustaining Scholarship in Business Schools". Special AACSB Report. Tampa, FL.

Andreu, R. 2009. "Knowledge, Learning and Competitive Advantage: Implications for the Management Profession". Conference on "Humanizing the Firm and the Management Profession". Barcelona, IESE,.

Barnard, C. 1938. *The Functions of the Executive*. Boston, MA: Harvard University Press.

Chandler, A. 1990. *Scale and Scope*. Cambridge, MA: Harvard University Press.

Collins, J. and O'Toole, J. 2005. "How Business Schools Lost Their Way". *Harvard Business Review* May: 96–104.

Drucker, P. 1974. *Management: Tasks, Responsibilities and Practices*. New York: Harper & Row.

Ferraro, F., Pfeffer, J. and Sutton, R. I. 2005. "Economics Language and Assumptions: How Theories Can Become Self-fulfilling". *Academy of Management Review* 30(1): 8–24.

Ghemawat, P. 2008. "The Globalization of Business Education: Through the Lens of Semiglobalization". *Journal of Management Development* 4: 391–414.

Ghoshal, S. 2005. "Bad Management Theories Are Destroying Good Management Practices". *Academy of Management Learning and Education* 4(1): 75–91.

Ghoshal, S. and Bartlett, C. A. 1997. *The Individualized Corporation*. New York: HarperBusiness.

Ghoshal, S. and Moran, P. 1996. "Bad for Practice: A Critique of Transaction Cost Theory". *Academy of Management Review* 21(1): 13–47.

Hamel, G. 2007. *The Future of Management*. Boston, MA: Harvard Business School Press).

James, H. 2001. *The End of Globalization: Lessons from the Great Depression*. Cambridge, MA: Harvard University Press.

Khurana, R. 2007. *From Higher Aims to Hired Hands*. Princeton, NJ: Princeton University Press.

Khurana, R. and Nohria, N. 2008. "It's Time to Make Management a True Profession". *Harvard Business Review* 86(10): 70–8.

Lorange, P. 2008. *Thought Leadership Means Business*. Cambridge: Cambridge University Press.

Martin, R. 2007. *The Opposable Mind*. Boston, MA: Harvard Business School Press).

Minztberg, H. 2004 *Managers, not MBAs*. London: Pearson Education.

Nohria, N. and Khurana, R. (eds) 2010. *Handbook of Leadership Theory and Practice*. Boston Harvard Business Publishing.

Pfeffer, J. and Fong, C. T. 2002. "The End of Business Schools? Less Success than Meets the Eye". *Academy of Management Learning and Education* 1: 78–95.

Roberts, J. 2004. *The Modern Firm*. Oxford: Oxford University Press.

Rosanas, J. M. 2008. "Beyond Economic Criteria: A Humanistic Approach to Organizational Survival". *Journal of Business Ethics* 78(3): 447–62.

Selznick, P. 1957 *Leadership in Administration*. Berkeley and Los Angeles: University of California Press.

Thomas, H. 2007, An Analysis of the Environmental and Competitive Dynamics of Management Education". *Journal of Management Development* 26(1): 9–21.

CHAPTER 1.2

Millennials and the Changing Landscape of Business Education

J. FRANK BROWN, Dean, INSEAD

In the past, when it came to the employer–employee relationship, it used to be that the employer had the upper hand. Today the situation has reversed – the employee has taken control from the employer. This relationship shift has had major implications for the role of business schools. What I shall offer in this chapter are my thoughts on how business schools can address the greater expectations of today's more demanding generation of managers.

Not so long ago, organizations could put together a schedule of things they wanted their employees to do and expect their employees to do them. This included educational programs. These programs tended to be more job-specific than merely adding to the overall skill portfolio of the individual.

They had obvious benefits for the organization, such as the ability to create, or train to reach, the desired profile and attributes of an individual that would benefit the organization, but not necessarily the employee. They did not always provide the training necessary for an individual to move upward within the organization. This is something the "millennial generation" – those employees who entered the workforce around the turn of the millennium – has picked up on.

Millennials are a demanding bunch. They speak out about what they want and they expect to get it, and if they don't, they move on. As Gloeckler noted in *BusinessWeek*, "They're [millennials] pursuing MBAs to change the world, but first they're forcing business schools to make changes in order to accommodate them."[1]

Otherwise known as "Generation Y" or the "Net Generation", millennials have high expectations, and their work–life balance is paramount. Moreover, new technologies such as blogs, podcasts and other social networking tools are normal for them. As a result, business schools and organizations have to adapt their tools and policies to their new employees' demands and keep up with their accelerating pace.

Ron Alsop (author of *The Trophy Kids Grow Up*) thinks the future looks bright, stating "Millennials were bred for achievement and most will work hard if the task is engaging and promises a tangible payoff."[2] There is also a lot of evidence which seems to prove that combining millennials and their less demanding predecessors, the baby boomers, can bring successful results.

Much more mobile

Recent research reveals that 60 percent of today's employees plan to look for a new job within the next year.[3] Millennials are much more mobile than past generations, both in terms of the organization they work for and the region of the world in which they work. And this is a global phenomenon, even in Japan, where people used to be locked into to an organization.

When top employees leave, mediocre ones are left behind, which is not a good thing for the organization. So the employer is faced with trying to come up with a balance between what is good for the organization and what is good for employees. And organizations are aware that they are all competing for top talent in a rapidly developing workforce in an age of eternal change. Organizations that don't focus on this will find themselves with high attrition rates and high replacement costs. And this is true even in the current economic climate. I believe that most people and organizations take a long-term view: they realize that retaining top performers is as important during an economic downturn as during an upturn – and probably even more so.

In this environment, the big question organizations need to ask themselves is what they can do to keep top talent on board. This fresh breed of learners works in an entirely new employment environment, shaped by new perceptions and principles. They want to have the opportunity to expand their skills and knowledge constantly to prepare for the inevitable challenges they will face.

Over the years as a partner at PricewaterhouseCoopers (PwC) and as Dean of INSEAD, I have kept an eye on the expectations of new generations of managers entering the workforce and think I have worked out what these employees want and what keeps them in an organization from year to year. This is not the result of any scientific study, it is just what I have observed by engaging with colleagues and acquaintances, other deans, students at business schools, CEOs and corporations. Here are the results of my observations.

Three main concerns of top employees

The number one concern of today's employees is "What am I learning? Do I really feel I am growing?" I think this is because young people today take a much longer view of their career than did past generations of employees. Of course, some are looking to get rich quick, but most of the people I encounter are looking for a place that will challenge and excite them through what they are doing and what they are learning.

The millennial high-achiever has a competitive temperament and values learning as a means of attaining objectives. Thanks to new technologies, millennials are surrounded by an almost unlimited amount of easy-to-access information. As a result they thrive on research, appreciating the opportunity to develop and learn more. They want to work for an organization that can quench this thirst for knowledge and learning.

Concern number two is "Do I respect and value the organization I am working in and the people I am working with?" This can be seen in any employee survey. The most important questions concern pride in the organization and the quality of the people who work for it.

As a recent article in *Forbes* said, "When leaders treat their people as their business partners and involve them in making important decisions, those people feel respected, and respect leads to trust. If you respect your people and they trust you as a leader, they will give their all to get the best results they can for your organisation."[4]

The millennials cross all boundaries – social, cultural and geographic. They can choose which company they want to work for, and they are demanding because they want to work for an organization that is open-minded, diverse and meaningful. They also want to be respected and helped by their colleagues. Today's employees do not just go to work because they have to.

And the third concern is "Am I making a living wage?"

I still think of things (probably too much so) from how I would have dealt with them in the corporate environment. But I am also learning how to think from an academic institution's perspective. What I conclude is that, as academic institutions, we should be trying to help our partners in organizations to make a dent in this problem. I see the retention of top talent as a shared goal between academic organizations such as INSEAD and our clients, be they corporations, governments or NGOs. Incentives are vital to keep top talent motivated and loyal.

With this in mind, I shall now discuss six ideas or trends in training and leadership development that I believe could be applied to achieve these goals.

Corporate degree programs

One of the most important trends I see is the need to provide advanced business training to mid-level executives to motivate them, make them feel that their time with a company is well spent and that they are gaining something valuable by staying with the company.

Macquarie is a good example of a company addressing this concern. At INSEAD, we initiated a three-year Master of Finance program with Macquarie Investment Bank in 2007.

Macquarie is a global institution which had the idea of creating a degree program for their investment banking cohort. The first three intakes have numbered between 80 and 100 people each, and there are about 250 people currently participating in the program. The participants continue in their current role in the bank and spend time undertaking residential modules, usually for three weeks twice a year. The modules are currently presented in Sydney, Singapore, Fontainebleau and New York. The cohort travels to each location at least once during the program.

Today, training is all about flexibility. Employees have many commitments, both personal and professional, and have to multitask, so though they wish for training, it has to fit into their lifestyle.

I think this program is brilliant from Macquarie's point of view because they are creating a game-changing academic experience for their people and building a tremendous amount of loyalty to the organization. I expect that this kind of model will be considered by many companies in the coming years and it is incumbent on academic institutions to create delivery models that will work in these programs.

Ian Woodward, Program Director for Macquarie's Master in Finance, feels that what we have set up is unique: "There are plenty of courses (run by other banks) but they don't confer a degree. It's the only investment banking-focused degree from a top ten business school. Our people study in multiple residential sessions while they work for us – gaining experience and learning together."[5]

Courses like this are the future, as top talent needs to gain technical skills but also to develop their leadership capabilities. With Macquarie, we have been able to build a program that is tailored specifically to meet their needs.

Other international corporations such as Apple, Pixar, Axa, Lufthansa and McDonald's have set up their own internal corporate universities to train and motivate their top talent in-house.

Coaching

Another trend that is addressing the demands of millennials is coaching. The value that MBAs and executives place on coaching can be seen in the fast-growing demand for coaching within organizations and business schools.

The reason for this may be that coaching itself has evolved to meet the needs of a greater number of people. Once considered "remedial" – a last attempt to salvage an underperforming executive – coaching is now a fully integrated part of many leadership development courses. Coaching not only contributes to improving individual performance, but can also have a trickle-down effect on the organization once the participant returns home and experiments with what has been learned.

It is clear that, in the next few years, the coaching profession will demand a higher level of training, qualification and supervision for people who want to work in this field, and INSEAD is already at the forefront in this respect. I was amazed when I joined INSEAD to learn that there are around fifty professional coaches on the staff or on *per diem*.

Like many business schools, we have even created a research centre dedicated to coaching. Called the INSEAD Global Leadership Centre, the Centre is dedicated to executive coaching and leadership development research. It works with coaches who have clinical training or graduate degrees in coaching, and years of experience in the business world.

Our approach to coaching, which draws on psychodynamic theory and business knowledge, helps leaders to reflect, experiment, change and find solutions within themselves and their own context. Participants find this approach particularly challenging and rewarding, since it remains firmly focused on their own issues and concerns, rather than on a generic case study. The Centre has also trained hundreds of coaches to use this method through the Consulting and Coaching for Change course.

At INSEAD, we developed an innovative group coaching approach, in which participants work in small peer groups of five to six people, with a coach–facilitator to share and analyze their own 360-degree feedback reports, discuss their career history and future goals, and create action plans to carry out with ongoing support from the group. In these turbulent times, we are finding that people are more open to discussing their background, assessing their behavior and style, and receiving critical feedback. INSEAD participants often tell us that they come to leadership courses not only to brush up their functional skills, but also to take time out from the demands of everyday professional life to reflect on their own desires and goals, and they value this "reflective space" very highly. We have had thousands of participants in group coaching sessions. The method is very effective in all cultures, and is also suited to specific groups such as boards, or specific contexts such as mergers or leadership succession.

Participants often state that leadership development and coaching courses have been one of the best experiences of their professional life. They give reasons that go beyond the obvious ones of gaining additional knowledge regarding organizational operations. Participants say that they appreciate the support (or push) that helps them to make changes in their own behavior, and better understand group dynamics. This new learning is particularly relevant for participants who are themselves in a career transition, or who are leading change at the organizational level. Group coaching is still quite rare but, as one of the largest providers of group coaching in the world, we are already aware of the benefits. The small-group coaching experience – a safe environment in which participants push one another to a level that is challenging but not uncomfortable, and where peers work together to realign career choices and analyze personal leadership style – is an extremely valuable experience, both for individuals and for their organizations.

Indeed, I believe this is where the future of coaching lies. As our Global Leadership Centre says in its mission statement: "Our objective is to create profitable, sustainable organizations that are great places to work." This addresses directly what we hear from our client companies: popular demand for the coaching element of our leadership development programs is driven increasingly by employer needs. I see organizational coaching as a huge value-added component for academic institutions, and expect to see this trend grow and develop further over time. From one-on-one coaching, and leadership development programs on campus, to company-specific programs taking place in-house, coaching is vital to help key people develop the competences and self-awareness to become more effective, and reflective, leaders – something today's employee is seeking, and today's organization cannot afford to ignore.

Building block degree programs

The third observation I shall mention is one that is not very well developed but I think it has potential for all of us, and when I say all of us I am talking about both the academic side and the organizational side. This is what I refer to as building block degree programs.

Every academic institution has a series of programs on offer. One of the things I wonder about is whether it would make sense for employees to follow a series of programs as they progress in their career? For example, at the age of 25 to 30 employees would undertake the general management program, developed for people taking on a supervisory role for the first time. Five years later they would enrol in a more advanced program for those taking on profit and loss (P&L) responsibility for the first time. This would be followed later by an advanced program for people running larger businesses for the first time. I am sure that building block programs could also be designed for HR professionals, finance professionals and others. Today's workforce wants an attractive future to aim for. This means that they want a career path that guarantees them personal and professional growth and learning to take forward themselves and their organization.

My other thought is that we should be offering something like a degree to people completing the entire course of study in a particular area. There is also potential here for joint-degree programs. For example, I have noticed on my travels and in meetings with alumni that many INSEAD MBA alumni go on to the Harvard Advanced Management Program, and many of the Harvard MBA alumni take part in the INSEAD Advanced Management Program. Perhaps a dual-degree could be developed for these people. Personal and professional networks are vital for today's leaders, who are conscious that their assets are even stronger once they are linked to the diverse strengths of others. The reason I say this is that I think it is up to us as academic institutions to develop programs and credentials that will be of the most benefit to our alumni and the organizations for which they work. I think we shall need to be much more proactive in the future to create and disseminate these value propositions.

This kind of continuous learning would also be responsive to one of the issues coming out of the financial crisis: lifelong learning. Today, it is not enough for an individual merely to get an MBA and assume he or she doesn't need anything more over a long career. I think business schools need to embrace this concept in a more organized way.

Virtual learning

Today, millennials have embraced technology in every sense of the word and in every part of their life, and now more than ever, it plays a significant role in their learning.

The online virtual environment is something I began to explore because I have a faculty member, Miklos Sarvary, who, with great foresight, decided a few years ago to build an INSEAD virtual campus in Second Life. If you have not yet had an opportunity to visit Second Life, it is worth taking a look as it is very interesting and, according to the experts, it is the kind of technology interface that will play an increasingly important role in the near future. You can create your own persona via an "avatar" that represents you in the 3-dimensional world of Second Life. Unlike other 3D game environments, however, in Second Life there are no rules so the users can create whatever they like. Anyone can buy virtual land (from Linden Lab, the creator of Second Life) and build what they want on it.

INSEAD has the reputation of being innovative and open to new ideas. We also have a long history of creating web-enabled business tools, such as simulations, that allow participants to "learn by doing". Second Life has provided us with a wonderful environment in which to explore new ways of delivering learning, of extending our reach, and even opens up new possibilities for carrying out research. As Miklos Sarvary says, "For a multi-campus establishment like INSEAD, Second Life is revolutionary."

Applications of our virtual environment

A number of our faculty and PhD students are doing research within the virtual environment. It can be much easier and less costly to set up experiments in Second Life rather than in real life, and this medium lends itself particularly well to research on marketing, consumer behavior or social norms. In conjunction with our behavioral lab in Paris, we have several academic research projects currently under way.

We have held classes in our Second Life campus for our MBA and Executive MBA programs. We have also created small meeting rooms adapted to peer-coaching groups or teamwork so that our participants can connect up at any time, avatar to avatar. Our receptionists, who are present on our campuses in France, Singapore and Abu Dhabi, are also logged on to our reception desk in Second Life in real time, so they can greet visitors, give information and act as hosts for our virtual events.

Second Life has proved to be extremely useful for events where our alumni cannot always attend. We have held alumni reunions with live video streaming in order to reach out to our friends across the globe who are unable to join us. The virtual amphitheater is also projected up in the real amphitheater so that both audiences feel part of the same event, and virtual participants can send in their questions to make it fully interactive.

About every two to three months we hold MBA information and master class sessions in Second Life, to communicate with potential candidates who are not necessarily able to visit our campuses in person. This also allows us to target some geographic regions we do not necessarily have the opportunity to visit as often as we would like, and to provide the information we would normally share during face-to-face meetings. There are even some advantages to virtual versus real-life participation. For example, in the virtual classroom, a participant does not have to be in the front row or be particularly extrovert to ask questions, and we find that it levels out the interaction as everyone is equal behind their computer. People who might be slightly reluctant to raise their hand in a real audience are able to type in a question and receive a personalized response in real time. During the session, prospective MBA participants also get the chance to meet alumni and current students and can ask them questions directly. This aspect is more easily organized in Second Life.

Nowadays, virtual worlds such as Second Life play a significant part in the digital marketplace and have a real impact on the economy. So, twice a year, we run B2B marketing classes, where MBA participants have to create an avatar and meet in the virtual classroom to present their teamwork. They have to research business applications within the virtual world by going there directly.

Many major international corporations, including some of our key clients, have a virtual presence and are actively using Second Life to develop their business activities. For example, Coca-Cola has a virtual island for marketing purposes, Alstom has used it for recruiting initiatives, and BP recently held a virtual awards ceremony in Second Life with senior managers across the globe, to avoid the cost and disruption of participants having to travel. So there are some obvious cost-effective applications, and despite recent disen-chantment with Second Life because some organizations have experimented and decided to withdraw their presence, it is still amazing to realize that over US$1 million are being spent in user-to-user transactions on a daily basis. Apparently, this money is being spent on goods (both real and virtual) and transactions within the virtual world, but in addition there is a huge amount of related business being generated, such as services to design and build the virtual spaces.

It is a fascinating and original way for students to understand business trends and learn about new technologies, by actually immersing themselves in the environment, rather than just reading about it: "Our campus on Second Life certainly puts us at the forefront of new technology and helps us to cut down on travel and physical building expenses".[6]

I am a firm believer that networking is a big part of any educational experience and therefore I do not anticipate that we at INSEAD will move to fully remote programs where the participants never physically meet each other or the faculty members. But I do believe that there is a lot we can do within our programs to supplement physical meetings. Virtual environments are a relatively easy and low-cost way to stay connected and for us to offer follow-up solutions.

Ethics

Millennials are also concerned about ethics. As a result, another main objective of business schools today is to make tomorrow's leaders holistic, sensible, responsible and genuinely concerned about their society and community.

As business changes, business schools must meet the demands of the workplace. We have to give more curriculum importance to social responsibility, ethical thinking and ecological content. It is vital that everyone realizes that good ethics equals good business. If business schools do not focus more on ethics now, the present concern we all have over business ethics will fade away. It is time to highlight the limits of financial reasoning and concentrate on whether companies make ethical decisions, and to scrutinize the unethical side of business. Our future leaders must set an example and we must adhere to corporate codes of conduct.

Some Harvard Business School students launched the MBA Oath[7] in 2009, which asked MBAs to sign up to take an oath. Whether one is for or against such an oath, this step shows the way that business schools are heading.

MBAs themselves are more aware about the world they live in and many are planning to join not-for-profit organizations or non-governmental organizations (NGOs) or even to set up their own social entrepreneurship business after graduating. Many recent graduates say that social innovation offerings and field courses have the strongest impact on them during their MBA course and are often the reason behind their choice of business school.

Many businesses are also competing to be on the annual list of the World's Most Ethical Companies.[8] Companies are contending through setting impressive examples by developing social objectives which become a part of their core business and lead to the development of new products, competencies, business models and innovative processes.

Business schools are also experimenting with innovative programs. Partnerships are being fostered which team private companies with NGOs, and our MBAs are integrated into project teams. These kinds of projects are unique and offer practical experience, which can be extremely valuable to future leaders.

In just a decade, business schools, along with business, have made exceptional progress to become socially responsible. These steps will be an important basis for future distinctive MBA programs.

Senior development

My final thought is represented by something I say to my children all the time: "You're probably going to live to be 100 years old. Your career doesn't have to end at 55 or 60 or 65, or whatever is the traditional retirement age." There are more and more seniors today and they need jobs. We should start to look at our career in compartments.

As a result of the recent financial crisis, more people are considering continuing to work beyond the traditional retirement age, or do not have the choice. Many of these people will need to be retrained or to train other people by sharing their skills. Business schools must adapt to be able to incorporate this generation into their curriculum to face the needs of business in the future.

What this means for academic institutions and organizations is that it provides a much broader recruiting field for both sides. I can see programs for people at age 60 looking to make a career change, or someone at age 70 saying "I haven't been a director yet. I want to do that." Or "I want to go into the not-for-profit environment now that I have had a fantastic for-profit career." So I think senior programs and transition programs with a much longer lifespan in mind are going to be another enormous trend.

Preparing leaders

I began by stating that organizations have entered a new phase where their control over employees is less firm than it used to be. In this new environment, business schools are uniquely placed to help these organizations provide the incentives their top employees are seeking to stay with the organization and continue to contribute to its long-term success. To do this, business schools must adapt to the new needs of organizations (and their employees) and develop programs and methods that address these needs.

Today's millennial managers are tomorrow's leaders. If businesses are to retain their top talent, they will have to meet the expectations of their managers, who are increasingly mobile and more hands-on. High achievers and competitive, millennial managers take a longer view of their career and demand an environment that will enhance their learning and promote their own evolution. Operating in a technology-driven, fast-evolving business environment, millennial managers need educational programs that will take into consideration their work and lifestyle.

In today's environment, business schools are presented with excellent opportunities to innovate and provide millennials with the education they are seeking. In this chapter I have outlined a few ideas and examples that are emerging or may contribute to changing the business education landscape. Corporate programs that are flexible in time and space and offer a degree to enhance the participant's credentials, meet a number of these requisites. Coaching will, I am sure, be more widely practiced as business schools respond effectively to the managers' demand for feedback and advice on their individual behavior and style. Building block degrees and senior development programs can be developed for millennial careers, which will evolve beyond the traditional retirement age. Virtual learning is already revolutionizing many aspects of education and networking. The years ahead will bring fascinating innovations that business schools will need to use to their advantage. And last but not least, business schools will have a fundamental role in educating millennial managers on integrating ethics and corporate social responsibility in their tasks.

Some of the ideas and trends I have discussed could be useful in developing such new programs. By focusing on the main concerns of today's generation of employees, organizations will be preparing managers with the skills and commitment to lead the organization into the future.

NOTES

1 Geoff Gloeckler, "The Millennials Invade the B-Schools", *BusinessWeek,* 13 November 2008.

2 R. Alsop (2008) *The Trophy Kids Grow Up: How the Millennial Generation Is Shaking Up the Workplace,* New York: John Wiley.

3 Salary.com (2008/09) Employee Satisfaction and Retention Survey and Reuters survey, November 2009.

4 Ken Blanchard and Terry Waghorn, "Make Sure Your Employees Trust You – Or Else", Forbes.com, 23 March 2009.

5 Jo Studdert, "Mac Bank's Masters", 5 November 2007, Available at eFinancial-Careers.com.au.

6 Francesca Di Meglio, "I Was a Second Life B-School Student", *BusinessWeek*, 16 April 2007.

7 The MBA Oath: http://mbaoath.org/.

8 http://ethisphere.com/wme2009/.

Collaborative Leadership: New Perspectives in Leadership Development

ARNOUD DE MEYER, President, Singapore Management University

Introduction

Business schools, and MBA programs in particular, are about leadership development. We are preparing our graduates to take on leadership positions in the world of business, government and NGOs. A cursory glance at the websites of many of the top business schools reveals that, one way or another, we put leadership at the core of our unique selling propositions. Developing for leadership, grooming for international leadership, educating leaders who will make a difference in the world, and so on, are just a few of the iterations one can find on our websites.

But what do these leadership qualities really stand for? Research on leadership has, of course, produced multiple varieties of leadership (Kets de Vries, 2000), ranging from traditional "command and control" leadership, moral authority, intuitive, charismatic or seductive leadership, through to the capability to become a global learner. This broad and, frankly speaking, sometimes disjointed literature on leadership does not help us to go much further in defining what business schools have to offer in their programs in order to prepare the graduates for the challenges in the professional world. And sometimes it seems that there is no clear difference in the programs of our schools with respect to what leadership on the one hand and management on the other is all about. Leadership and management are indeed often confused with each other.

In my opinion the best approach to what business schools need to do, is to prepare our graduates to become effective innovators and managers of change. This is very much in line with how Kotter defined leadership: management is about coping with complexity, leadership is about coping with change (Kotter, 1990). Organizations need to change constantly to survive, and it is the capability to provide leadership for this process of change that will make our MBA graduates attractive to recruiters and successful in their professional development.

Providing leadership to manage change is to some extent contextual. It is dependent on the culture in which one operates (Schneider and Barsoux, 2003), is contingent on the objectives of the organization – for example, nonprofit versus a profit orientation – and has to adjust to the changing challenges of the economic environment. I shall build the case in this chapter that in many circumstances today a *collaborative approach to leadership* is better adapted to cope with the emerging environment in which our MBA graduates will have to operate.

Collaborative leadership

All too often leadership is associated with "having power over" people, as opposed to having power *with* people about the change process. In such an approach, leadership is associated with formal command and control, or with a charismatic leadership style, where the leader may seduce groups of followers to, sometimes blindly, execute his or her wishes. I am deliberately presenting a rather extreme view, but I am doing so to contrast it with a style of leadership I would call responsible and collective.

Mary Parker Follett, the early-twentieth-century social worker and management guru *"avant la lettre"*, described management as "the art of getting things done through people". She was a specialist on social communities and education, but her analysis has been influential in management literature, in particular through the human resources school of management. She believed essentially in the power of people working together, and that, to get things done, one needed to form a community. She distinguished between operating change in a coercive manner versus operating in a coactive manner, and considered a community as a creative process that can be effective through constantly reframing the issues at hand.

I am convinced that we may have to revisit this, because "working through" people, who are often your peers, is more aligned with the needs of change management today. Current-day leadership may require more than the coacting that Mary Parker Follett argued for, but it is very much based on it. I shall argue that effective leadership in the current climate requires collaboration, listening, influencing and flexible adaptation, rather than command and control. This

I define as collaborative leadership. But let me first suggest why such a new approach to leadership is needed.

What is changing in our environment?

Managing change today is not what it used to be. Or rather the environment in which we need to innovate and implement change has changed dramatically. Before the difficulties in the financial sector in 2007 and 2008, and the ensuing economic downturn, I might have attributed this change to eight important trends. These were, in no particular order, the growing internationalization of organizations; the fragmentation of value chains; the creeping increase in numbers of knowledge workers; the demands that civil society puts on companies to be drivers of social change; the diffusion of sources of knowledge production and innovation; the increasingly networked nature of multinational organizations; the need for risk management in a world where the gradual reduction of borders and trade barriers has led to an increasingly level playing field for companies; and the role of information and telecommunication technologies in networking. I shall summarize below what I mean in each case.

Globalization

We are living in a world that has become truly international, and where organizations themselves have also become truly international. It may be a sweeping generalization, but there are very few "national" companies now: companies are either regional or international.

We know that internationalization is not totally new. There have been previous waves of internationalization, notably the one started in the industrializing nineteenth century before being halted by the First World War. This should remind us that globalization movements can be reversed. And current globalization is not without its flaws. Critics of the free market attitude to internationalization often point out the short-term negative effects of globalization – for example, the exploitation of labor in low-labor-cost countries; the faster spread of diseases (as illustrated by the H1N1 virus); the increasing difficulties associated with migration; or the shift of operational and production jobs to emerging countries. And they warn about the risk of industrial desertification of Europe and the United States. Our own research suggests that this not necessarily the case, and that the growth of

manufacturing in emerging countries such as China is more a response to
rising demand there, rather than a systematic transfer of production capacity
(Vereecke and De Meyer, 2009). Others may argue that China does not
always play by the rules of the free trade game, and that internationalization
is one-sided. As a consequence one hears in Europe a number of voices
among politicians calling for a better-managed globalization, if not for more
protectionism. But while I think that the future shape of globalization may be
different from what it is today, and may go through some serious challenges
and upheavals, I remain convinced that globalization is a trend that will be
difficult to stop and that our organizations must develop a greater capability
to operate on an international scale.

This may be relatively straightforward and accepted by large companies
and organizations, but even small and medium-sized enterprises and nonprofit
organizations are often networked and integrated into international networks
of suppliers, subcontractors, distributors and partners. Many of these smaller
organizations have also become truly international. As a consequence they
have to manage diversity, both culturally and geographically. And they have
to understand how international supply chains operate and how global
geopolitical trends influence their markets for talent, resources and outputs.

This increased globalization requires increased networking. A purely
transactional approach to doing business may work in some specific business
cultures – for example, the USA – but is not the general standard. Partners in
internationalization rarely accept that one of them is dominant. As I mentioned
above, there is no one-size-fits-all solution for leading change. It is contextual,
and has to be adapted to the key characteristics of the cultural, religious and
geographical environment in which it operates. This cultural sensitivity must
become an order of magnitude more sophisticated than it used to be in the
1990s. This is illustrated by a growing body of literature on international
alliances and the role of culture in their performance, which indicates the
necessity of managing the cultural differences extremely carefully to achieve
value creation through joint ventures and alliances (Sirmon and Lane, 2004).

Fragmentation of the value chain

A corollary of the internationalization of business and commerce is the
increased fragmentation of value chains resulting from outsourcing and
collaborative networks for the design and delivery of goods. Few, if any,
companies still control their whole value chain. Vertical integration seems to

be out of fashion. In fact, the recommendation to focus on the core business of the organization and to outsource or subcontract all nonessential activities has been one of the most successful messages from both business schools and consultants since the mid-1990s. As a consequence, companies have outsourced many activities and have fragmented their value creation. They have created collaborative networks for value creation.

The outsourcing occurs on an international scale, and often involves partners that are lot bigger than the company itself. Some medium-sized European companies have outsourced their supply chain management or their IT division to organizations that are an order of magnitude bigger than they are themselves. This leads to major changes in the natural power equilibrium in the value chain. Some suppliers have become true partners. But some outsourcing partners may be in a position of power *vis-à-vis* their principal, and in a position to dictate terms and impose their systems. Managing change and providing leadership in these collaborative networks cannot rely on traditional power relations and hierarchies, but requires a style of management that is again based on seduction and persuasion (Mukherjee, 2008).

More knowledge workers

For many organizations the main production factors remain people, capital and, in the case of manufacturing, raw materials and components. But knowledge has become a production factor of growing importance. In recruiting we now often look for brains as well as a pair of hands. A large proportion of the workforce now consists of knowledge workers: people whose major contribution to value creation is their creativity and expertise. Modern knowledge workers often have a rather different attitude from their traditional counterparts; they are often more independent, more loyal to their area of expertise than to their organization, and dislike authority unless it is based on expertise. In short, they require a somewhat different style of leadership, one that is based on seduction and convincing on the basis of rational arguments, rather than on command and control (De Meyer *et al.*, 2001).

One can argue that this is not really new. There have always been a small number of knowledge workers in organizations, and many organizations had research and development (R&D) departments that were full of experts and knowledge professionals. And professional businesses such as those of consultants, accountants or lawyers have always been built around people who invest in knowledge production and deployment. But as long as the knowledge workers remained a relatively marginal group in the organization, or if professional businesses were relatively small, it was possible to lead them on a quasi-individualized, ad hoc basis.

The growing importance of knowledge workers and the increasing size of professional businesses require systems to be developed to lead them, and this needs in many cases a true transformation of organizations.

The increasing demands of society

Society has a growing expectation about the contributions from companies to the social sphere. Since the 1980s we have seen the triumph of shareholder-value-based organizations. One of the underlying assumptions of this approach was that the main, if not the only, role of a company was to create value for its shareholders – and, by doing so, the company would create wealth for society. No more was expected of them. The redistribution of wealth was the state's role, or in some cases this was left to philanthropy. This is a somewhat stylized view, and many companies did engage in socially-focused activities, thus embracing some corporate social responsibility.

But the growing trend of corporatization and privatization of public services has changed this extreme view. Many companies are now expected by their governments to engage in public–private partnership to support education, health provision, public transport, and in some cases even security and protection – all services that were traditionally provided by the state. Society does not care necessarily about the mantra of shareholder value and expects profit-oriented organizations to behave as corporate citizens (Jones *et al.*, 2007). Interestingly enough, even Jack Welch, the former CEO of GE (General Electric Company), who was often closely associated with the implementation of the shareholder value concept, has recently questioned its relevance (*Financial Times*, 2009). And one should not forget that companies in emerging countries have always been expected to help in nation-building.

As a consequence of this trend, leadership more than ever requires integrating and working with local and national communities to preserve the integrity of the company's image and brand. This is more than a watered-down program for corporate social responsibility, which is often seen by senior managers as a form of soft reputation- or brand-building. The new leadership requires that the integration with the community is at the heart of what the company sees as its way of creating value.

Dispersion of the sources of knowledge and innovation

In contrast to the twentieth century, the source of innovation today is no longer limited to a fixed set of sources in the industrialized world. In the 1970s the world looked relatively simple. In most of the areas of innovation, in particular if such innovation was enabled by technology, the sources of innovative ideas were rather limited and concentrated. Innovation based on microelectronics and software in the 1960s and 1970s virtually all came out of Silicon Valley, Boston or Texas in the USA. Pharmaceutical innovation was perhaps spread a little more extensively, but there were only a few major centres of innovation – in the USA, the UK, Switzerland and Germany. Innovation in the automotive industry was also concentrated in just a few places, again in Germany, in Italy and in Detroit in the USA. This has gradually changed and the sources of ideas and knowledge, but also the sources of innovative consumer behavior have become much more dispersed (Doz *et al.,* 2002). To follow what is going on today in genetic engineering you have to access what is discussed on the west and east Coasts of the USA, Cambridge (UK), the South of Sweden, Munich, the north of Italy, Bangalore, Singapore and Seoul.

At the same time we are witnessing the emergence of a lower middle class with specific and different consumer preferences in the emerging countries such as China, India, South East Asia and Latin America. By my own approximate calculations, on the basis of statistics provided by the Asian Development Bank, there are at least about 580 million people living in the South, South East and East Asia at this level of lower middle class (defined as a spending power for an average family of at least €5,000 per year) or above. This is almost twice the number of consumers in the USA and one and a half times those in the European Union. One can see this group as a target for products developed in Japan, the USA or Europe. However, they are also a formidable source of new ideas (De Meyer and Garg, 2005). Recently we have seen many examples published of innovations created for the "bottom of the pyramid", and it has been pointed out that when it comes to innovation with mobile phones, operators in emerging countries such as India, the Philippines or East Africa have been leading the world.

Leading change in a world where the sources of ideas for innovation have become so dispersed will require people who can pick up ideas from all over the world, and can combine these ideas into new products, services and organizations, and roll these out in a very effective way.

Changes in the structure of multinationals

Multinational organizations are moving from a triangular organizational structure (with the boss at the top) to a networked structure. Multinational, transnational or global organizations might well have had different structures, but most of them had a clear reporting path to one headquarters (HQ). They may have operated on an international scale, but they often had a very clear national image, and binational organizations such as Shell or Unilever were a great exception. This "master–slave" organization, whereby the regional organizations and subsidiaries reported to a master at the HQ, is gradually slipping away, not least because of the commercial and financial success of some of the subsidiaries in emerging regions, that demand a more equitable balance of power in the organization (Palmisano, 2006). This is reinforced by the technological developments that allow for international coordination and integration of employees without having them colocated in one place. This flattening of organizations and distribution of organizational power may better reflect the current reality of these multinationals, but it has the disadvantage that it reduces clarity. Managing change in such networked and flatter organizations, where the core management group is not necessarily in a single location, and where power is more evenly distributed, will require managers that can live with ambiguity and can trigger action through collaboration.

Increased importance of risk management

Good leaders will be those who can calculate and cope with risk. As I argued earlier, the internationalization of the world economy goes through cycles and is likely to keep on doing so. But unless there is a major geopolitical catastrophe, I dare to predict that we shall continue to see in the long term a growing internationalization of trade, a reduction of trade barriers and a decrease in the importance of national borders. This reduces the protection of the individual firm by its national authorities and increases the interdependence of the players in the world market. It also means that shock waves will spread faster throughout the world, and that the amplitude of shocks may increase. The speed with which the demise of Lehman Brothers influenced the rest of the financial world was a simple illustration of this. It means higher risks.

In such a world, the quality of both management and leadership becomes more important for the success of an organization than does the protection offered by staying behind trade barriers and the advantages provided by artificial information asymmetries provided by helpful governments. Managers will become more exposed and high quality leaders will be those who can estimate risk and uncertainty, and are better at coping with it through experimentation and quick learning (Loch *et al.*, 2006). Such experimentation and learning will require people who are more sensitive to weak signals in their environment, and have the ability to avoid small disruptions becoming amplified once they start rolling though the networks.

The role of ICT in networking

It has become a commonplace that information and communication technologies (ICT) are changing the world. In reality the world of business has adapted quickly and remarkably well to the opportunities that are offered through better electronic communication. But I am convinced that there are two areas where we are only seeing the start of the challenge: how do we exploit the value and the format of the weak ties that are created in the social networking sites; and how do we cope with information overload?

Social networking as we observe it in Facebook, LinkedIn, Baidu, Orkut or YouTube has increased by several orders of magnitude the number and the nature of weak ties (Fraser and Dutta, 2008). As we know from research carried out since the 1970s, these weak ties are of high importance in getting things done, and in asserting leadership (Granovetter, 1973). I am convinced that we have yet to scratch the surface of how to manage and obtain an advantage from these new types of relationships in the business world. This is a significant challenge, not least because we still do not know which social networking concept will be the winner: the dominant design of social networking has still to emerge. I have seen several companies which experiment with internal social networking sites, but who seem perplexed as to how to manage or leverage the enormous activity that has developed so quickly over these internal networking sites. The leader of tomorrow will need to use this abundance of weak ties to his or her advantage in the management of change.

Moreover, as a consequence of these new networks and many other developments in the internet world, we have moved from a situation of information scarcity to one of information abundance. Most of our decision analysis and management tools were developed for a world with a scarcity of information. Satisfying behavior when it comes to information processing has been one of the mantras in the management literature. We do not yet have the tools to lead and decide in a world where everybody has access to an abundance of information, and where every decision can be challenged, based on evidence available on the World Wide Web. Once again, the ability to exploit this abundance of information and the mobilization of the experts who own this knowledge will be the hallmark of a good leader.

And all these changes in a very different context for the markets

As I mentioned above, a year ago I would have argued that these eight categories captured to a large extent the changes in the context in which we need to exert our leadership. The financial turbulence in 2008 and the ensuing economic crisis have in fact created an additional difference. We are coming out of a period of almost thirty years where "business was good". The most eagerly pursued jobs were in business, business leaders were upheld as role models, and the top talent wanted to have a job in finance or business. Entrepreneurship had become popular entertainment on TV. Governments were lectured by business people on how to run their affairs. Running public services required a business attitude. Public–private partnerships were often well-accepted disguises for privatization. Regulation could be better replaced by self-regulation and codes of conduct. Business was good for you!

The recent crisis and scandals in which some business leaders have shown incompetence and an inability to self-regulate satisfactorily may well change this attitude of society in a dramatic way. I fear that the pendulum is swinging back and that in the coming years the business world will constantly have to justify its actions to an increasingly skeptical society. That in turn will impose new requirements on business leaders in terms of interactions with the societies in which they operate. They might be admired less as "captains of industry", and increasingly vilified as incompetent schemers. Let us hope that this will not be true, but we cannot avoid preparing for the possibility. A cursory reading of any mainstream newspaper is not allaying my fears.

Business leaders will have to become active marketers for the values of good management and leadership. And they will need to convince society that it can pick up a few ideas from them on how organizations should be run. True leadership will require us to collaborate with other stakeholders in society and improve communication about the role of business in society.

The new collaborative leader

I admit that the trends I have indicated are fairly general and to some extent speculative. Many of them are also correlated. But when you put them together, the picture that emerges suggests that the future leaders we train at business schools will require a different portfolio of skills compared to those in the first decade of the twenty-first century. What we need is more "responsible, collaborative leaders".

This is a different breed of leader from the one who leads through sheer power, expertise, charisma, or leadership based on dogma. It is a leader who can sometimes be at the same level as those among whom he or she wishes to implement change. And who wants to achieve results in innovation and change management by stimulating collaboration with peers. The four key words I would like to propose to describe the skill set that these future leaders will need are *collaboration*, *listening*, *influencing* and *adaptation*.

Collaboration

In many of the nine trends discussed above, the word network was used. Multinationals become networks, value is created in fragmented networks, knowledge workers prefer to work in networks of peers, ICT leads to networks of weak ties, and sources of new ideas come from combining ideas from different geographical and cultural networks. In these networks, management becomes "getting things done through a community of peers". Action requires *collaboration* with people – that is, to coact with others in order to implement change.

Good leaders should be able to operate within these networks and to become the drivers of them. This will require a willingness constantly to make significant strategic investments in networking and collaboration, and create a virtuous cycle of collaboration. Collaboration is in itself not always natural. Under pressure and faced with shortages of time and money we may prefer to isolate ourselves from a network, fall back on command and control, and implement all the changes ourselves. But collaborative leadership requires that one constantly makes the trade-off between going it alone and working through others, in favour of the latter.

Listening

Collaboration will not be effective unless we develop other capabilities. A good collaborative leader needs to sense what is going on with the peers. Often the signals these peers are sending are very weak and not codified. Knowing what is going on in the networks forces one to be alert to these weak signals. Providing collaborative leadership often requires being able to get under the skin of the peers, and mastering the art of responding quickly to their needs and uncertainties. Collaboration also requires a strong capacity to trust the peers and leave them the opportunity to develop their own entrepreneurial action in the face of change. All this requires an enhanced capacity to listen, both to internal and external signals and messages. But we need to recognize that the coveted capacity to listen should not lead to procrastination or immobility in decision-making.

Influencing

Change in these networks will not come through command and control. It requires evidence-based *influence*. Peers in social networks, knowledge workers, equals in the multinational networks, stakeholders in society all want to be convinced. Influencing rather than informing will become the required modus operandi. These peers often have their own insights, strong expertise and entrepreneurial drive, and prefer to act in teams of equals. If told what to do they may have excellent reasons and sufficient knowledge to disagree, in particular in a world where information has become abundant, and where information that exists outside one's organization is often as valuable as the information inside it. Their insights may well be as valuable as yours. And they will try to influence you. A good collaborative leader is the one who is able to influence and convince his or her peers without falling into the trap of becoming manipulative.

Adaptation

Finally the world is becoming more uncertain, and one that contains more risks. And there is less protection in the form of governments, artificial information asymmetries or trade barriers. Change and change management have become at the same time more complex because of the dispersion of sources of knowledge and innovation. Therefore the environment in which change needs to be implemented is becoming less predictable. The successful leader will be the one who is able to *adapt flexibly* and very rapidly to these changing circumstances. She or he needs to be able to appreciate and manage the increased risks in the environment. Agility is a must, but not at the expense of costly shortcuts in decision-making.

But beware, this is not a panacea

I am not arguing that all leadership should become collaborative. There may be good reasons why and circumstances where leadership should be of the old type of command and control. The transaction costs of collaborative leadership can be pretty high and there may be circumstances where the simplicity of the situation does not allow for the investment in collaboration. And one needs to recognize that, in the short term, collaborative leadership is not always the fastest. One can imagine that, for example, in the management of catastrophes one would prefer straightforward command and control. Or faced with a highly complex situation requiring a very high level of expertise one may prefer to revert to leadership based on technical expertise. But in cases where some of the trends I described earlier do apply, I would argue that collaboration should prevail.

And as I have already hinted, collaborative leadership may also have its dark side: listening may become procrastination, influencing may become manipulation, and flexible adaptation may come at the expense of thoroughness. One of the important elements of collaborative leadership is also restraint, and an ability to walk the fine line between the light and the dark side of its characteristics.

What does preparation for collaborative leadership require?

What needs to be done prepare young people for such collaborative leadership? A lot is about process, which I will discuss in the next section. But there are six insights to which those who aspire to be collaborative leaders should pay attention and understand.

Getting the right mindset

Collaborative leadership is partially about having the right attitude and mindset. It is about understanding that others have capabilities and are prepared to share these in order to achieve change and innovation, and this on condition that both leaders work on an equal basis. It is up to one leader to leverage this willingness to commit to the change that the other leader proposes. It is about being willing to make the tradeoff in favor of collaborating rather than going it alone. It is about being willing to invest in relationships. It requires being prepared to recognize the contributions of peers.

Corporate change these days is often about the continuing renewal of the business model. In the large majority of cases, new business models involve many partners, and getting the models implemented requires the collaboration of the partners and the suppliers, who can help to structure the information linkages that are needed to deliver the business model. It is necessary to recognize that operating alone one can achieve a little, whereas in a network one can achieve a lot.

Reducing transaction costs

Collaborative leadership is not free of charge. Collaboration requires interaction, has its coordination costs, and often requires the provision of leadership outside the boundaries of your own organization. You could even argue that collaboration may sap a lot of energy and thus be tiring for some of us.

To be successful, collaborative leaders must be good at recognizing the differences in values and organizational structures between profit and nonprofit organizations, between large and small organizations, and between firms and organizations with a different cultural anchorage. Organizations that collaborate may have very different, sometimes opposing objectives. This is all the more so when one collaborates with organizations from different countries, or with a fundamentally different value system. NGOs, government and business organizations need increasingly to work together. Collaborative leaders need to understand how one can share common action between organizations that have incompatible objectives and value systems. A good collaborative leader will know how to reduce transaction costs, mainly by building trust and investing in the informality of relationships. If successful, this will lead to a true collaboration, which may reduce the transaction costs in many ways.

Seeing beyond the borders of the organization

A good collaborative leader needs to understand that his or her domain of action does not stop at the borders of the organization. Organizational boundaries often become fuzzy in a collaborative world, and both authority and accountability do not stop at the border of the organization. Companies can be made accountable for what their subcontractors do, or how their partners communicate. Leadership has to go beyond the borders of the organization. Persuading other parties to build value together will be essential to any effective collaboration.

Building consensus

Action that is implemented through a community of peers requires consensus building and the creation of ownership to implement the decision among the widest group of peers.

But consensus building carries a big risk: it may lead to the acceptance of the lowest common denominator of the group and thus to suboptimal decisions. We need to understand how to build a consensus, but at the same time how to get the optimal and best-performing decision with the group.

We know from earlier research on culture and management that diversity can enhance the quality of decision-making, on condition that we confront the cultural and contextual differences (Schneider and Barsoux, 2003). The least effective thing to do is to cover up differences between individuals with a different cultural background, out of a misplaced sense of politeness, respect or political correctness. We do know that multicultural teams, compared to monocultural groups, either regress to a lower performance in the face of decisions, or perform significantly better. The worst-performing groups are those that cover up the differences, while the better-performing multicultural groups are those that confront and address the differences. Groups that are able to do so perform better than monocultural groups, because they benefit from the creativity and differences in perspective that the diversity offers.

It may still be a conjecture, but I would like to offer the hypothesis that collaborative leaders need to build consensus, but do this in such a way that they bring out the differences and tensions in the team, thereby enhancing the creativity and avoiding a reduction to the lowest common denominator.

Ability to network

Collaborative leaders need to be good social networkers. The creation of a wide network of weak ties will enhance significantly their ability to perform. We can and should teach potential leaders how to build and maintain these networks.

They need to understand how to build the perception of their identity with their peers, how to manage status and power relationships in the network, and how to develop the capabilities that the literature on R&D management describes as technological gatekeepers or boundary spanners (Allen, 1977). Gatekeepers are not necessarily the core social networkers in the internal team, or the eternal organizers of group activities – for example, social events or sports outings. But they are usually high performers, have social skills, are well connected both inside and outside their organization, and are capable of translating the information and knowledge that is abundantly available outside the network, into the jargon that is recognizable and actionable within it. This ability to spot such important information and translate it back into the internal network is no doubt their key value-added feature.

Again, I would like to venture the hypothesis that collaborative leadership has much in common with this ability to develop social networks, but also with infusing them with know-how that others may not have spotted, or where the relevance for the change to be implemented is not as clear. This role of translation is no doubt a key element in collaborative leadership, because it is part of the building-up of the credibility of the leader.

Managing the dualities

The world is full of dualities (Trompenaars and Hampden Turner, 1998). The right approach is often not "either/or", but rather "and/and". We need to conform to the group and yet think creatively outside the box. We need to be both formal and informal. We need to listen to experience and at the same time challenge it through experimentation. We want to make money, and we need to be socially responsive. We need to compete and we need to collaborate.

It is uncomfortable to live with such dualities. But in a collaborative world we have no choice.

Can you prepare young people for such leadership?

Can you teach this type of collaborative leadership? The answer is similar to that related to many other skills and capabilities that require some innate talent. You cannot transform a person with no talent into a successful collaborative leader, but you can take a rough diamond and polish it. You can hone the skills of those who have some aptitude for it.

Adult learning in a professional environment is always a combination of five major areas of activity: on-the-job training, mentoring, special projects, job rotation and formal education. The formal education is a very important element, because it helps to make sense of all the other activities.

Preparing a young person with high potential for a role as a collaborative leader also requires a combination of these five aspects. Formal education at a business school is a tremendous opportunity to help people to expand on the experiences they have had in collaborative leadership, conceptualizing these experiences, and giving them the confidence that these concepts are not idiosyncratic but can in fact be generalized and applied in many different circumstances. Business schools can and do play a very important role in speeding up this process of adult learning.

At the Judge Business School at the University of Cambridge we have been experimenting with collaborative leadership for almost a decade. It is probably partially in our genetic heritage as a collegiate university. The University of Cambridge consists of more than forty independent institutions that have to work together in the Cambridge ecosystem. A collegiate university is probably an age-old experiment in collaboration and collaborative leadership, because nobody has really strong power: we are only effective by working together and sharing strong values. Similarly, the ecosystem of small and medium-sized entrepreneurial high-tech companies clustered around the University of Cambridge seems to operate within a similar collaborative approach. One of the successful companies in Cambridge, ARM, a producer of reduced instruction set computing (RISC) processors for the mobile phone industry, is also an extreme example of working within networks (Williamson and De Meyer, 2009).

But even so, educating for collaborative leadership is still a new area for us and I do not pretend that we have here in Cambridge all the techniques to do this successfully. To stimulate a debate on how we can help to groom collaborative leaders for the coming decade I would like to make five propositions.

Leadership development is essentially experiential: adult learning is often about making sense of an individual's own experience gained through projects, on-the-job learning and so on. We need to provide our students with the opportunity to become masters of their own leadership destiny. Therefore our programs need to include a significant element of experiential learning. We do this, like many other business schools, through a great deal of group work, and classroom interactions with leaders. But we have also found it most helpful to include in the program two major group consulting projects: one with a small local organization (often high-tech entrepreneurial companies); and one with a globally operating large organization. These projects provide a relatively low-risk environment in which to experiment with collaborative leadership.

Learning about collaborative leadership requires *dialogue*. Rather than sticking to a single pedagogical method at the Cambridge Judge Business School, we believe in mixing lectures with cases discussions, *interactions* with leaders, group work and so on, and above all, that interaction between all involved in the learning process is at the heart of adult learning. I do believe that, ultimately, we learn when we can formulate our own insights. Dialogue is probably at the heart of what collaboration is all about.

Collaborative leadership development requires interdisciplinary interactions, beyond the boundaries of a business, and of business in general. It requires strong interactions and learning from scientists, social leaders, politicians, philosophers and so on, to create openness in one's thinking and an ability to listen to information coming from unexpected areas. In a sense, we are blessed by being a business school operating at the heart of the University of Cambridge, and one that has resolutely chosen to be integrated with the other departments. Beyond the opportunity for interdisciplinary research opportunities that this creates, it is also a way of bringing a wide range of colleagues from other departments into the learning activities.

Collaborative leadership requires our students to learn *how to manage the difficult triangle of simultaneously listening, influencing and keeping an action orientation*. Collaborative leadership requires all three, and it is all too easy to fall into the trap of overemphasizing only one or two of them. Listening alone may be good for a coach or a counsellor. Influencing alone is good for a teacher or a consultant. And action alone is perhaps good for a crisis manager. But true collaborative leadership requires a careful balance between all three. The balance is also important because it is the best way to exercise the restraint I mentioned earlier. Collaborative leadership has its dark side, and striking the right balance between listening, influencing and action is perhaps the best way of exercising restraint.

Leadership is about *managing constant change*. Collaborative leadership requires that such change is managed through others. But constant change is tiring, and the collaborative leader needs to find the energy to keep on driving through the change, as well as developing the energy for his or her peers to do the same. I find this at once the most challenging and the easiest task in helping students to learn about collaborative leadership. We need to inspire our students to find and create energy for themselves and for others. It is difficult because energy is not that easy to create, but it becomes easy when we can make students see that there is energy in working with others and in doing things you like to do.

It may appear from the description of my five propositions that I consider this type of leadership development to a large extent experiential. This is partially true, but a lot of what we do is anchored in concepts we studied in our research, and translated into theory and practical concepts. Formal knowledge-sharing and capability development are part of each of these five areas (de Rond, 2008).

Finally, we need to accept that leaders in a risky, networked world cannot predict and control everything, and that a *measure of luck* is needed. Tongue in cheek, I would like to argue that we need to believe in the logic of luck. Successful action is not only about cold analysis and structured decision-making. *Once you are lucky you have to be able to spot it* and exploit it quickly. That is another trick we think our students can learn.

Conclusion

There is an old adage that says leadership styles have to "fit" the context in order to be effective. The case I wanted to present is that the changes in the environment of our enterprises and nonprofit organizations is such that a more collaborative style of leadership is currently perhaps more appropriate than some of the more traditional styles of leadership. I defined that type of leadership with four key words: collaboration, listening, influencing and adaptation, and described what the focal points should be for those who want to adopt such a leadership style.

As a leader of a business school I have to think constantly about the role we can play in grooming good managers and good leaders. I am strongly convinced that business schools have a very important role to play in helping young people with high potential to recognize and conceptualize their own experiences with collaboration. And we can also help them in making the concepts actionable and useful in their own professional environment.

But in order to do this effectively I am sure that we in future-oriented business schools need to adapt our processes of adult learning. Most of us have gone away from a style of learning that is pure classroom teaching, or a quasi-dogmatic adherence to one particular pedagogical method. Our approach in Cambridge is nondogmatic and one of stimulating dialogue. And there is a lot to be said for more experiential and interdisciplinary learning, as well as showing students to keep action, listening and influencing in balance – as long as it is anchored in rigorous, relevant and revealing research.

REFERENCES

Allen, T. J. 1977. *Managing the Flow of Technology.* Cambridge, MA: MIT Press.

De Meyer, A., Dutta, S. and Srivastawa, S. 2001. *The Bright Stuff.* London: Prentice Hall.

De Meyer, A. and Garg, S. 2005. *Inspire to Innovate: Management and Innovation in Asia*. London: Pearson.

de Rond, M. 2008. *The Last Amateurs: To Hell and Back with the Cambridge Boat Race Crew*. London: Icon Books.

Doz, Y., Santos, J. and Williamson, P. 2002. *From Global to Metanational: How Companies Win in the Knowledge Economy*. Boston, MA: Harvard Business School Press.

Financial Times. 2009. "Welch Denounces Corporate Obsessions", 12 March.

Fraser, M. and Dutta, S. 2008. *Throwing Sheep in the Boardroom: How On-line Social Networking Will Change Your Life, Work and World*. New York: Wiley.

Granovetter, M. 1973. "The Strengths of Weak Ties", *American Journal of Sociology* 78(6): 1360–80.

Jones, I. W., Pollitt, M. and Bek, D. 2007. *Multinationals in Their Communities: A Social Capital Approach to Corporate Citizenship Projects*. Basingstoke: Palgrave Macmillan.

Kets de Vries, M. 2000. *The Leadership Mystique: A User's Manual for the Human Enterprise*. London: Financial Times/Prentice Hall.

Kotter, J. 1990. "What Leaders Really Do", *Harvard Business Review*. May–June.

Loch, C. J., De Meyer, A. and Pich, M.T. 2006. *Managing the Unknown: A New Approach to Managing High Uncertainty and Risk in Projects*. London: Wiley.

Mukherjee, A. 2008. *The Spider's Strategy: Creating Networks to Avert Crisis, Create Change, and Really Get Ahead*. Upper Saddle River, NJ: FT Press.

Palmisano, S. 2006. "The Globally Integrated Enterprise", *Foreign Affairs*.May–June.

Schneider, S. and Barsoux, J. L. 2003. *Managing Across Cultures*. London: Prentice Hall.

Sirmon, D. G. and Lane, P. J. 2004. "A Model of Cultural Differences and International Alliance Performance". *Journal of International Business Studies* 35(4): 306–19.

Trompenaars, F. and Hampden Turner, C. 1998. *Riding the Waves of Culture: Understanding Cultural Diversity in Global Business*. New York: McGraw-Hill.

Vereecke, A. and De Meyer, A. 2009. "The Dynamic Management of Manufacturing Networks". Working paper. Judge Business School, University of Cambridge.

Williamson, P. and De Meyer, A. 2009. *ARM Holdings plc: Ecosystem Advantage*. Case study. Judge Business School, University of Cambridge.

The Enduring Value of the MBA Degree

DIPAK C. JAIN, Professor and Dean Emeritus, and **MATT GOLOSINSKI**, Executive Editor
Kellogg School of Management, Northwestern University

B
usiness schools are at a crossroads, and business itself is suffering from an image problem. Or even a *vision* problem.

In the wake of the recent global economic tsunami, many are questioning whether these institutions have lost their way and forgotten how to contribute to civic life. Concerns about the teaching, research and ethics of business have provided grist for high-profile media features and scholarly journals. The very purpose of business schools has come under scrutiny, thanks to conflicting and sometimes vague notions about their academic mission and how to fulfill it.

For example, do business schools have the same social obligations as schools of law or medicine? If so, is this obligation spelled out clearly and consistently? Without an established professional code – a prospect discussed, fruitlessly, for decades – can business even be considered a profession? More technically, are the institutional, curricular and market dynamics of business schools in fact similar to those associated with these other professional schools?

There is no universal agreement on the answers, but for management to make a lasting contribution in the years ahead, there needs to be consensus around such issues. Critics, meanwhile, have pointed out what they see as problems.

"Where business schools went wrong was starting to see themselves as business and not enough as education," Harvard professor Rakesh Khurana has said.[1]

McGill University's Henry Mintzberg laments what he views as a tendency of these schools to rely too much on quantitative tools when preparing students for messy real-world scenarios that don't necessarily play out "by the numbers". He even doubts whether managers can be trained in the classroom at all.[2]

Others question the ethics of business, directing their concerns in particular at Wall Street and wondering if the world wouldn't be better off without the esoteric financial engineering credited with spurring the recent market crash. The schools that produced these executives have also come under fire for at best being irrelevant and at worst, dangerous.[3]

In contrast to this, considering the dearth of leadership today, we believe that business schools have never been more important than they are at present. These schools, occupying as they do the space at the convergence of many fields – from the social sciences to the physical and life sciences – can thrive if they think *beyond the conventional framework* and recognize their potential to become interdisciplinary knowledge hubs within universities. In fact, this model of working with a range of scholarly peers is one aspect of a broader vision of partnership among academic institutions. We see a central role for business schools as they strike up innovative relationships, even among traditional rivals, in an effort to solve problems. Some of these relationships may seem odd at first, as opponents realize the power of working together to find win–win ways to harness each other's strengths. In truth, *the future of competition looks a lot like collaboration.*[4]

But that is the future. At the present time, many of the complaints made against business schools are serious and deserve attention if the MBA brand is to be revived and remain relevant. After all, because of numerous isomorphic factors, including the close relationships between business schools and recruiters, most schools are not interested in upending orthodox market views or seriously challenging standard operating procedures – even when these models may benefit from revision.[5] Some schools have been more willing to reflect on past achievements than on the ways that their research and teaching could shift to make a larger impact. In this regard, it is best to recall the words of the playwright George Bernard Shaw: "We are made wise not by the recollection of our past, but by the responsibility for our future."

The current economic crisis is good in this way at least: it focuses the mind and is too serious to dismiss with breezy assurances. Solving a problem of this magnitude will require action from multiple parties, including business schools. If anything, the fallout from the banking crisis argues for a *redoubled* commitment to management education, since, now as never before, global market complexity requires exceptionally talented leaders. Yet, there needs to be a frank discussion about the overall context in which these schools operate, and the expectations stakeholders have for business education.

While profits are important – and they clearly are one way that organizations can create social value – excessive focus on short-term material gain, rather than on finding meaningful ways to advance broad, sustainable social good, have led too many executives and educators into a blind alley.

In the aftermath of this disruption, savvy business schools will renew themselves to stay relevant. They will think beyond conventional boundaries in three key ways. They will seek to look *beyond business* to find ways to make social contributions. They will also look *beyond material success* to find opportunities to cultivate significance. And they will look *beyond the USA* to take a global view. It's not difficult to find ways for MBAs to make an impact in a world challenged by great problems. Poverty, hunger and environmental degradation are among the issues demanding sharp minds and compassionate hearts if we hope to address these blights.

Viewed in this way, the stakes have never been higher, and the need never greater, for a business curriculum that transcends traditional definitions of what leadership education can be and can achieve.

Getting back to basics: why are we here?

This enormous potential for a leadership renaissance won't happen without a conceptual structure that gives rise to strategic planning and implementation.

For this to occur, management education must gain clarity about its mission by asking some key questions, the answers to which offer the chance to revitalize the MBA curriculum and degree. Some points to consider:

- Are we preparing capable graduates who will bring a passionate, humane and expansive understanding of how the tools of professional management can effect significant positive change?

- Are we setting the right incentives – for both students and faculty – to achieve that goal?

- Will we design curricula that embrace leadership's full possibility, both in familiar corporate settings and in novel, emerging situations such as those confronting social entrepreneurs?

- Will our graduates be ready to combine both analytical and "people" skills in effective ways to produce solutions that matter? Or, instead, shall we be content with business as usual, adhering to traditional notions of simply maximizing shareholder value, hoping that conventional market theories remain viable in an evolving global context that offers no assurance that they will.

Undoubtedly, some will believe that this latter option, by "playing it safe", is the best course. In reality, there is nothing safe about it. Conventional thinking at a time that demands innovation leads down the path of obsolescence. If management education does not reinvent itself to remain in the forefront of innovative institutions, then business schools as we understand them will decline – and rightly so. This outcome, though, would be unfortunate, and not only for those affiliated with the schools; it would also be a missed opportunity for society at large.

However, if management education can effect a large-scale revamping of its mission, credibly asserting its social value, then this "road map" can help to design another principle element for business schools to succeed: a professional code.

Today, the absence of a professional business code sows confusion, for both practitioners and for the public, which is then likely to hold unreasonable or vague expectations for business. Doctors and lawyers, for example, follow a code that provides clear expectations about the knowledge they should have mastered, as well as a way of *certifying* that knowledge. These practitioners also adhere to an ethical code that reinforces their profession's fundamental commitment to the public good.[6] If anyone runs foul of the rules, they face peer rebuke and formal censure, which can include losing one's license to practice.

No such clarity surrounds business, despite decades of effort to establish a professional framework.

For example, at its 1908 inception, Northwestern University's business school had as its ultimate purpose developing a curriculum that would provide students "with standards and professional aims comparable with those of the older professional schools", according to founding dean, Willard E. Hotchkiss. Individual schools, including Northwestern, made progress in this area; yet half a century later, in 1959, the Ford Foundation and Carnegie Corporation would each publish comprehensive surveys of US business schools. The findings' largely negative assessment of management education included concern about the lack of professionalism among practitioners and educators. While top-tier institutions fared better in the surveys than did their lower-ranked peers, the reports highlighted what the researchers saw as underlying problems with curriculum, research and even the industry's *raison d'être*.

Even before the 2008 recession, some critics faulted business schools for being out of step with the times, teaching the wrong subjects in the wrong way, and often with lackluster results. The Ford and Carnegie surveys touched off widespread debate, but a recent article in the *Financial Times* offers a typical contemporary argument. Compared with professional schools such as medicine, law and engineering, business schools fail to produce research that matters to practitioners. According to the article: "When law schools publish journals, lawyers read them. When law schools put on conferences, lawyers turn up. Chief executives, on the other hand, pay little attention to what business schools do or say."[7] The same article quotes Columbia Business School's Rita Gunther McGrath, who says, "Most of what we publish isn't even cited by other academics."

For too long, both too much and too little may have been asked of business. On the one hand, the public, and certainly many in the investing public, has demanded that corporations do whatever necessary to meet quarterly earnings expectations. This impoverished and unimaginative perspective has resulted, too often, in business leaders who push (and sometimes blunder over) the boundaries of legal or ethical practice. It has not encouraged a more expansive view of the role that management and management education could play in the twenty-first century. This must change.

The MBA degree: poised for a renaissance

Whether one considers the needs of corporations, nonprofits, the entrepreneurial community, government agencies or universities themselves, all stand to benefit from a revitalized business curriculum. Of course, so do the students, enrolled in full-time, part-time or executive MBA programs, who define value along professional and personal-growth dimensions. These groups share some traits, but each also presents unique challenges for management educators. All of them, though, offer proof of the expanded landscape within which trained leaders, and the business schools producing them, can contribute today.[8]

Still, capitalizing on opportunities to enhance the MBA's value requires analysis and action to address weaknesses in how educators prepare management students. It is critical to understand both today's students and market needs in order to design relevant programs. At the same time, it is also important to anticipate future trends and to look beyond simple, exclusive notions of "market utility" to foster a more imaginative view of management's potential social contributions. The key throughout is reinforcing the elements that are already working well to advance a principal goal of management education: *structured critical thinking*. This involves teaching students how to provide a structure for complex, unstructured business problems and exposing learners to problem-solving skills, tools and concepts.

This traditional objective will also be melded with new ones, as tomorrow's business schools have the chance to become *interdisciplinary innovation hubs* within universities. These schools should bring science and philosophy together to enable students to make well-founded arguments developed by data that result in *actionable processes*. If philosophy represents a search for explanations via intellectual frameworks, science offers structured ways to derive actual value from those frameworks. Using both, management education should cultivate a student's ability to see people and business challenges with clarity and depth. In so doing, they discover how to motivate others to advance organizational goals while at the same time helping them to harness their own potential for excellence. Most important, students cultivate the desire and ability to pursue a career that is both *materially successful* and *broadly significant* in making the world a better place.

The complaint

Critics have argued that too many MBA programs today err both in what they teach and how they teach it. Management training, they say, is too academic and divorced from practitioners' needs. Equally troubling, this inferior curriculum is not even taught correctly: by focusing too much on theory rather than giving students opportunities that test leadership skills, business programs doubly fail their clientele.[9]

And faculty tenure systems are designed to reward research, not teaching, and then only credit publication in academic journals, not in periodicals directed at practicing managers.[10] This presents a huge incentive challenge for administrators, one that demands to be realigned with updated goals. Indeed, designing incentives to produce the desired outcome – a more expansive role for business and business education – requires a fundamental rethinking of premises. Management education leaders will have to assess what research and teaching they believe is most beneficial to advancing the industry's mission. If business should have a larger part to play in solving social issues (and, incidentally, not everyone holds this view, which is why consensus has been so elusive) then rewarding research that bridges theory and practice in a way that leads to real-world results is an important signal.

It may also be time to expand the context in which that work is disseminated, giving credit to publications in nontraditional forums (for example, conference proceedings) and practitioner-oriented journals, as well as in traditional academic journals. This move is likely to present a design challenge for administrators involved in tenure and promotion, but the effort is worthwhile. Clearly, what is of central importance is knowledge dissemination itself; the details of how that knowledge is shared is a secondary matter. Innovation should be a watchword for management education professionals, just as it is for practitioners competing in the marketplace.

Some observers also say that MBA students lack passion for what a business career should be – a professional adventure that can effect significant change in the commercial world and throughout society. What is more, these students too often lack the desired ethical foundations, and instead focus on "earning rather than learning". They should be "digging deeper" to develop the insights, knowledge, perspectives and experiences that produce leaders.

In a related criticism, others point out that the cost of an MBA since 2001 has outstripped its market value. Salaries have not kept pace with tuition. For example, in 2001, the cost of a year of management education totaled US$30,200. An average starting salary at that time was US$85,400. In 2006, tuition was US$41,100, with salaries averaging US$92,400.[11] These figures indicate that the MBA's value requires restructuring (see Table 1). Nevertheless, "the value of an MBA degree seems undiminished by current economic turmoil – 98 percent of respondents from small to multinational businesses alike were satisfied with their MBA employees", according to research by the Graduate Management Admission Council (GMAC). Their 2009 survey analysis revealed that "employers consistently paid MBA graduates almost double the average starting salary offered to undergraduate school students and 30 percent to 35 percent more than they paid graduates with other management degrees".[12] That said, GMAC data expected 2009 average starting salaries to dip by 4 to 6 percent compared with a year earlier.

Overall, these assessments are too bleak, and hardly unique to the past decade.[13] Yet many people with a vested interest in the MBA degree are

Table 1: Tuition increases have outpaced salary increases – cost/value of an MBA (trends)

Year	One year tuition (thousands US$)	Average starting salary (thousands US$)	Starting salary/ two-year tuition ratio
2001	30.2	85.4	1.41
2002	32.0	77.5	1.21
2003	34.3	79.5	1.15
2004	36.4	78.6	1.08
2005	38.8	88.6	1.14

Source: Based on data from the Graduate Management Admissions Council (GMAC).

concerned, rightly, with management education's shortfalls. Fortunately, remedies exist, such as those we include below. Among the points to remember is that the MBA career is not monolithic – the same always and for everyone – but is a *multistage cycle* extending over a lifetime. The life cycle's trajectory produces different demands at different times, needing particular talents to excel depending on professional circumstance. The success of business schools depends in part on their understanding these varying market needs and providing the appropriate knowledge, at the appropriate times, to support their graduates' advancement.

Any correctives do not arise in a vacuum. Understanding the road that management education has traveled since the early twentieth century offers an appreciation of the MBA's transformations and shows why our proposed structure will help this degree to remain valuable.

A century of market change

Curricula, teaching and the very purpose of management institutions have been called into question periodically since the start of the twentieth century. This fact is unsurprising, given the rapidity with which modern industrial markets have developed, challenging schools to keep pace with changing professional needs.

Still, for more than fifty years these institutions have made contributions to management, even though many began life as little more than trade schools teaching the rudiments of accounting, alongside filing and other clerical tasks. Typical early teaching relied on case studies and practitioner "war stories" (though, for some schools, economists played a major part). The focus was almost entirely on business *relevance*, with little academic scaffolding to support claims. *Intuition*, more than research, grounded decisions (see Table 2).

As indicated earlier, historians of management education will recall the landmark surveys conducted independently by The Ford Foundation and Carnegie Corporation, with results highly critical of business schools.[14] While the studies' authors (Robert A. Gordon and James E. Howell wrote the Ford study; Frank C. Pierson the Carnegie effort) approached their subject from the vantage point of academic economists, not practicing businesspeople, they nonetheless leveled a scathing indictment of the typical business curriculum, addressing concerns shared by practitioners. Among other things, they found that too many schools lacked academic rigor, producing graduates who might demonstrate a functional facility but who failed to impress as leaders educated in the fundamentals required to manage complex, modern organizations. Those trained under this model risked having their skills become irrelevant.

To combat this deficiency and to build on the case study pedagogy, many schools again made accommodations to include more analytical subjects,

Table 2: Evolution of management education

Time period	Up to mid-1960s	Late 1960s to late 1990s	2000–2008	2009 and beyond
Pedagogical tools used	Case studies	Theoretical frameworks driven by academic research	Analytical frameworks and experiential global learning	Analytical frameworks, experiential global learning and renewed risk management models
Decision-making driven by	Judgment and intuition	Data analytics	Business insights and corporate ethics	Business insights, corporate ethics and global challenges
Focus on	Business relevance	Academic rigor	Academic rigor and business relevance	Academic rigor, business relevance and social impact

Note: Across time, each category grows cumulatively, incorporating earlier models and methods into later approaches.

hiring research-oriented faculty members to teach quantitative skills and to create the intellectual product now familiar in peer-reviewed management journals. The schools developed into rigorous entities housing talent from the fields of economics, mathematics, operations research, sociology, physics, anthropology and psychology, among others. By the 1970s and until the century's end, business schools turned to theoretical frameworks and academic research.

Today, some critics say management education has suffered from too much of a good thing. In its pursuit of academic credibility, seeking to become a discipline that could call itself a science of commerce, schools may have moved their academic focus too far from practitioners' needs, infatuated by a "physics envy". This scenario represents an inversion of the earliest critiques of these institutions.

Most recently, some academics have objected to elements in the MBA curriculum and its delivery.[15] Mintzberg argues that managers cannot be created in the classroom, but should "remain in [a professional] context" while studying. Furthermore, the object of that study should be organized around "managerial mindsets, not business functions". We believe that the classroom remains valuable for management training so long as it is used in conjunction with an action-oriented curriculum that provides leadership opportunities. In addition, too often critics ignore or minimize less obvious aspects of the MBA experience, including the network of alumni contacts that can enhance people's professional life. Equally important are the benefits noted by Professor Anthony Hopwood, former dean of Oxford University's Business School. He said that the MBA degree could afford graduates both geographic and professional mobility, "creating people who can operate in diverse and interdisciplinary contexts".[16]

Despite legitimate critical concern, some schools are already ahead of the pack in implementing strategies to keep their programs relevant. Top-tier management education is again reinventing itself. One driver influencing this process are professional rankings conducted by observers such as *BusinessWeek*, *The Wall Street Journal*, the *Financial Times*, The Economist Intelligence Unit (the research and advisory firm affiliated with *The Economist*), and others. Though sometimes disparaged, especially for their methodology,[17] such reports can serve a valuable purpose, so long as administrators keep the results in perspective and refrain from being "rankings-driven" in their approach to the curriculum and teaching. Instead, the value of rankings is as an *overall holistic guide* or a helpful diagnostic tool. The rankings, while individually emphasizing somewhat different elements of the MBA experience and weighting these factors to derive a "best–worst" evaluation, generally encourage schools to direct attention and resources toward innovations that, with due diligence, can prove beneficial. Rankings serve another function too: they help to establish a school's reputation. This is especially important for business education, a field that, unlike medicine or law, does not have a licensing body to impart its professional imprimatur.

Professional values

This fact raises a significant issue for discussion: the merit of establishing a professional code for business. We agree that instituting a clear code for ethical and professional behavior, as well as a mechanism for certifying credentials and punishing inappropriate conduct, would create a helpful framework for practitioners. At the same time, this code would also send a powerful signal to other stakeholders, including most broadly the public, about the values, and the value, of business. The fact that such a code has not appeared over the last century indicates something about the associated challenges of enacting it. Some will contend that the only proper focus of business is creating shareholder value, defined narrowly and in exclusively monetary terms. This follows the traditional libertarian market view championed by Milton Friedman. But in a globalizing world that is increasingly complex, management experts must at least consider the ramifications of a professional code – especially given the recent global liquidity crisis that almost brought down the world's financial system.

As Rakesh Khurana and Nitin Nohria have written, a professional code could also help to define the core curriculum and expectations at business schools, leading to more rigorous and useful leadership education. They write, with urgency, that "the harm to society that untrained managers could cause – particularly in a more complex, globalizing world – cannot be underestimated".[18] A professional code could help to restore the legitimacy of business in the eyes of the public.

Perhaps the most important aspect of the professional code would be its potential benefit in terms of sharpening the focus and strength of curriculum enhancements. Those institutions willing to compete must provide creative experiential offerings that balance academic rigor with practical relevance – a perennial ideal, but one that today is critical. Also vital is *how* schools achieve this goal: new models should emphasize a multifaceted approach to management and leadership.

Yet recent trends indicate that fewer students are seriously considering rankings per se when making their choices about where to pursue their management education.[19] A survey of 6,000 potential business school applicants by TopMBA.com was reported in *Asia Inc.*; the findings showed that several other factors, such as overall reputation, the strength of the school's placement office, available financial aid, and breadth of curriculum were all emphasized above rankings.[20] Some experts advise applicants to consider the data behind the rankings to determine if the criteria are aligned with the candidate's objectives and expectations.

Reason for hope: a cure for what ails

Business educators can find coherence and direction in what we call the Four Pillars, a framework to advance what should be the mission of management schools: developing responsible global leaders who pursue materially successful and socially significant careers (see Figure 2). The Four Pillars

Figure 2: The Four Pillars model indicates key supports for the ideal of responsible leaders operating in the modern global business environment

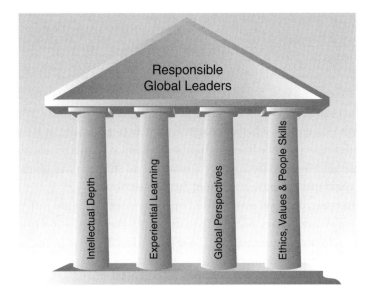

outlines the holistic skills necessary to achieve this goal. Intellectual depth, experiential learning, global perspectives and ethics, values and people skills are the keys to achieving success. Individually, these qualities offer tools that can take students partway toward leadership, but only together, and within an environment that encourages creativity and collaboration, can they provide a full complement of necessary skills.

Intellectual depth (thought leadership through coursework)

This requires students to pursue studies rigorously, working closely with faculty members as colleagues to make discoveries that bridge theory and practice while *learning by doing* (for example, in experiential settings such as the practicum or internship, and through initiatives that include student-led conferences and clubs with a leadership component). Students are "cocreators" of knowledge, not passive bystanders. They also develop the ability to envision the next important trends, and understand how to anticipate change. Key to achieving this objective is taking students outside their comfort zones, with professors who inspire and liberate them from the constraints of routinized thought – which is critically important for leaders who hope to drive success through innovation. Doing so requires faculty prepared to grade academic work tough-mindedly, a practice not always implemented in schools where the "student-as-customer" model is taken to extremes, partly as a result of market pressures.[21]

Enhancing this kind of scholarship is critical – for business schools and their students, but also, ultimately, for the organizations spanning the corporate, nonprofit and public domains where this knowledge will be put to work. Research-based frameworks are what have enabled modern global management practices to meet the challenges posed by increased competition and complexity, and have helped business schools to grow into academic centers offering a versatile liberal education. The root of this scholarship lies in management-focused doctoral programs whose students will often serve as the next generation of business school faculty members.

Unfortunately, doctoral programs in business institutions are suffering from an enrollment crisis. According to data from the Association to Advance Collegiate Schools of Business (AACSB),[22] a marked decrease in doctoral candidates is creating serious long-term implications for schools and organizations. AACSB cites research that indicates US business doctorates declined from 1,327 in 1994–5 to 1,071 in 1999–2000, a drop of 19 percent. By 2013, AACSB estimates a 2,500 shortfall of US doctoral candidates. The number is startling, given the importance of these graduates in instilling intellectual rigor, since academic, business and public policy institutions all rely on these scholars. Figures from the Graduate Management Admissions Council (GMAC)[23] also indicate a 20 percent decrease in applicants to doctoral programs for 2007–8, compared with the previous academic year.

AACSB notes that "a significant number of potential doctoral candidates do not fully understand and appreciate the opportunities and rewards of a business doctoral program", indicating that schools might benefit from enhanced outreach to market themselves to this audience. At the same time, schools and the government can work together to support doctoral programs by directing more funds from sources such as the National Science Foundation to management education. Recent numbers indicate a gross disparity between NSF funding of science, engineering and social science initiatives compared with business.[24]

Given this diminishing supply of doctoral graduates, recruiting and retaining superior professors and students will significantly influence the MBA's value proposition. In fact, such intellectual property now proves central to competitive advantage. Schools able to attract top talent will position themselves as global leaders, with their campuses being hubs of intellectual activity that span disciplines as they remain connected to actual business concerns. In this role, business schools will work more closely with their universities in ways that continue to deliver on the traditional mission – *knowledge creation*, *knowledge dissemination* and *knowledge certification* – but also adding another critical component: *knowledge monetization*. Management education will assist universities in creating real-world value and garner actual return on investment that will help to support the overall academic environment on campus.

Experiential learning (team leadership through collaboration)

This should pervade the entire MBA education process and influence each of the pillars. Hands-on learning provides real opportunities to test classroom insights, giving students the chance to strengthen their leadership within contexts that approximate actual management situations, a circumstance analogous to medical residencies. Some of these opportunities may involve leadership simulations, internships and field excursions, as well as orchestrating professional academic conferences and similar events that bring together practitioners, professors and students in ways that advance leadership discourse. As valuable as classroom lessons are in establishing intellectual perspective, it is crucial to complement this with actual "frontline" encounters that force students to synthesize and apply their insights.[25] As a recent article in *ISB Insight* put it: "The principal objection that appears to have emerged in the past few years is that B-Schools provide a closed, non-dynamic environment for decision-making that equip students poorly for the fluid, unpredictable realities of real-life business." Further, the business school experience can create a "false notion of how to manage" by leaving out considerations of implementation – the actual practice of management, which demands team skills and leadership.[26]

One way that business schools cultivate this experiential knowledge is to provide rewarding collaborative learning opportunities for students – indeed, students today expect and seek out this kind of environment.[27] Working in teams, both inside and outside the classroom, prepares managers for the challenges of the professional world, where colleagues work closely with one another even though they may be spread across several countries. The ability to lead diverse teams is essential, and this training should be one of the ways that the MBA experience benefits those pursuing the degree.[28]

There is already evidence that today's students are embracing this shift. *The Economist* has reported that, as schools "start to teach more ethics and practical skills, enrolments are climbing again". The paper notes that applications and salaries offered to graduates are again rising, thanks in part to more emphasis being given to the application of theory and a renewed focus on the values that should guide leadership.[29] Among those credited with exemplary curriculum change is Stanford, which has approved the most significant revision to its courses in almost thirty years. Stanford elected to create more flexibility for students by minimizing the number of core courses required and instead to allow students to chart their own paths. The school has also placed more emphasis on "analytical critical thinking, general management and the development of leadership skills".[30] Yale too has revised its curriculum dramatically, aiming for a multidisciplinary approach when revamping courses. Yale is trying to communicate across departmental silos so that faculty members know what their colleagues are teaching and researching. This boundary-spanning is critical to transforming the MBA curriculum from one focused on narrow intellectual domains, often disconnected from practitioners, into a balanced portfolio that is both rigorous and relevant. Nurturing these boundary-spanners helps to mitigate the excesses of what Ranjay Gulati has termed "polarized tribes" setting up camps across the rigor– relevance divide. In his view, "we should aim not to restructure our programs and processes, but rather to reconfigure our identities as more fluid and inclusive, allowing us to be comfortable performing research for application and real-world impact but also to enhance academic understanding. This means freeing ourselves from the familiarity and blinders of either/or, to integrate rigor with relevance."[31] Such a model is similar to traditional medical residencies. What business schools must implement is a kind of *executive residency*.

The effort to integrate offerings within schools, while aligning schools with the business community, suggests an important shift toward a holistic framework for management education. Understanding the context in which business schools operate should increase the ability to understand how the curriculum's parts function – or should function. This is a view shared by Russell Ackoff, professor emeritus of the Wharton School. Ackoff's book, *Management F-Laws: How Organizations Really Work*, details the failings of current business school training, including a central problem of teaching subjects in relative isolation from each other, rather than demonstrating how they interact.

He also emphasizes the importance of *learning by doing* in an environment that encourages appropriate risk-taking: "You never learn by doing something right, because you already know how to do it," says Ackoff. "The only opportunity for learning is to identify mistakes and correct them."[32] While many organizations cannot afford an excess of risk, and so often discourage employees from taking the risks that can result in mistakes (but also real learning), schools are in the valuable position of permitting students to experiment and learn.

Global perspectives (market leadership through cross-cultural diversity)

Schools must provide students with the chance to appreciate and understand the complexity of international commerce, gaining the ability to perform in a diverse context alongside colleagues who offer diversity of thought and experience. This global focus should be part of every course, since one cannot discuss business today in provincial terms. Classroom experiences should be augmented with excursions that put students face to face with practitioners.

A course that achieves this is a global practicum combining a quarter/semester of intensive classroom preparation and research with a couple of weeks of fieldwork in one of several countries. Students meet with leaders from business and government, going behind the scenes for a look at how commerce works.

Increasingly, schools are recognizing the need to provide students with a chance to study abroad for part of their MBA experience.[33] More fundamentally, the network of faculty and students in the modern business school should be expansive, reflecting the cultural diversity of a global business community, with resources directed toward attracting international students. One way to achieve this goal is by recruiting the best international students and ensuring that they make up a significant part of the student body. Increasingly, we are discovering the importance of diversity and studying it scientifically to understand how it functions within global business. The work of organizations in the twenty-first century will be conducted across continents by culturally diverse teams that form (and dissolve) rapidly, and are expected to deliver results instantly. Preparing students to compete in this environment is among the objectives of top business schools.[34]

Ethics, values and people skills (civic leadership through community outreach and social responsibility)

These are competencies easily misunderstood or overlooked as ancillary to the primary function of business schools. In truth, this pillar is as critical as the others. It does not displace the analytical skills required to run an enterprise; it complements them. Business leaders must act *ethically* if they are to regain and maintain public confidence in the aftermath of corporate accounting scandals in the early 2000s and the reputational damage caused by the more recent financial sector meltdown. These abuses sent a powerful negative signal to the public about business and, while introducing ethical and social concerns to the curriculum helps to offset an undesirable public image for business schools, the most important reason to include this discussion is that doing so helps to safeguard the trust that is the bedrock of our financial markets. Not only is ethical behavior intrinsically right to pursue; it is also essential to create widespread prosperity. MBA programs are positioned to make important contributions to society by advancing this discourse and instilling the proper values in their graduates. With this civic leadership focus, ethical behavior is paramount for business schools and must be diffused throughout the curriculum.

Ethical behavior must be reflected in the civic arena but also within organizations, where it plays a part in building trust and morale. Managing people effectively means understanding how to motivate them to achieve their best performance. Respect and fair-mindedness are virtues in themselves, but they also serve progressive functions within an organization to create an inclusive culture where teams are challenged and engaged. Demonstrating genuine concern for building the staff's abilities will serve those individuals and the entire organization. Effective leaders understand that accomplishments require many people pulling together, motivated by a common goal to which they lend their talents.

Such a people-centric culture helps to build talent and provide recognition through feedback. It empowers people to act while holding them accountable and letting them make a difference. Schools should cultivate many ways for students to build these skills by creating an environment with clubs (particularly those with an academic agenda) and engagement with the community through civic leadership opportunities, such as those available through the national Net Impact organization. Another way students gain leadership through collaboration is by organizing and running academic conferences. This allows them to refine their team-leadership skills while providing a forum for testing classroom insights through interaction with practitioners and other conference participants.

Effective communication is equally important – particularly across national and cultural borders. These so-called "soft skills" make hard impressions that influence success. Anyone who has negotiated an important deal understands this challenge. Add cross-cultural complexity to negotiation and one quickly sees how important these people skills can be. Business periodicals regularly feature articles outlining the necessary steps to ensure optimal negotiations; and, without fail, a critical element is the ability to understand human psychology and cultural differences.[35] These skills are often lacking in business school graduates, even as the skills' importance increases. A *Fortune* article outlined the problem, and indicated how some schools were complementing their analytical courses with team-oriented offerings that provide a forum for honing communication.[36]

Through an approach like the Four Pillars, business curricula can kindle students' imaginations, encouraging them to dream big and igniting a desire for action that makes significant positive contributions to the world. Through inspiration, schools can foster the drive necessary for leaders to harness their people's energy and instill a culture of action in their organizations.

The values implicit in the Four Pillars relate to another point raised by some critics of the MBA curriculum: the age and diversity of the entering students. Some have argued that the average student enrolled in a full-time MBA program is too young to benefit from the experience. These students, whose average age is 27, typically enter the program after five years of professional experience. In fact, five years is *too long* to wait before pursuing the MBA. Three years on the job is more than sufficient to gain the necessary perspective and experience–but not so long that undesirable habits (that is, learning impediments) form. Today's "millennial" students, born between 1980 and 2000, study quickly and are very bright, having grown up with computer technology in environments that forced them to manage multiple challenges simultaneously. These students are capable of benefiting from the leadership models advanced here. In fact, top US business schools are starting to pay more attention to younger students, with some even targeting 10 percent of their enrollment from among those arriving directly from undergraduate programs (see, for example, Della Bradshaw, "The Rise of the Younger Student", *Financial Times*, 17 September 2007).

Still, in one important way, student age is indeed a major consideration for business schools, in that curricula must respond to the various needs of what we call the "MBA Lifecycle," a framework that helps illustrate, and maintain and enhance, the MBA's lifetime value (see Figure 3).

Figure 3: The typical career trajectory of today's MBA graduate

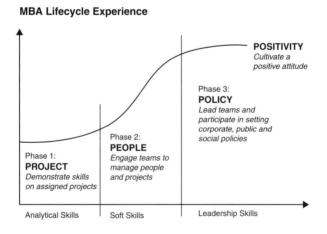

In addition, the market greeting today's graduates looks different than that confronting graduates in the 1970s. At that time, the MBA had more obvious value, since those holding the degree went to work for people who did not themselves have an MBA. Today, some might suggest that management education is a victim of its own success: more people now have the degree, producing typical supply-and-demand pressures. Answering this challenge calls for increased innovation, superior execution and product differentiation, considerations that inform the MBA Lifecycle model below. Understanding the life cycle, and recent trends in applications and recruitment at business schools, supports the view that the MBA's value remains significant and unique. In fact, according to the 2007 "Global MBA Survey" conducted by GMAC, 61 percent of all respondents "considered their degrees to be outstanding or excellent value".[37]

"MBA Lifecycle": long-term learning for a changing market

Rather than viewing management education as a one-size-fits-all proposition, we see the MBA experience *as lifelong learning*, possessing various dimensions over time. Just as there are different skills and objectives associated with different career steps, so too are there different academic offerings to meet individual needs at different times.

Early in the typical career, during the *initial stage* of the MBA Lifecycle, one is called upon to *manage projects*. Doing so requires using many of the skills, tools and concepts taught in a conventional MBA program: key functional disciplines, such as accounting, competitive strategy, finance and marketing are especially important, as are statistics and economics offerings that appear in the core curriculum at many schools. This stage may last for five to six years after graduation.[38]

The MBA Lifecycle's *second stage* begins with the individual being called upon to *manage people*. This period can last for another five years until ten to twelve years post-graduation. In addition to functional skills, this stage draws on leadership abilities to create teams and an environment conducive to achieving the organization's mission. These are "soft skills" that create "hard impressions". Business school courses that address subjects such as the behavior of organizations, leadership in organizations, managing a diverse workforce, and human resources management are among the offerings of particular value for this career stage.

Finally, the MBA Lifecycle's *third stage* finds the graduate involved in *designing policy*. In addition to functional skills and people skills, this advanced stage demands superior leadership and strategic vision as the person must drive higher-level organizational change and, in many cases, change within a larger community. Here, business schools have an opportunity to offer graduates value through executive education programs that refine and update skills to bring them in line with current market demands. Schools can design and deliver various custom programs to meet *specific client needs,* alongside other offerings providing insights in areas such as creating and managing strategic alliances, or corporate governance. Schools can tailor programs to the needs of executives whose MBA degrees were earned ten or twelve years earlier, and which now require fresh frameworks to enable continued success.[39]

Certainly, the ability to manage teams is valuable throughout one's career, and there will be crossover among these three categories. Nevertheless, as a framework that identifies the general trajectory of most graduates, the MBA Lifecycle shows how schools should address their clientele's evolving needs in a way that reflects a commitment to *lifelong learning.*

In addition, the curriculum at each level of this life cycle, from full- or part-time MBA study through advanced executive education, must balance academic rigor and business relevance. Research-based insights without application are likely intellectual exercises of limited value, while practical strategies divorced from underlying theory offer only anecdotal, hit-or-miss possibilities. Either without the other is a rudderless ship, though many within management education continue to favor research silos that exclude work of particular importance to practitioners. As Harold Leavitt has contended, the typical MBA curriculum has too often created students "with lopsided brains, icy hearts, and shrunken souls".[40]

Another element that helps safeguard against such an unfortunate outcome is one that runs throughout all the life cycle stages – *a positive attitude.* Cultivating an attitude that is enthusiastic and that embraces challenges and opportunities with a genuine desire to make a difference is a necessity for moving through the life cycle.

Demand for professional managers: the numbers

Despite criticisms of the MBA curriculum – including the claim of market saturation and "degree dilution", given that US business schools produce more than 120,000 graduates each year[41] – the demand and associated metrics for management graduates remain strong, suggesting that students and recruiters continue to perceive value in the MBA. Recent trends related to applications and recruitment support this claim, as do survey results assessing student satisfaction of their management education experience, particularly as it pertains to long-term potential for creating value.[42]

First, however, it is helpful to establish perspective on these data by considering macro trends in the market since the end of the 1990s to understand why admissions wax and wane. These reasons often have more to do with larger economic realities than with problems associated with business schools per se.

During 1994–5, applications and Graduate Management Admissions Test (GMAT) volume increased as the US economy rebounded following the 1990–2 recession. GMAT volume surged in 1996–7, as candidates were eager to take the paper test before the introduction of the computer-based exam. Between 1998 and 2001, business school applications rose as a result of the booming economy and companies seeking management talent.

In 2001–2, business school applications and GMAT volume rose to record levels, in part because of the 11 September terrorist attacks that contributed to a sharp economic downturn. Professionals exited the weak economy and turned to graduate programs, including MBA programs, taking advantage of the difficult market to enhance their skills and to position themselves in readiness for opportunities once the market turned up again. This dynamic mirrored a similar trend during the recession of the early 1990s.

The 2001 surge, however, masked the start of another key transition: a smaller number of 29–31-year-olds (the typical age of those applying to full-time MBA programs). This demographic shift is attributable to fewer births overall at the time (in the early 1970s) when these students were born. In the early 1990s, undergraduate university programs suffered because of this shift. By 2002–5, this trend was becoming obvious in the MBA applicant pool, producing a predictable decline. Indeed, throughout the management education industry, the applicant pool "bottomed out" during 2003–4.

In 2004–5, the pool was still declining, but not as steeply, as the US economy was rebounding and applicant demographics were shifting. The entrance of the earliest segment of a new student population, the millennials, also helped to turn the tide.[43]

Admissions for 2005–6, as well as GMAT volume, began to climb once more, as forecast by the Graduate Management Admissions Council. Increased confidence in the economy, as well as the arrival in earnest of the millennial population, both influenced this turn. More recently, GMAC noted a 36 percent application increase year-on-year for full-time MBA programs in 2007. In 2006, the year-on-year increase was 41 percent.[44]

In 2010, it is expected that overall business school applications will continue rising as an additional 90 million millennials reach the target age (25 to 29) for pursuing full-time MBAs.[45] Specifically, the forecast is for an increase in applications from the USA and Asia; applicants from Europe have declined since 2005, a trend that is so far continuing.

According to 2006 GMAC survey data, business school applications are up year-on-year across all programs, full-time, part-time and executive MBA. Part-time and EMBA programs showed the biggest jump: part-time applications increased from 46 to 62 percent in volume for 2006, while EMBA applications increased from 38 percent in 2005 to 69 percent in 2006. The same survey, which reflects responses from 230 MBA programs at 147 graduate business schools, also reports an increase in female and minority applications for all MBA programs.

GMAC reports that "the rebound in MBA application volume reflects steadily improving prospects for MBAs", including a rise in average starting salaries for graduates. Salaries for new MBA graduates in 2006 averaged more than US$92,000, according to GMAC, and two-thirds of these people obtained job offers that included signing bonuses. This figure represents an increase of 4.2 percent over 2005 starting salaries, reported as US$88,626. In addition, the survey indicates, more students are finding jobs before completing their MBA degrees. This is a multiyear trend, with 52 percent of respondents in 2006 reporting that "they had received or accepted a job offer before graduation", according to the GMAC Global MBA Graduate Survey. That number reflects an increase of 2 percent over 2005, a 10 percent increase over 2004 and a 16 percent increase over 2003. Figures reported by a 2006 *Financial Times* survey echo this trend. In particular, the paper reported a US$10,000 increase in base salaries in the banking sector, resulting in starting pay being pegged at slightly more than US$95,000. Consultancies, according to *FT*, raised their base salaries by US$5,000, with average pay starting at US$109,586.

In tandem with this trend, corporate recruiters report more optimism about overall economic prospects, resulting in their visiting more business schools, according to GMAC.

While these figures are important and support claims of the MBA's enduring market value, we appreciate a related concern raised by some critics, notably Pfeffer and Fong. In a 2004 paper[46] they lament that too many management schools and their students place undue emphasis on the MBA degree as "simply ... a road to riches and better jobs". Some schools create a culture that values earning more than learning. As suggested earlier, such a focus can prove academically toxic, which is why schools should insist on recruiting and educating students who demonstrate an *intrinsic passion* for making a difference, and who intend to use their MBA skills in that mission. Adequate compensation for talent is hardly to be shunned, but management education, and those served by it, benefits most when students and faculty commit themselves first to enriching the knowledge base for researchers and practitioners.

Business education should stir the souls of those involved, producing innovation and action that makes genuine social contributions. Schools must find ways to inspire this outcome – that is, link *success* and *significance* – by recruiting superior talent, making curriculum innovations and pursuing an overall culture that encourages students to use their intellect to solve problems that make the world a better place.[47]

Among undergraduate majors reported by those taking the GMAT, the largest sample, not surprisingly, comes from a business/commerce background. More than 92,000 such students tested in 2004–5. The next-largest sample came from the sciences (approximately 41,000 applicants), followed by the social sciences (about 26,000), economics (13,000), and humanities (8,400). Significant applicant numbers came from other disciplines, including political science, psychology, law, anthropology, government and art history. These figures indicate that an array of students continues to perceive value in enhancing the undergraduate experience by considering an MBA degree. Further, the range of undergraduate studies represented suggests that the average incoming business school class today is composed of people who possess eclectic intellectual perspectives. This trend indicates that business schools, while certainly focused on the core management-training mission, are also places where the liberal arts and ideas flourish.

The right stuff: easier said than done

Not all business schools are likely to execute strategy that delivers along all the dimensions recommended here.

Top schools have more resources and strategic advantages – facilities, faculty, brand recognition, prestigious alumni networks, global alliances with other institutions and so on. – than those in the middle and bottom tiers.

They are also better situated to deliver a *portfolio* of offerings that meets the needs of various market segments (for example, full-time, part-time, EMBA, non-degree executive education). Superimposed on the MBA Lifecycle are other possible innovations and points of differentiation to increase value for the MBA. Joint degrees, such as the JD-MBA or the MD-MBA, are one way to build additional strength and relevance into the academic experience.

Then too there is the dichotomy between public and private institutions and their associated revenue streams (for example, funding from taxes and tuition primarily supporting public schools; tuition and philanthropy supporting private schools). Not all programs will survive the contraction that will find the best players, already well positioned, competing for resources such as exemplary talent (professors and students, mainly, but also staff who play important roles in alumni relations, career management and other areas). In some instances, schools in the middle ranks will need to redefine their markets and create specialized offerings, such as an MBA in health care, technology, real estate, nonprofit management and so on. In one case, Babson College has created a niche for itself by fashioning a curriculum focused on entrepreneurship.[48]

Management educators must not focus their attention exclusively on the MBA program, since market demand for undergraduate business degrees Bachelor of Business Administration – BBA) has enjoyed a resurgence since 1995, accounting for about 69 percent of all business degrees awarded in the USA.[49] What is more, undergraduate programs are adopting aspects of the MBA curriculum, such as leadership, entrepreneurship and supply chain management courses. (The classroom experience will differ markedly between the two programs, because undergraduates lack the professional background and maturity of their MBA program counterparts.)

While some schools with sufficient resources may choose to offer both graduate and undergraduate programs, other schools may, out of strategic choice or necessity, specialize in one or the other. Neither program will replace the other, but instead they will be complementary. The MBA historically has provided graduates with the skills to change careers more easily – something likely to continue, even as graduate programs may be forced by BBA offerings to adopt new formats. Undergraduate business education, on the other hand, appeals to more employers today, in part because businesses perceive such graduates as being malleable: they possess sufficient business knowledge and can be molded to fit a particular organizational culture than can some older MBAs.

In addition, those holding a BBA degree will be offered a more modest starting salary – less than an MBA graduate. In lower-level positions, an undergraduate business major may perform quite well, while sophisticated roles will continue to demand a more experienced professional who brings a portfolio of skills that only an MBA program can provide.

The future may see schools presenting a more blended portfolio, involving programming to provide customers with the service and value they seek – whether that means the two-year MBA program, a one-year MBA, executive MBA offerings, non-degree executive education, the part-time MBA, or the undergraduate BBA curricula. Options other than the BBA could include undergraduate certificate programs that provide targeted training in areas such as finance, giving younger students a taste of management education so that they eventually return to complete an MBA. Rather than resist change, schools should listen to the market and embrace the change necessary to flourish.

High-stakes global complexity demands MBAs who aspire to be, and to give, more

> "If you want to build a ship, don't drum up the men to collect wood, divide the work and give orders. Instead, teach them to desire the vast sea."
> *Antoine de Saint-Exupéry, French author and aviator*

In the next fifty years, humanity's challenges will be enormous: poverty, longevity, disease and environmental crises all loom. Energy, prosperity and national security are linked, presenting CEOs and heads of state with thorny problems of vast consequence. AIDS and avian flu, or other emerging threats, will intrude on global corporate strategy as surely as they will influence the decisions of politicians and NGOs. Hypercompetitive global markets make even traditional management complex and daunting. Leaders must marshal diverse talents and knowledge, bringing them to bear in an arena that blurs the lines among business, government and broader social actors, such as consumer activists. What is more, leaders must operate from a position of unimpeachable ethical integrity; anything less will erode the collective trust at the core of market-based enterprise.

Clearly, leadership matters more than ever and the job is going to grow more difficult. This is why the MBA curriculum must remain in the educational vanguard as it prepares the next generation for success. Business schools can stay at the forefront by strengthening their relationships with universities and becoming interdisciplinary innovation hubs.

Modern challenges across all fields will see business faculty members and students aspiring to achieve more and to *be* more. "Make no little plans; they have no magic to strike man's blood": these words, attributed to architect and urban planner Daniel Burnham (1846–1912), responsible for the development of the first skyscrapers in the USA, might today also capture the imagination of those looking to expand management education's scope. Participants in this journey will be many – players touching all domains and disciplines.

Current research must not shrink from taking risks and asking big questions. Faculty members should focus on problems pertinent to corporations (such as growth), and on issues confronting public/social policy-makers (for example, social security, health care). In so doing, management education can recalibrate itself along another essential front – the aspirational. Such research will have a direct impact on the business world, while also benefiting society overall. Beyond the intrinsic importance of this work, another benefit is that business schools will enhance their reputations.

Students pursuing the MBA degree should aspire to make significant social contributions. Their focus should be on learning as much as possible to achieve this goal, and not pursuing an astronomical salary. Earnings are important, but too often they eclipse the more crucial mission that should occupy a leader: *daring to make the world a better and safer place.*

Overcoming major social hurdles and stimulating prosperity using intellectual tools at the intersection of many disciplines should inspire all members of the management profession. Reason and creativity each have parts to play in this effort, and MBA training should engage a person's whole spirit.

Management training can do this through a commitment to experiential learning coupled with a curriculum that delivers business fundamentals, including analytical skills. Students must learn inside and outside the classroom, enjoying vigorous, bi-directional interactions with faculty members to extend the boundaries of management research that produces innovative solutions to real problems. The goal, always, is combining *intellectual rigor* with *business relevance.*

It is only a slight exaggeration to say that twenty-first-century leaders will find the strength and insight to go forward by looking back at earlier ideals. And the MBA curriculum should make room for such broadminded discoveries, even as it prepares future leaders to master discipline-based standards such as finance, operations and marketing.

The Renaissance ideal of the polymath – the person who learns continuously, acquiring knowledge in many subjects – is one that surely would serve contemporary leaders well as they negotiate today's multicultural, "nanosecond" global culture. Leaders might also benefit by referring to an even earlier model, the "philosopher king" in Plato's *Republic*. Here the author describes the proper education for this person:

> And when they are 50 years old, those who have lasted the whole [educational] course and are in every way best at everything, both in practice and in theory, must at last be led to the final goal, and must be compelled to lift up the eyes of their psyches towards that which provides light for everything, the Good itself. And taking it as their model, they must put in good order both the polis [city-state] and themselves for the remainder of their lives.[50]

As well as making a respectable argument for executive education and lifelong learning, Plato emphasizes key elements that today's MBA training must provide: *knowledge rooted in theory and practice, and informed by ethical virtue that respects and cultivates the community.*

These are the tools that will change lives by drawing MBA students to their real calling and responsibility. And these are ideals to inform the curricula of business schools that wish to remain vital by creating not merely the means to nudge the Dow Jones up three points, but to produce leaders who transform the world and themselves. After all, *to the world you may be just one person, but to one person you may be the world.*

We wish for each MBA graduate to build on personal success and turn these accomplishments into action that makes a significant difference to the lives of those around him or her. In this way, the value of the MBA endures and the world thrives.

NOTES

1 "The Future of Business Schools", *BusinessWeek* online, 26 May 2009.

2 Della Bradshaw, "Deans Fight Crisis Fires", *Financial Times*, 7 June 2009.

3 See, for example, T. T. Ram Mohan, "Crisis: Are B-schools to Blame?", *The Economic Times,* 11 June 2009. Also, Philip Delves Broughton (2008) *Ahead of the Curve: What They Teach You at HBS*, New York: Viking, an unflattering account of his two years in that school's MBA program.

4 For example, a top business school can join forces with a top medical school to produce a partnership that benefits both: managerial students gain insights

about the world of medicine, while medical students learn more about business. Each institution benefits by playing to its strengths, rather than having to create – from scratch – the means to deliver the knowledge that a capable partner can provide.

5 For a rather pointed critique of current market practices, see Amartya Sen, "Adam Smith's Market Never Stood Alone", *Financial Times*, 10 March 2009. "Despite all Smith did to explain and defend the constructive role of the market, he was deeply concerned about the incidence of poverty, illiteracy and relative deprivation that might remain despite a well-functioning market economy," writes Sen, a Harvard economist and Nobel laureate, "He wanted institutional diversity and motivational variety, not monolithic markets and singular dominance of the profit motive." See also the critique made by N. Adler and A. W. K. Harzing in "When Knowledge Wins: Transcending the Sense and Nonsense of Academic Rankings", *Academy of Management Learning and Education*, March 2009.

6 In the case of physicians, for example, the Hippocratic Oath asserts "Above all, do no harm."

7 Michael Skapinker, "Why Business Ignores the Business Schools", *Financial Times*, 7 January 2008.

8 Metrics, discussed below, support this claim. After a brief downturn linked to larger economic trends, business school applications are again up, as are recruitment and average starting salaries for MBA graduates. While we wish to argue for a broader social role for leadership education, avoiding merely framing matters in market terms, nevertheless this market demand is one important indicator of value.

9 See Henry Mintzberg (2004) *Managers, Not MBAs: A Hard Look at the Soft Practice of Managing and Management Development*, San Francisco: Berrett-Koehler, for his argument about why he agrees with Drucker, that "Management is a practice … not a science."

10 For example, Warren Bennis and James O'Toole of the University of Southern California have stated that while many business schools have become expert in pursuing scientific research, the fruits of this work offer little value to practitioners. In their May 2005 *Harvard Business Review* article, "How Business Schools Lost Their Way", the authors state that schools "simply must rediscover the practice of business".

11 Average starting salaries for graduates of some top-tier MBA programs, however, reflect the premium value recruiters place on those schools. Graduates sometimes garnered salaries more than 13 percent higher than the industry-wide average. Again, we wish to argue for management education's broader value creation, using both market and nonmarket criteria. But these salary data also represent a relevant input.

12 Graduate Management Admissions Council (GMAC), "Corporate Recruiters Survey 2009 General Data Report" p. 3.

13 See below for the historical precedent in critiquing business school that dates back a half-century and proves that management educators are capable of adapting to meet market and student demands.

14 Both the Ford study, *Higher Education for Business* (New York: Columbia University Press, 1959), and the Carnegie research, *The Education of American Businessmen: A Study of University-College Programs in Business Administration* (New York: McGraw-Hill, 1959), offer detailed portraits of the management landscape of the time.

15 Critics include Jeffrey Pfeffer and Christina Fong ("The Business School 'Business': Some Lessons from the US Experience", *Journal of Management Studies,* December 2004); Mintzberg (*Managers, Not MBAs, 2004*); and Bennis and O'Toole ("How Business Schools Lost Their Way," *Harvard Business Review,* May 2005).

16 "Potent in a Global Market", *Financial Times*, 29 January 2007, p. 10.

17 Some surveys, for example, ignore recruiters' opinions while heavily weighting factors such as starting salary. Others focus on research, doctoral programs, or else consider student perspectives, while discounting or minimizing other aspects of the MBA experience. It is difficult for the same school to excel across all these dimensions, resulting in different ranking outcomes depending upon the criteria most valued in the assessments.

18 "It's Time to Make Management a True Profession", *Harvard Business Review,* October 2008.

19 Even some senior school administrators find the rankings' imperfections frustrating. This frustration extends even to those who benefit by the rankings, such as former Wharton dean, Patrick Harker, who told *TopMBA*: "Some people believe that if the rankings help us, who cares if they are flawed or give a limited view of the school? But we can't have it both ways. We either endorse a defective, inconsistent practice, or we speak out and ... work with the media to enable them to report with more useful, objective data."

20 Nunzio Quacquarelli, "B-schools Look Beyond Rankings", , *Asia Inc.*, May–June 2007, pp. 81–2.

21 Customer focus is essential for all successful commerce, but schools that over-indulge this concern can lose track of their educational mission. Focusing on student needs is important, especially when doing so creates valuable learning experiences. When schools cater to every whim, however, they abandon their primary function and perform no great service to their customers – neither the students nor recruiters. "Customer focus" can devolve into undesirable byproducts, including grade inflation.

22 "Sustaining Scholarship in Business Schools: Report of the Doctoral Faculty Commission to AACSB's Board of Directors", 2003.

23 A nonprofit organization founded in 1953 to advance management education by helping schools develop metrics, such as standardized tests, to evaluate candidates. Additional details about these and the figures above may be found on GMAC's website.

24 AACSB cites that some US$2.2 billion in NSF funding was directed to the sciences and engineering in 2002–3, while only US$10 million went to business schools.

25 Increasingly, management educators recognize this. Richard Schmalensee, dean of the MIT Sloan School of Management, for example, said that schools must "engage thoughtful practitioners in research-based, problem-driven endeavors to improve both teaching *and* practice of management". See "Where's the 'B' in B-Schools?", *BusinessWeek*, 27 November 2006, p. 118.

26 See "Do B-Schools Add Value?", *ISB Insight,* June 2005, pp. 4–10.

27 "Global MBA Graduate Survey, 2007", Graduate Management Admission Council, p. 2: "Rather than attending class and passively learning from their professors, graduate business student respondents sought engaging classroom settings where their fellow students contributed to the learning process."

28 *The Wall Street Journal* ranked the most-valued attributes of MBA students from the recruiters' perspective. Topping the list with 89 percent of recruiters calling it "very important" was communication and interpersonal skills. Right behind that attribute was the ability to work well within a team (86.9 percent), and analytical and problem-solving skills (84.3 percent). See "Ranking the Attributes" in 20 September, 2006 edition.

29 "New Graduation Skills", *The Economist*, 12 May 2007, pp. 75–6.

30 See "Permanent Innovation", *América Economía*, August 2006, pp. 2–4. The flexibility demonstrated by Stanford and other top schools, including Harvard, Wharton, MIT, Kellogg and INSEAD, can help to align curricula with business needs, while also attracting top talent from a broader pool of students, including those whose backgrounds include government studies, philosophy and the arts who are "looking to develop careers in business, investment banking or management consulting, sectors that are ravenous for ever more new and creative talent".

31 Ranjay Gulati, "Tent-poles, Tribalism, and Boundary-Spanning: The Rigor–Relevance Debate in Management Research", *Academy of Management Journal*, August 2007, pp. 775–82.

32 "Back to School for Business Schools", Peter Day, BBC Radio 4 and BBC World Service, 5 March 2007.

33 See, for example, "More US Students Go Abroad for Their MBAs", *USA Today*, 7 June 2007, p. 5B.

34 Just as students benefit from cultivating global perspectives, top schools themselves may discover value in expanding their global footprint through collaborative ventures, such as strategic alliances, academic partnerships or "train the trainer" arrangements. Alternatively, they can expand abroad through new campus development. Resources, clearly, are the key determinant of the success of such global expansion. Some schools may find that a hybrid approach, combining the above options, works best.

35 For a recent example of such an article, see Chan Chao Peh, "The Art of the China Deal: Eight Tips for Successful Negotiations with Chinese Business Partners," *Asia Inc.*, May–June 2007, pp. 58–9.

36 Anne Fisher, "The Trouble with MBAs", *Fortune*, 30 April 2007, pp. 49–50.

37 The survey, available on GMAC's website, indicates that a majority of students across all programs find many dimensions – faculty, curriculum, classmates, admissions – of their MBA experience "outstanding/excellent". For example, some 73 percent of executive students report that their faculty members were exemplary, while 68 percent and 62 percent of full- and part-time students, respectively, reported the same. One area seemingly in need of attention across all programs is career services: no cohort ranked this part of the experience higher than 40 percent "excellent". Part-time students found most fault with these services, ranking them "outstanding" only 31 percent of the time.

38 These estimates are necessarily approximate. Individual talent and circumstances influence the exact duration of each stage, but most managers will find their careers tracing a path roughly as indicated here.

39 The July 2005 edition of *CEO Magazine* noted that executive education's value proposition included academic insights, often tailored to meet the custom needs of a client – and at a lower cost than bringing in outside consultants – as well as the relational return on investment (ROI) obtained by companies through interaction with business schools. In addition, said the article's author, "[L]eaning on a business professor or dean for regular professional advice can be more economically palatable than bringing in a high-priced management consultant for a one-shot quick fix."

40 H. J. Leavitt (1989) "Educating Our MBAs: On Teaching What We Haven't Taught", *California Management* Review 31(3): 38–50.

41 Current US Department of Education figures in the agency's National Center for Educational Statistics HEGIS survey capture data through 2002.

42 See the 2006 GMAC "Global Graduate Survey", p. 7. Students strongly reported believing that their MBA education would result in long-term potential, in part because it would give them the ability to think strategically and integrate information while also enhancing their leadership and quantitative skills. In the 2007 version of this survey, GMAC noted (p. 9) that graduates reported great improvements in areas such as knowledge of general business functions, managing strategy and innovation, managing the decision-making process,

strategic systems skills, generative thinking and interpersonal skills. (Fewer respondents expressed satisfaction with their program's ability to impart a lot of technology, design and production knowledge, or knowledge of media communications and delivery.)

43 GMAC reports that, as of 2007, the average annual growth among test takers under the age of 24 is 8.5 percent, "higher than the rate of growth calculated for older test-takers". See GMAC's 2007 "Global MBA Survey", p. 20.

44 Graduate Management Admission Council, "Application Trends Survey, 2007".

45 The figure is from US Bureau of Census data.

46 "The Business School 'Business': Some Lessons from the US Experience", *Journal of Management Studies* 41(8) December 2004.

47 In this category we include difficult business problems whose solution creates value for customers, for organizations and for their employees. More broadly, the benefits accrued by solving such challenges extend to the larger community affected by the organization and its people, products or services.

48 See, for example, Chrystia Freeland, "Doing Well or Doing Good?", *Financial Times*, 23 June 2007. Also, Marlene Habib, "MBA 2.0: A Stepping Stone to Tech Management", *Globe and Mail* (Canada) 26 March 2008; and Marie Field, "Nonprofit MBAs – No, This Isn't an Oxymoron", *TopMBA*, 2 February 2008.

49 Sharon Shinn, "Bachelor No. 1", *BizE*, November/December 2006, pp. 26–31. Traditionally, most business schools began exclusively as undergraduate programs, with the MBA flourishing after the Second World War and facilitating career changes. Hence, the renewed interest in the undergraduate business degree simply reflects a market shift similar to those that management education has seen in decades past. Schools adapted to market needs then and should now be capable of adapting again. At the same time, the decade of the 2000s has seen the market for executive education decline overall, as numbers of the traditional demographic for these non-degree programs – midcareer executives, and generally males aged 35 to 39 – has dwindled by about 1 million. While such programs, particularly custom ones, remain in demand, this trend accents the need for schools to consider their overall portfolio of programs when their devising competitive strategy. See Irwin Speizer, "Back to School: Exec Programs See Resurgence", *Workforce Management*, 15 January 2007.

50 *The Republic*, Book VII.

Business Schools and the Demands of Business Leadership

JAY O. LIGHT, Dean, Harvard Business School

T he financial crisis of 2008 and the global recession that followed – as deep and painful as any since the early decades of the twentieth century – have created profound new challenges for business leaders and raised funda-mental questions about the role and responsibility of business schools in produc-ing these leaders. The collapse was the result of a collective failure, not only of financial safeguards and institutions, but of leadership at many levels. This was true in corporate executive offices, in government, as well as in business schools.

The crisis that has consumed us for much of the past two years, however, is only the most recent instance of events in the larger world requiring business leaders and business schools to reexamine their fundamental purposes and ways of proceeding. The Great Depression, the Second World War, the rise of shareholder capitalism in the 1980s, and the corporate scandals of the early 2000s are all examples of disruptive events that had a deep impact on how executives and business educators thought about their roles. In this chapter I shall use the recent financial crisis as a way of raising and answering, for the present, two questions that have arisen before and will no doubt arise again: How have business schools fallen short in the past? And what must they do to rise to the challenges they now face in the light of present urgencies?

My answer to these questions will focus on the history of the MBA degree in the United States, because it is in America that the university-based business school of today originated and the MBA degree evolved. As many readers of this volume will recognize, however, there are parallels and similarities between the situation I will describe in American business schools and what has been happening in their counterparts in Europe (and elsewhere in the world) over the last fifty or more years.

The early evolution of the MBA

Management education has its roots in the private, for-profit schools of commerce that began to be established in the USA in the 1820s and expanded in number throughout the nineteenth century. These were vocational schools that primarily taught bookkeeping, inventory control and selling.

For-profit business colleges were supplemented and eventually supplanted by university-based schools of business that began to appear in the late nineteenth and early twentieth centuries. In the USA, the first collegiate business school was the University of Pennsylvania's Wharton School, founded in 1881 as a three-year undergraduate school and grounded in the liberal arts. Dartmouth's Tuck School of Administration and Finance, established in 1900, had a 3+2 structure in which students took a three-year undergraduate program in the liberal arts followed by two years of graduate study in business, for which they received a master's degree.

My own institution, Harvard Business School, was founded in 1908 as the first strictly graduate school of business: students had to have already earned a bachelor's degree in order to be admitted to its two-year program. Harvard's Graduate School of Business Administration, as it was then called, invented the title Master's in Business Administration, or MBA, for the degree it awarded, and was the first to grant that degree. Relatively soon, several other business schools were founded that had two-year programs and also awarded an MBA.

It is important to reflect on what the founders of these schools thought they were doing, and what was the special purpose of these university-based business schools. To put this in historical perspective, the early decades of the twentieth century, when these schools were created, were tumultuous. Business enterprises of unprecedented size and scope had emerged in industries such as railroads, oil and chemicals. These very large companies created a need for new and far more sophisticated management skills than had been required in the past. Moreover, they brought tremendous changes to American society, and for the first time placed great power and influence in the hands of professional managers who were not the owners of the business. Before that time, it had been the owners of businesses who held the power and influence and were accountable, both to their employees and to society at large, for what went on within their organizations.

In light of the recent crisis, it seems especially worth noting that dramatic swings in the business cycle and the instability of the financial system that became evident in the late nineteenth century and the first decade of the twentieth also formed an important part of the backdrop to the founding of graduate business schools and the rise of the MBA. Historical accounts of the Panic of 1907 read eerily like a prediction of today's economic circumstances. Liquidity problems, high levels of debt, and a complex, interconnected system of financial innovations led to a plunging stock market, the failure of major financial institutions, and a world on the verge of economic collapse – all after a long period of rapid economic growth. The parallels are striking, and point out the fact that business schools were founded with a mission to serve society by producing enlightened leadership for its major economic institutions.

In keeping with this particular sense of mission, the early business school founders and deans sought to create MBA programs that did at least two things. First, they were to impart new, higher-level knowledge and skills for the new top managers of firms, reflecting the increased complexity of these organizations and of the business environment. Second, and perhaps more important, the new MBA programs were meant to cultivate attitudes and values, and to develop character and integrity. They set out to equip their graduates with not only the tools for business success but also an appreciation of the role business played in the larger society and, along with that, a clear sense of purpose and responsibility. As Edwin Gay, the founding dean of Harvard Business School, described the school's purpose, HBS was to develop among its students "a habit of intellectual respect for business as a profession, with the social implications and heightened sense of responsibility that goes with that".

Thus early business schools sought, by teaching both skills and values, to develop what came to be known as general managers, and the institutions became known as schools of general management. Both teaching and research aimed for managerial relevance with a focus on practice. This emphasis was reinforced by the recruitment of practitioners – often drawn from the key industries of the time – as well as academics for teaching roles. These practitioners brought experience and insight into the classroom, teaching students about using management knowledge and skills in real business situations and about putting values into practice amid the competing interests and pressures that real business leaders face.

Changes in the postwar period

Graduate business education continued to expand in the decades after the founding of Harvard Business School in 1908. New institutions, such as the business schools at Columbia University and Stanford University (founded in

1916 and 1925, respectively) were founded, while older ones developed fully-fledged curricula and stronger faculties. (The Graduate School of Business at the University of Chicago, which grew out of an earlier institution founded in 1898, established the first PhD program in a business school in 1920.) Even so, by the end of the Second World War, there were still relatively few schools offering graduate management education, and those that did were very similar: all the schools had two-year MBA programs and all were schools of general management. One could move from school to school and recognize the curriculum, what the faculty was trying to do, and what the objectives of the institution were.

In the postwar era, all this began to change significantly under the impact of a number of forces. In the successful Allied war effort in the Second World War – to which American business schools leant significant support – new concepts in statistics, applied mathematics and economics were shown to be tremendously effective in dealing with the problems of managing large-scale enterprises. The war itself was the great triumph of what later became known as operations research. Analytical techniques and methods such as linear programming not only proved to be very effective in the war effort, but also appeared to have significant application to business organizations and operations. As a result, business schools began to experiment with their curricula to see how these new concepts and techniques might be incorporated into them.

A second major influence on business schools in the immediate postwar era was the economic boom that brought about explosive growth in American business, greatly increasing the demand for executive talent just as the GI Act was creating opportunities for returning American veterans to attend colleges and universities.

Finally, and most important, business schools began to come under fire from critics who saw them more as vocational schools than professional ones. Academic standards that had been developed and put into effect in fields such as medicine and law in the 1920s and 1930s had never been implemented in business schools, whose critics saw them lacking in at least three key areas. First, business schools were said to have insufficient academic rigor – in particular, it was charged, they paid little attention to scientific method in the study of management, or to developing scientific theories of management. Second, it was noted, few business schools had a research emphasis, in large part because of the heavy use of practitioners as instructors. (In the early

1950s, in fact, fewer than half of the full-time faculty even at leading business schools held doctorates, and fewer still did any research.) Third, doctoral education in business schools was deemed to be inadequate: the few programs that did exist were small and of relatively low quality, and the best students to graduate from them often chose high-paying jobs outside academia rather than joining the faculties of growing business schools.

In 1959, the Carnegie Foundation and Ford Foundation in the United States released reports that strongly criticized US business schools for their lack of academic rigor and advocated a much more scientific approach to the study of management. Change was crucial, the foundations said, not just to address the problems they had identified but also for equipping business schools to face the new challenges that would come as the "baby boom" generation entered college and graduate schools, including business schools. Beginning in the 1960s, with extremely generous support from the Ford Foundation and some others, change began to occur – slowly at first, and then relatively quickly. (This was the same period in which business schools also began to develop in larger numbers in Europe, where a similar process was at work.) Business schools raised the standards for admissions to their graduate programs. They hired and developed faculty members, who increasingly were discipline-based. They strengthened their doctoral programs, which also became much more discipline-based. New frameworks and models were brought to bear on management issues. Fields including finance, operations management and research, and marketing were greatly enhanced by the introduction of more rigorous and scientific methods of research and analysis.

While many of these changes were for the better, they were not without unintended consequences. As more and more business schools began to develop academically-oriented programs organized around disciplinary specialization – particularly in the behavioral sciences and quantitative disciplines – this new focus began to dilute the functional specialization of earlier decades. This change, in turn, pointed to a potential conflict between academic rigor and managerial relevance, a conflict that has become real, as some business schools and business school faculties have diverged from the criterion of managerial relevance in the pursuit of academic rigor. For example, financial theory has postulated a set of risk-and-return relationships whose applicability to corporate finance is unclear (as is their contribution to understanding what could and did go wrong in the recent financial crisis). Operations research has diverged rather sharply from practical notions of operations management, and the use of statistics in market research has strayed some distance from the concerns of practitioners in the field of marketing. In all these fields, it is doubtful that practitioners could understand many or most of the articles now published in peer-reviewed academic journals by business school faculty members – which was not the case in the 1960s and 1970s, before the changes initiated by the foundations had taken root in business schools around the country.

Moreover, even when the sophisticated new concepts and techniques taught in business schools are capable of being put into practice, they can become dangerous, as we have recently learned, when business leaders lack the judgment and values to use them for the right purposes. One lesson from the financial crisis is that many institutions had very sophisticated risk-management systems that did not lead to sensible risk management. This happened because financial executives were unable to determine when these systems were performing their intended functions and when they were just spitting out numbers. Lehman Brothers, for example, thought it had its risk management covered because it had all the right mathematical models; yet someone with judgment might have questioned whether, given the changes in the home mortgage market as lenders handed out loans to borrowers who were unable to repay them, the historical numbers on which Lehman's models were based were any longer relevant. The poor judgment exhibited here was partly a failure to think systemically about the firm and its environment, and partly, perhaps, a case of intelligence becoming clouded by short-term greed.

The lesson here is that while it is important, in examining what led up to the recent financial crisis, to include things such as the risk-management practices in large financial institutions, any serious inquiry into the causes of this economic disaster must inevitably look not just at concepts, models, techniques and practices but also at behavior and values. If various flaws in global financial markets and institutions encouraged individuals to become less focused than they should have been on systemic risks and more focused on the potential upside and their own personal gain, we must still answer the question of why so many individuals made the decisions that they did and – given that some of the actors involved are business school graduates – why the business schools they attended did not instill in them better judgment and sounder values.

Part of the answer to this question lies in the effects of recruiting discipline-based faculty members who are involved in discipline-based research.

The emphasis on this has increased only since the era when the Ford Foundation reforms began to take effect in business schools. (Interestingly, in a self-fulfilling cycle, more and more students are now entering discipline-based PhD programs rather than broad-based business administration programs, and business schools' promotion criteria have evolved to reward more discipline-based work.) As well as the conflict between academic rigor and managerial relevance noted above, the new academic orientation, with its emphasis on quantitative analysis and technique, has tended to crowd out attention in the MBA curriculum to larger business and contextual issues that business leaders (as opposed to managers) must understand. In short, the same reforms that helped to strengthen business schools in an era when they were still relatively unformed institutions have resulted in the undermining, in certain ways, of their dual mission of imparting knowledge and skills that are relevant to business practice while also instilling the judgment, character and values needed for wise and responsible business leadership.

Another factor has been the adoption of a "student as customer" model that, in some cases, has caused schools to be swept up, along with their students, in the temper of the times while neglecting certain unchanging realities. To return to the subject of risk management and the recent financial crisis: Amid the difficult economic times of the late 1970s and early 1980s – a period when American business was focused on the need to manage the downside, which is a crucial facet of general management – Harvard Business School offered several courses on the financial system and risk management that drew large numbers of students. Yet these courses disappeared from the curriculum as the economy revived and students became more focused on the upside. Today's MBA students, understandably, are much more focused on risk than were their predecessors just a few years ago, though it remains to be seen how business schools will react when the next boom arrives and their students are looking at a different horizon.

Both of these issues – the academic orientation of business school faculties, and the ways in which they respond to their students' demands for relevance – raise the question of what new reforms business schools must undertake in order to reaffirm and perform more effectively their historic mission in the environment in which we find ourselves today.

Meeting the new challenges: how business schools must adapt

Given that business schools must accept at least some of responsibility for the crisis that has brought so much pain and created so much uncertainty about the future, they must also be more committed than ever to being part of the solution. Although the need for competent and wise business leadership is today as great as, or perhaps greater than it has ever been, the challenges now faced by traditional, university-based business schools with MBA programs focused on general management and dedicated to producing business leaders are many – starting with the fact that the very idea of the MBA as anything more than vocational training is under widespread attack.

Management education as it has developed in the United States and abroad since the 1940s and 1950s is an unqualified success story in certain respects. In the United States, for example, the number of MBA degrees conferred each year has risen from approximately 3,000 at the end of the 1950s to approaching 150,000 today. Yet the MBA degree itself has come to stand for many more varied things than it did prior to the reforms of the postwar period in America.

As previously noted, American business schools and their MBA programs looked very similar to one another in their basic structure and content at the end of the Second World War. Yet the development of academic rigor promoted by the foundations beginning in the 1960s did not take the same form in all MBA programs. Faculties, for example, began to differ from one institution to another as some business schools became more discipline-based, others remained more functionally-based, while still others became more managerially-based. Some MBA programs became specialized while others remained more oriented toward general management; some were more global in focus, and others more national or even local. The character of the research pursued by faculty also began to diverge across schools. The teaching and learning process – be it centered around the case method, other kinds of participative processes, or lectures – also began to look different from one school to the next. The types of students sought by different schools began to change. Executive education, introduced in the 1950s primarily by the Harvard Business School, came to represent a very large and growing component of many business schools' activities.

Today, the MBA "industry", both in the United States and abroad, has become highly fragmented, while the degree itself has become increasingly commoditized. For example, there are now one-year MBA programs, two-year programs, 15-month programs and 27-month programs, many of them focused on specialties such as finance or information technology. There are evening and weekend programs. Business schools now award both executive degrees (EMBAs) and traditional MBAs. A portfolio of executive education offerings for managers at every stage of their careers has been developed. There is now a whole industry of "custom" executive education – a fast-growing segment of management education – where individual companies hire business schools to deliver tailored programs to their organizations. Most large US companies also now have an internal campus and hire faculty members – typically from business schools – to deliver things that look suspiciously like MBA courses to their employees, and only their employees. Meanwhile, undergraduate programs in the United States have begun to teach large parts of what used to be taught within MBA programs. Finally, online MBA education has become a sufficiently big business that people can buy an "MBA in a box", while the publishing industry has begun to get on the bandwagon with a whole variety of offerings with the "MBA" label on them.

To the extent that such innovations draw students away from traditional MBA programs by diluting the meaning and value of the initials "MBA", they pose a threat to any business schools that can offer no more than a path to a better-paying job in the short term. For traditional MBA programs to survive and flourish, it may not even be enough to appeal to those who seek from management education only a path to a more lucrative career over the long term. Business schools that really wish to differentiate themselves in the face of the fragmentation and commoditization of the MBA need to recommit themselves to their foundational purpose of educating general managers and leaders for a world that needs skilled and responsible business leadership now more than ever. They must do this by reexamining the way they carry out both aspects of their mission: imparting knowledge and teaching skills; and instilling judgment and values.

At the level of knowledge, skills and techniques, the first step that traditional business schools must take is to examine the way they develop and evaluate the faculty. Given that an emphasis on academic rigor in a disciplinary context conflicts increasingly with the need for managerial relevance in faculty research, business schools need to spend significant time and energy developing junior faculty members. Young faculty members coming out of PhD programs have typically not worked in business and often know little about it. This makes it important for them to be exposed to practice and practicing managers – through teaching executive education courses, or team-teaching with practitioners, or casewriting, for example –to learn about the problems facing practitioners.

Having been helped in this way to orient their thinking and research towards managerial practice, junior faculty need to be evaluated for tenure based on the quality and relevance of their research for practitioners, not just on the number of articles they publish in peer-reviewed journals. For improved development and evaluation of young faculty members, in turn, business schools should not only have a significant number of practitioners on the staff, but also have them as full-time, senior members who are embedded in the institution and able to influence how other faculty members think about issues. This is not now the case in most American business schools, where practitioners, though well represented in the teaching corps, are rarely full-time faculty members (whereas, as we have seen, they represented over half of full-time business school faculties in the early 1950s).

A second step that business schools must take to ensure that the knowledge and skills they impart remain relevant to the education of general managers and business leaders is to reexamine their curricula in the light of recent events in the financial world and beyond. As business schools develop new tools for managers to use, so as to anticipate and avoid catastrophes such as the one we have just experienced, one immediate challenge will be to balance a sense of urgency about this task against the knowledge that effective solutions will come only from a deep understanding of the crisis and its causes and effects. As we have all witnessed, the diagnosis here is extremely complicated. Developing the deep understanding we need will require us to reexamine virtually everything we teach in our MBA programs for years to come – particularly when it comes to teaching our students to look at the big picture, as business leaders must be able to do.

Two new courses developed by faculty at HBS illustrate how business schools can address the particulars of the recent financial crisis while also developing a broad and deep understanding that should remain relevant to the circumstances that future business leaders will face. One of our professors of management practice (who spent twenty years with J. P. Morgan & Co. before earning a PhD in sociology and embarking on a teaching career) now teaches a second-year elective called "Managing the Financial Firm". The course explores the challenges faced by leaders in financial firms at a time of unprecedented disruption to industry and business models, of historic regulatory and political intervention in markets and firms, and of a fundamental reconsideration of the roles and responsibilities of these firms and their leaders. Another of our faculty members, an historian, has launched a course entitled "Creating the Modern Financial System", which examines the historical development of key financial instruments and institutions worldwide and the behavior of financial actors and groups (particularly in the context of financial bubbles and crashes). In addition to creating such new courses in the area of finance, we are also reconsidering topics such as the oversight responsibilities of directors, and revisiting the kinds of incentives provided by executive compensation packages. These examples are just the tip of the iceberg in a curriculum that will continue to evolve as what will probably be a new global financial system emerges.

Such innovation in the curriculum is something that business schools have always done and will always have to do to adapt their teaching to changing environments and prepare their students for the real world of practice. Beyond these issues of curriculum and content, business schools that remain committed to a mission of educating leaders will need to instill in their students not just ideas but also particular perspectives, habits of mind and attitudes. As we have seen all too clearly in the past year, leaders in the twenty-first century will need to be able to operate more effectively in a world defined by closer relationships among government, business and other stakeholders. We shall therefore need to equip our graduates to operate at the increasingly connected interface of business, government and society on a global basis, so that our graduates will in effect speak many "languages" at a time when fluency is an essential asset for our leaders. By the same token, we need to respond to the expanding interests of our students, who are planning careers not only in traditional business settings but also in healthcare and science-based organizations as well as nonprofit and other social enterprises.

Another critical task for business schools that aspire to prepare their students for leadership roles is to cultivate the intangible but indispensable quality we call judgment. The leading business schools have always seen the cultivation of judgment in their students as one of their most important objectives. Yet the continuing evolution of the business world, along with its social and political environment, toward ever greater complexity makes it all the more important for leaders to be able to think through and make decisions in situations where no perfect understanding is possible, and no clear right answer exists. In addition to the judgment required to make wise decisions amid complexity and uncertainty, business leaders continue to need a strong sense of values, particularly now that the integrity of so many has been called into question and the roles and responsibilities of business are up for redefinition.

By rededicating themselves to such core objectives while adapting to meet the new economic, social and political realities, and the wide-ranging ambitions of their students, traditional business schools can and, I believe, will be part of the solution to the global crisis that has so threatened confidence in our economic institutions and their leadership.

At my own school, this means that the core of our teaching will be more important than ever before. We shall help our students to see the big picture and anticipate the impact of their decisions as well as to offer them a deeper understanding of the financial crisis and its implications. We shall do so through the daily classroom interactions that are the signature of the case method, with its emphasis on framing the issues and asking the right questions as opposed to simply giving the right answer; indeed, we believe that such interactions, more than any particular curriculum, must be at the heart of any effort to educate leaders who will make a difference in the world. We shall continue to do research that is close to practice and offers genuinely innovative ways of thinking about business, managerial and leadership issues. And we shall recommit ourselves to cultivating the qualities at the heart of leadership: an entrepreneurial point of view that can see longstanding problems through fresh eyes; judgment that leads to sound decision-making in complex, often ambiguous conditions; values and ethics; the ability to listen and communicate; and a penchant for turning analysis into effective action.

For all of us in business schools, whether in the United States or elsewhere around the globe, it is by reaffirming our most fundamental and deeply held values that we can best adapt to an ever-changing environment and produce the kinds of business leaders that our world will always need.

The Contribution of Business Schools to the Twenty-first Century

PEDRO NUENO, Bertran Foundation Professor of Entrepreneurship, IESE Business School, University of Navarra, and President, China Europe International Business School (CEIBS)

The first question anyone who chooses to write under such a title is likely to be asked is: Will business schools still be around at the end of the twenty-first century? Whether my great-grandchildren's grandchildren or their contemporaries will want to do an MBA is hard to predict, but if trends are anything to go by, the most likely answer is that, yes, business schools will still be here at the end of the century.

Two of the most prestigious schools, Harvard and Wharton, have been going for over a hundred years and continue to grow. On 12–14 October 2008, Harvard Business School celebrated its 100th anniversary with an event attended by 2,000 alumni. Participants were electrified by a line-up of speakers that included Bill Gates and Meg Whitman. Then they split into groups and trooped back into classrooms that some of them had last seen more than fifty years earlier to discuss, with faculty moderators, the issues that interested them most from among a large selection: corporate governance, the future of Dubai, the growth of the real estate industry, the depth of the economic crisis, the future of entrepreneurship, China among the global economies and so on. The alumni sat in a half-circle, while the professor, chalk in hand, moved around in the middle of the half-circle between the first row of students and the blackboards on the front wall.

At first sight, the classrooms themselves had changed very little in the intervening period and what went on inside them was essentially the same as in earlier days. An observant alumnus would immediately notice a lot of electronic equipment that had not been invented when he/she last sat there, perhaps twenty-five years earlier. Yet in those classrooms, the professor still called on students to speak by pointing at them or by name (read from a name card on the desk in front of each person), setting one opinion against another, provoking reflection, dialogue and controversy, and writing on the board the key points to be brought out from this skillfully orchestrated discussion.

Harvard Business School has a supervisory board appointed by the University, known as the Visiting Committee, of which I have the honor to be a member. In a recent session I asked Dean Jay Light, "What will a classroom be like here in 2020?" Without hesitation he replied, "It won't have changed much; there will probably be more technology, but what happens in the classroom will be very similar to what happens today."

I teach at Harvard Business School several times a year and usually take the opportunity to attend classes given by internationally renowned colleagues. Today's classes are very similar to the ones I attended as a student almost forty years ago, except that at some point technology may come into play, as when Prof. Srikant Datar, for example, in a session in which the Novartis case was discussed, arranged a live debate between the students and Novartis Chairman Daniel Vasella, sitting in his office in Switzerland, who could see the students as clearly as they could see him and, as a Harvard alumnus, enthusiastically joined in the discussion. The same happens at Wharton, the London Business School and IESE.

A hundred years of history

Despite some schools having existed for a hundred years or more, business education can be said to have developed in the United States and Europe after the Second World War – that is, starting in the 1950s. Some MBA programs were begun in the United States before the Second World War. The format varied, but the most common was the two-year program for young people with a university degree and some professional experience.

Training for more experienced managers took off in the 1940s at Harvard Business School, when Frank Folts was given the task of transforming the training opportunities offered by Harvard to the companies engaged in the war effort through a program for senior executives. The result was the Advanced Management Program (AMP), a type of course that is still very successful today and has inspired similar programs at the world's top business schools.

It was in the 1950s and 1960s, often with academic support from the United States and imitating US models, that the first schools with an international outlook and scope appeared in Europe, including IMEDE in Switzerland,

INSEAD in France, the London Business School in the UK and IESE in Spain. The first schools in Latin America, Africa and Japan date from the same period. Many of the schools established in Latin America – in Mexico in the 1960s, Argentina in the 1970s and many more countries in the 1980s – received – and still receive – crucial support from IESE. The first business schools in Africa appeared in South Africa in the 1970s, and again IESE provided vital support to schools in many countries, starting with its close collaboration with Lagos Business School in Nigeria in the early 1990s. In Japan, the Harvard Business School backed the development of the Keio Business School, but the business school model has never really taken root in Japan.

During the 1970s and 1980s, many European universities created management departments and launched MBA and Ph.D. programs, while many other projects were developed under private initiatives.

The first to establish themselves seriously in China were the European schools, led by their association, the European Foundation for Management Development (EFMD), with the start-up of an MBA in Beijing in 1984. In 1994, the EFMD decided to transfer the project to Shanghai, recasting it as a joint initiative of the European Union and the Shanghai government, implemented through the China Europe International Business School (CEIBS). The intellectual and economic dynamism of Shanghai and the spectacular development of China provided the conditions for extraordinary growth in student numbers and quality, so that CEIBS came to be considered the top business school in the Asia-Pacific region. During the 1990s and early 2000s, business schools proliferated in China, some achieving a high level of excellence by international standards. Much the same occurred in India, where schools such as the Indian Institute of Management achieved the very highest level of quality.

The 1960s and 1970s saw a new concern to develop custom programs for individual companies, building on the ability of business schools not only to impart management knowledge but also to adapt it to the specific circumstances of particular firms. Most large companies use all the training options at their disposal: they hire young MBAs, send their managers on different types of "open programs", and arrange for specific training tailored to the particular circumstances of their development.

The process of a business school

It is generally agreed that the leading philosopher in the field of management so far has been Peter Drucker. He visited IESE a couple of times in the early

1980s and always had fond memories of Barcelona and IESE. Shortly before he passed away, he shared his views with me on the process methodology of a business school, a subject on which my dean, Jordi Canals, had asked me to give a presentation to IESE faculty members. I approached Peter Drucker for help and he generously taught me the following: management, he said, is not a science but a practice; and the best model for a business school, he suggested, is that of a university hospital.

In a university hospital you have patients (companies), doctors (professors), and students (participants in management programs). Doctors visit patients and write patient histories (cases). They discuss these cases with their students, assess the situation and evaluate possible treatments. Some of these treatments are part of new drug testing and so are state-of-the-art. As doctors start to feel comfortable diagnosing and treating diseases, they draw up protocols (frameworks for action), which then become standard practice. Their case teaching helps them and their students to understand the problems, and to develop treatments and protocols. Doctors present their findings at doctors' meetings and progress in their profession as a result of the recognition of their peers.

In the field of management, professors must step into the real world, study the problems that managers face in different areas of corporate activity and write cases on these problems. Once they have written several cases and have a good coverage of the real world, they can bring this knowledge and experience into the classroom and discuss it in an organized way. In the process, they learn and develop frameworks to facilitate analysis and decision-making in the chosen problem areas. Once they have acquired expertise in dealing with management reality, professors can put it to use as consultants or directors.

The itinerary, therefore, that Peter Drucker recommends for management professors is this: go to the real world and collect its problems in the case format; bring reality into the classroom with the case format and discuss it with program participants to generate problem-solving approaches; go to the office and develop "problem-approaching frameworks" based on the results of the discussion of different cases dealing with similar problems; bring these frameworks to professional meetings with peers to contribute to the development of management knowledge; bring this knowledge to reality as a consultant or director, using it directly to solve problems; keep going through this cycle again and again.

There is no doubt that Peter Drucker made an excellent contribution, bridging the gap between theory and practice, between teaching, research and action, between the world of ideas and the world of relevance. For him, these two worlds are one, and management knowledge cannot isolate itself from the practice of management. Most leading business schools have accepted this model of thinking and the best-known professors of management have openly practiced this approach.

Competition among business schools

Business schools stand out among academic institutions in the way that they compete with one another. They do so by trying to attract the best human capital, both faculty members and students, be they young MBA students, high-flyers taking an EMBA, or managers at different levels attending a wide variety of programs.

This competition influences and shapes faculty careers. Good faculty members must have earned a PhD at one of the best universities; but they must also compete successfully against several other candidates, all of whom must demonstrate their potential as teachers and researchers. There will be various promotion opportunities during their career, subject to meeting ambitious goals in terms of published contributions to management knowledge and teaching performance, evidenced in part by the assessments made by their students. All this takes place on an international stage.

When it comes to selecting program participants, careful evaluation of CVs, standard international tests and, in some cases, interviews with personnel selection experts are used to ensure that candidates have the right motivation, are clearly choosing the future they want and are likely to do very well in the program and in their subsequent career.

Do business schools add value to society?

If we take the period of recent history in which business schools have developed (basically, the period since the Second World War), there is no denying that the quality of life around the world has improved in an extraordinary way. Hundreds of millions of people have achieved a quality of life characteristic of developed economies. This enormous and indisputable improvement, unlike anything experienced in any other period of history (considering the number of people affected), has been driven by what we call innovation and entrepreneurship.

Innovation is the application of new knowledge to existing reality. Entrepreneurship consists of organizing the necessary processes to satisfy a new need (what we call an opportunity), aiming to do so profitably and accepting a certain risk. Innovation and entrepreneurship go hand in hand. It does not take a very rigorous analysis to realize that what is available to us today in terms of food, health, communication, transportation and housing, and all that this entails in terms of industry and services, has improved spectacularly over the period referred to, across borders and across continents.

A slightly deeper analysis would show how business schools help to catalyze this process. Their working method is to bring the latest developments into the classroom, study them, discuss them and find ways to structure their key aspects, all with a view to improving economic development and spreading the knowledge of how to do so. Different periods have brought new subjects into the classroom: personal motivation, marketing, quality control, "just-in-time" operations, private equity, global management, diversification, acquisitions, restructuring, and the creation of technology-based firms.

Certain management professors are closely associated with the basic knowledge that has been used to build the economic wealth we enjoy today, which they put into a usable form. I could mention here Theodore Levitt and marketing; Elton May and Fritz Roetlisberger and motivation; Wilbur England and purchasing; Michael Porter and strategy; James Bright and technology management; Howard Stevenson and entrepreneurship – among many others. Georges Doriot created the American Research and Development Corporation (ARDC), the world's first venture capital firm. Doriot was a professor at Harvard Business School and would bring his innovative ideas into the classroom by discussing with his students such early deals as the financing of Ken Olsen's Digital Equipment Corporation. ARDC was a success and its French-born founder played an important role in establishing INSEAD as the leading business school in France and a major player worldwide.

Concepts such as "quality circles" developed out of the interaction between companies and the classroom. A early as 1944, Frank Folts tried to disseminate these concepts in his book *The Production Conference*. Curiously, Folts found more receptive audiences in Japan, a country he visited frequently, where the idea of continuous improvement and employee participation was applied successfully to manufacturing and other industries. In the 1980s, Japan emerged as an unbeatable industrial power. Its companies invested in Europe and the United States, quickly making a place for themselves in the market. Western business schools reacted swiftly and effectively: Japanese know-how was translated and popularized; schools organized study trips to Japan; early applications of the concepts of continuous improvement, quality circles and just-in-time working were converted into case studies and widely discussed and disseminated. By the end of the decade Japanese companies had lost their competitive edge and the industrial processes of the West had made these concepts their own.

Business schools have been pioneers in assimilating successive waves of knowledge and changes in society. They engaged with, absorbed, studied and disseminated the technology explosion of the 1990s. They explored the globalization of companies in search of new markets, and the resulting problems of how to manage people in different cultures and how to manage complex logistics efficiently. Many leading schools have looked for ways to form alliances with new schools in emerging countries in order to study these developments "on the ground".

Business schools and values

Ethics, corporate social responsibility and fair distribution of wealth are foundational concepts of business schools. They feature in the speech Antonio Valero, IESE's founding dean, gave at the school's first MBA graduation ceremony in 1966. Yet these are cross-disciplinary subjects that have been part of the curriculum for business school students since such schools first came into existence. In the early 1940s, Elton May studied *The Social Problems of an Industrial Civilization* from a global perspective, which even then included China. Texts such as Clarence Walton's *Corporate Social Responsibilities* (1967) and William Frankena's *Ethics* (1963) were compulsory reading for PhD students at the Harvard Business School in the 1970s.

If we look at the courses offered in the second year of the MBA at the Harvard Business School in the early 1970s, we find courses such as: *Low Income Housing*; *Business and Society in Africa*; *Business, Society and the Individual*; *Comparative Business and Culture*. Courses were delivered on environmental management issues such as energy, sustainable business growth and balanced urban development. Many of these subjects are still as topical as ever, but by applying management knowledge we have been able to make extraordinary progress in this unprecedented international economic development.

The future of business schools

The world's best business schools have something in common: the support and affection of their alumni, with whom they maintain close ties. Most of their alumni pursue successful careers as entrepreneurs (who must be good managers) or managers (who must be entrepreneurs). The career success of their alumni, creating value for society, is proof that business schools have made a positive contribution. This is corroborated by the grateful support they receive from their alumni. Given this relationship, the continuity of business schools is assured.

Institutions have long life cycles and great inertia. Some business schools that once led the world have now fallen into obscurity; they gradually declined, perhaps without realizing it. Others have come from nowhere, earning a high level of recognition in a very short time. Institutions develop through sustained effort – something that surely will not change in the twenty-first century. We shall have to carry on learning, day by day; living in the real world and improving it with new applicable knowledge. We shall have to monitor the results very closely and establish effective feedback to ensure that the impact on the social and economic environment is as intended. We can safely predict that business schools will still be with us at the end of this century, though if we look at the list of the top schools, we may find that some we expected to find there have disappeared, while others that do not even exist today figure prominently.

PART 2

New Challenges in Leadership Development and Executive Education: The Scholars' Perspective

CHAPTER 2.1

From Action Theory to the Theory of the Firm

ANTONIO ARGANDOÑA, La Caixa Professor of Corporate Social Responsibility, IESE Business School, University of Navarra

Introduction[1]

Traditionally, economics has concerned itself with the efficient use of scarce resources used for alternative purposes (Robbins, 1934). The prime locus of economic efficiency is the market, where subjects conduct transactions that, under certain conditions, optimize the use of resources. Coase (1937), however, finds that, in this context, there are certain organizations in which voluntary market exchanges are replaced by decisions made by means of authority. This is the starting point for the neoclassical institutional theories of the firm that now dominate the economics departments of universities and business schools.

It is not my intention here to explain these theories, or their variants.[2] Together they make an excellent, well-founded and well-developed body that has contributed decisively to our understanding of the firm and the large questions surrounding it – which are, principally, why the firm exists, its boundaries and its internal organization (Holmström and Tirole, 1989). The institutional theories have been criticized on conceptual and methodological grounds (Foss and Klein, 2006, 2008, 2009; Foss, 2007) and because of their practical consequences (Ghoshal and Moran, 1996; Donaldson, 2002; Ferraro *et al.*, 2005). Yet this does not diminish their theoretical and empirical importance. Whatever one's conception of the firm, any theory of the firm must take into account transaction costs, property rights, agency problems, information asymmetries, moral hazard, asset specificity, rent-seeking, incomplete contracts, opportunism and hold up, team production, shirking and many other aspects of institutional theory. That is why these are considered to be mainstream theories.

There are other, alternative theories, which could be termed cybernetic institutional theories.[3] They differ from the neoclassical institutional theories mainly in their conception of the economic agent as an open system (hence the term "cybernetic") and of the rationality of human action, which, in their conception, is not complete and closed to outside influence but is open to learning. Included in this category are evolutionary theory (Nelson and Winter, 1982); the theory of competencies or capabilities (Penrose, 1959; Richardson, 1972); and the Austrian theories (Foss, 1994; Dulbecco and Garrouste, 1999; Ioannides, 1999; Yu, 1999; Lewin and Phelan, 2000).[4] Nelson and Winter pay particular attention to the strategy of the firm in its dealings with the environment, the firm's structure or institutional "memory", and firm capabilities, thus tying in with a second group of theories which conceive of the firm as a nexus of capabilities that are to a greater or lesser extent shared by the firm's members, effectively making the firm a means of coordinating the knowledge possessed by its members. The Austrian theories, in contrast, emphasize, among other aspects, the actions of the entrepreneur, the subjective nature of such actions and the fact that the actions takes place under conditions of ignorance and uncertainty *à la* Knight (1921).

Economics always starts from a theory of human action (though it does not always make that theory explicit). Mainstream theories about the firm adopt a limited view of human action, as they concern themselves with what distinguishes exchange-oriented action from the action that takes place inside firms, which is characterized by authority.[5] The first question Coase (1937) asks is why are there "islands of conscious power in this ocean of unconscious cooperation, like lumps of butter coagulating in a pail of buttermilk?" (Coase, 1937, p. 388, citing D. H. Robertson). In theories of the firm, therefore, the market is the model; and the human action with which these theories are concerned is the action that manifests itself in exchange, be it in the market or in the firm. This is particularly important when discussing the subjects' motivations. In the theories we are considering, the motivation that is most important – and in some cases the only motivation that counts – is what is usually known as extrinsic motivation; that is, what rational subjects pursue when they exchange goods in the market; other types of motivation are irrelevant to them.

Limited as they are to exchange, these theories are not intended to explain human organizations in general, only for-profit business firms. Other organizations will require a different explanation, which may coincide with the theory of the firm in so far as it describes how these other organizations seek to achieve economic efficiency, in the same way as companies (Posner, 2010).

On the other hand, if what differentiates a firm from the market (at least at first sight) is the existence of relations of authority or hierarchy, the theories of the firm will conceive of decision-making in terms of a principal who gives orders and one or more agents who obey. What they will try to explain is how the agents can be induced to cooperate in achieving the goals set by the principal, what contracts can be written, what incentives can be offered, how the agents can be monitored and controlled, and other similar matters. All this revolves around the contract as the central institution, in both the market and the firm (though the contracts will be structured differently in each case). What matters, therefore, is the formal organization, the assumption being that the informal organization is immaterial (Pérez-López, 1993, p. 16). This also implies that theories about the internal organizational structure of the firm will be left to other disciplines.[6]

The purpose of this chapter is not to pick holes in mainstream theories of the firm, but rather to show how a broader action theory may help to overcome some of their limitations. In the following section we shall briefly explain the basics of that broader action theory and its implications for human organizations. After that, we shall make some suggestions about what the broader action theory might entail for the theory of the firm – not a proposal, just some general indications of where the conventional theories could be improved – and ending with our conclusions.

An action theory

Our starting point will be a fairly general theory of rational action.[7] Let us assume that the subjects act in order to move from a less satisfactory situation to a more satisfactory one (here we shall deal exclusively with actions that involve interaction between a personal subject, the "active agent", and another subject, the "reactive agent"). The effect or outcome the active agent hopes to achieve may be extrinsic (the satisfaction he or she derives from the reactive agent's response) or intrinsic (an internal effect that does not come from the reactive agent – for example, what the active agent learns – or the satisfaction he or she derives from the action itself) or external (an effect on the reactive agent, but only in so far as this effect does not have extrinsic or intrinsic effects on the active agent) (Pérez-López, 1991).

This gives rise, in turn, to three possible motivations for action, depending on the outcome the active agent hopes to achieve: extrinsic (as a result of the effect the reactive agent's response has on the active agent), intrinsic (caused by what the active agent does and the effect it has on him or her) and transcendent (as a result of the effect the active agent expects the interaction to have on the reactive agent).[8] All three motivations are relevant and may occur simultaneously; there is no reason why one should predominate over the others. While, in economic activity, extrinsic motivation is the first to appear, we cannot ignore the other two, not even in exchanges that take place in the market or actions that take place inside the firm.

The active agent could be, for example, an entrepreneur who wants to seize a business opportunity to obtain an economic profit (extrinsic motive), win social recognition (extrinsic), have the personal satisfaction of achieving what he or she set out to do (intrinsic), help other people (transcendent), have the personal satisfaction of helping others (intrinsic) or receive recognition for helping others (extrinsic). The active agent could also be a manager (agent), who serves an owner (principal) and manages an employee out of motives that may be extrinsic (to earn a salary, including the possibility of appropriating the rents generated by the business, within the agency relationship with the principal), intrinsic (learning, satisfaction) or transcendent (customer service, professional and human development of the employee, fulfillment of a duty to the principal). As the action theory is general in scope, the employee too can be seen as an active agent, whose motives may be extrinsic (pay, promotion, recognition), intrinsic (learning, enjoyment of the job) or transcendent (serving customers, satisfying his manager, helping his co-workers).

Actions have consequences, the extrinsic outcomes intended by the active agent, but also other effects on both active and reactive agents. When a person acts, he or she acquires operational learning (knowledge, capabilities and skills that make him/her better at what he/she does and that make what is done more enjoyable – or less so, if it becomes repetitive). And when a person seeks external results, he or she acquires evaluative learning (the ability to value people and actions, in so far as they affect people, and as a result, motivation to perform tasks and the ability to solve other people's problems). In either case, what the person learns changes his or her preferences and rules of action, which means that he/she might decide differently in the future.

Every action produces the results mentioned above, which are always present to some extent, whether deliberately sought or not. We therefore have three criteria for evaluating the active agent's action: the satisfaction obtained as a result of achieving the expected or desired extrinsic outcome (which we shall call effectiveness); the satisfaction obtained as a result of achieving the internal outcome (efficiency), which will make it easier or more difficult for the active agent to achieve similar extrinsic outcomes again in the future; and the changes that take place in the reactive agent as a result of the interaction, which will make it easier or more difficult to interact with the same reactive agent again in the future (consistency) (Pérez-López, 1991, pp. 36–8).[9]

Effectiveness, efficiency and consistency can act in different directions. An action plan may be effective (the employee does what the manager orders him or her to do), but inefficient (the manager becomes increasingly reluctant to give orders) or inconsistent (implementing the action plan makes it more difficult, or even impossible, to implement a similar action plan again in the future with this reactive agent).[10] An inconsistent plan results in negative learning on the part of the active agent, in so far as it makes the agent, probably without realizing it, less able to see what is really important in the interaction until it is too late (Pérez López, 1991, p. 55).[11]

Evaluating an action is therefore not a trivial task. There are three reasons why it is not:

1. One has to take into account not just a single criterion (effectiveness), as is usually the case in economics, but three, which may act in opposing directions – and there is no law to tell us how and when they will differ.

2. The relationships between the three criteria are not obvious. There is a certain trade-off between effectiveness and efficiency: an employee with high intrinsic motivation will perform better and probably need less extrinsic motivation; similarly, a greater financial reward is likely to be sufficient to induce the employee to accept a more unpleasant job. But that will not always be the case: given an assignment he or she does not like, the employee may react by accepting the assignment because it is what the firm requires of him/her, or he/she may protest because he/she feels mistreated, or may demand a pay raise, or may adopt an attitude of refusal – and this reaction might change over time.

3. The relative importance of the three outcomes is not obvious. The active agent will naturally do his or her best, perhaps spontaneously, to take the extrinsic effects (effectiveness) of his/her action into

account, and possibly also the intrinsic effects (efficiency); but he/she will not consider the external effects (consistency) except by making a conscious, positive effort. And the changes in the effectiveness, efficiency and consistency of his/her action will change the agent's decision rule, "the set of operations ... by which an active agent chooses an action" (Pérez-López, 1991, p. 28).

The rational action theory outlined here may serve as a basis for a general theory of organizations.[12] An organization is "a group of people who coordinate their actions to achieve objectives in which they all have an interest, albeit for different reasons" (Pérez-López, 1993, p. 13) – objectives they would not be able to achieve, or would find it more difficult to achieve, if they did not work together and coordinate their actions (Rosanas, 2008, p. 447).[13] Organizations therefore exist to achieve certain common goals in a way that is compatible with the "different reasons" of their members, at least as far as the available resources allow (Finnis, 1998).

Whatever the aims of an organization may be, managers must achieve them, and to do so they must secure the cooperation of the members of the organization – that is, of the people (owners, employees, suppliers, customers and other stakeholders) who possess the human and material resources the company needs.[14] The neoclassical institutional theories assume that this is achieved through a set of contracts that provide the necessary incentives for the agents to act in the principal's interest. The action theory, however, suggests that the problem is somewhat more complex than this. If the subjects can act out of three types of motivation, managers must monitor three state variables:

1. Effectiveness, which represents the difference between the economic results obtained by providing a service to consumers and the resources employed, roughly equivalent to profit – which is why this variable could also be called profitability.

2. The organization must also be attractive to its members, which it will be if it develops skills among its members that enhance their satisfaction or reduce the cost for them of doing what the organization requires – that is, if it develops the distinctive abilities that enable it to solve problems more effectively, or to solve more complex problems, because its members have a better knowledge of the needs to be met and are more capable of meeting them.

3. The organization must also achieve consistency in its actions, which it will do when its members identify with it and start to trust one another.

The significance of these state variables in the organization is similar to the significance they have in the subjects' behavior, as the subjects learn through their actions; and what they learn changes their future behavior and therefore also their relations with the other agents; that is, with the organization. The immediate consequences of these actions will therefore not coincide with their long-term results, and an organization must strive not only to achieve immediate results but, above all, to build the capacity to continue to obtain results in the future (consistency) and ensure that those results are the best ones possible.

These three variables are therefore necessary for the survival and development of any organization, especially firms. Profitability is a necessary condition for a firm's long-term survival because it allows a firm to satisfy its members' extrinsic motivations. The firm must offer its employees a salary that is greater than their opportunity cost (the salary they could earn in comparable alternative employment); and it must offer its owners remuneration equal to or greater than what they could obtain in the capital market for the same level of risk. For this to be possible, the combined cost of the contributions of all the firm's suppliers of resources must not be greater than the revenue the firm obtains from the sale of its products or services.[15]

However, profitability is not the key condition for the existence of the firm, nor the measure of its success as an institution: "The necessary and sufficient condition for an organization to really exist is that there be a group of people who are motivated to belong to that organization, with all that such belonging implies for them. The organization's objectives must be oriented to conserving and increasing those motivations, as otherwise the organization would disintegrate" (Pérez-López, 1981, p. 5).

In order to achieve this, the organization must fulfill at least some of the requirements, in terms of attractiveness, that motivate people to contribute. First, the job that each person does in the firm (as owner, manager or employee) must not be unpleasant for him or her, or at least not so unpleasant as to make the person put in less effort than is needed for production. Second, it must allow job-related operational learning that will make the person's future actions more effective (Pérez-López, 1991, p. 90), bearing in mind the possibility of negative learning – for example, if the work is boring and repetitive. Up to a point, therefore, there is a trade-off between profitability and attractiveness, in so far as a firm must pay more for unpleasant than for pleasant work.[16]

Finally, the organization must also take into account the consequences for consistency, which in the long run could modify the outcomes achieved. Profit maximization does not guarantee a stable, long-term solution because the decisions a manager makes today will influence what people learn, and thus how attractive they find the idea of collaborating with the organization again in the future; above all, the manager's decisions will influence people's willingness to collaborate as well as the manager's own ability to persuade them to collaborate. These are three interrelated aspects of reality; they are not independent, they cannot be reduced to one another, and they cannot be processed using a single, common unit of measure (Pérez-López, 1990, p. 180).[17]

Accordingly, while every decision within the organization must necessarily respect certain minimum levels of profitability and attractiveness, this does not guarantee the achievement of a sufficient degree of consistency in the long run. For that, everybody must act with at least a minimum of transcendent motivation, taking the needs of others into account – not because of the consequences this may have for the utility of the active agent, but because of the consequences it will have for the others. This means that the agents must be capable of evaluating the consequences of their actions not only for themselves (in terms of effectiveness and efficiency) but also for others (in terms of consistency). This is an imperative not only for those in positions of command, but also for those that obey.

In summary, every human action has three types of effect – extrinsic, intrinsic and external – which in turn sustain three types of motivation – extrinsic, intrinsic and transcendent – and establish three state variables of profitability, attractiveness and consistency that every organization must satisfy in the long run. We have also pointed out that the three types of motivation are independent; each relates to the other two, but none dominates. All three are necessary and a complete lack of any one of them may result in the failure of the organization. The three state variables therefore cannot be summed up in a single variable.

From the action theory to the theory of the firm

As we explained earlier, the purpose of this chapter is to outline an action theory that is broader than the neoclassical and Austrian ones, and to show

how such a theory could in some cases broaden, and in others correct or qualify, but not replace the institutional theories of the firm. What follows is a set of conjectures, which, to the extent that they are well-founded, suggest a wide-ranging program of research.

Action theory and motivations

Our starting point is *a unified action theory*. The starting hypothesis of the neoclassical theory of the firm is "in the beginning was the market" (Williamson, 1985, p. 87). Alternatively, we propose a general human action theory ("in the beginning were the agents, acting in relation to one another") that explains both market exchanges and relations of authority in the firm as particular cases of the agents' actions in relation to one another.[18] This action theory would start with the subject acting on his or her own (the theory of the consumer, for example, but including operational and evaluative learning); it would continue with occasional relations between agents, before moving on to lasting relationships that demand some kind of coordination (organization theory), and it would end with a particular case – the theory of the firm.

This theory includes *different types of motivation*, namely extrinsic, intrinsic and transcendent. This is not new: neoclassical theory also accepts a diversity of preferences, both selfish and altruistic, in the same utility function; intrinsic motivation has been elaborated on in the social psychology, sociology and economics literature;[19] and various theories of altruistic, prosocial or other-related behaviors have been developed.[20]

However, the action theory presented here adds at least three clarifications to that diversity of motivations: (i) there are no precise relationships between the different motivations and no tradeoffs that can be exploited to reduce one to another: they cannot be treated as part of the same utility function; (ii) organizations must satisfy at least extrinsic and intrinsic motivation to be viable even in the short term; and (iii) there is a certain order of motivations: for example, extrinsic and intrinsic motivations tend to receive more attention in the short run, but, for an organization to survive in the long run, (all) the agents must be capable of acting with at least a minimum of transcendent motivation. To put it another way, it is not enough to add intrinsic and transcendent motives "from outside"; the theory must explain how all three are coordinated.

A broader theory of motivation would also clarify or broaden some aspects of the theory of the firm. The concepts of transaction costs, rent-seeking and opportunism, among others, may emerge more clearly if the existence of different motivations in the agents is taken into account, as well as the state variables that must be considered in the firm as conditions of long-run stable equilibrium of the system.

The agency conflict between the principal (the owner) and the agent (the professional manager), for example, would take on new dimensions. As presented by Jensen and Meckling (1976), if the agent acts out of extrinsic motivation, seeking only his or her own economic benefit, conflict is inevitable (assuming the other conditions, especially information asymmetry, are given). And yet, as we have seen, other motives come into play and the relationships between them are not elementary. If the agent acts out of intrinsic motives and those motives are aligned with the interests of the principal, there will be no agency conflict. But agents learn, so those motives may weaken (for example, the work may start to seem routine).[21] And if the agent acts out of transcendent motives (in the interests of the principal and the firm, but not necessarily of other employees, suppliers and customers), there will be no conflict. Agency conflict is therefore a particular – probably very widespread but none the less particular – case of a range of possible behaviors.

This is not to say that transcendent motives are a substitute for the monitoring and control procedures put in place by the principal, or for incentives designed to align the interests of the two parties: transcendent motives cannot be created at will (they belong to the sphere of the virtues: see Pérez-López, 1991) and any attempts to do so may be interpreted by the agent as attempts to manipulate his or her motivations. In any case, the action theory presented above would allow us to address issues such as why agency conflicts occur; why they do not always occur; why they change over time (because of the nature of evaluative learning);[22] what conditions must be met (in the principal and in the agent, and in the relations between them and in the organization), for such conflicts to occur or not to occur; and what are the most likely consequences of the incentive systems and monitoring methods used to combat them.

In the conventional theory, the interaction between the active and the reactive agent is intended to achieve the goals set by the active agent; the employees are seen mainly as a constraint and have to be offered compensation to avoid impeding the desired outcome (Rosanas, 2001). A general action theory should be bi-directional in order to explain, within a common framework, both the behavior of the person who gives the orders and that of the person who obeys.[23] The motivations of both will be the same, possibly combined in different proportions; the other components of their behavior (knowledge, capabilities, attitudes, values and so on) will probably also be different.

This may shed some light on other issues related to the theory of the firm, such as those regarding *employee participation* in decision-making or regarding decentralization. For example, if an employee acts out of intrinsic motivation, he or she must find a meaning in the action she performs (solving a coordination problem requires understanding the action of the other: Yu, 1999).[24] Similarly, if a manager acts out of transcendent motivation, he or she needs to be able to put him/herself in the other person's position in order to understand what that other person needs and how those needs can be satisfied, so as to be able to persuade him or her to collaborate (Pérez-López, 1991).[25]

The firm as a community of people

In neoclassical institutional theory, a firm is a collection of (physical or human) resources or assets (or of property rights on such resources or assets), which work together efficiently to produce goods and services for sale on the market; or a nexus of contracts or routines. The fact that there are three types of motivation suggests that the emphasis should be on the people who own those resources: *the firm would be better understood as a community of people*. This is not about adding a "humanistic" touch to the theory, but of acknowledging at least three facts: (i) resources have no value without knowledge: "without the 'knowledge' of how to profitably use a resource, it is not a resource, it has no value" (Lewin and Phelan, 2000, p. 71);(ii) knowledge is inevitably personal, unlike information, which has an objective existence (Fransman, 1994); and(iii) motivations cannot always be linked to ownership of resources, whether physical or human.

If the employees' motivations are to be taken into account, a certain *identification of their motivations with the firm's goals* is needed.[26] As we have already explained, the employees' participation in the firm is justified by the need to achieve extrinsic, intrinsic and external outcomes, which may satisfy the employees' needs. Extrinsic outcomes belong to the category of incentives, as defined by neoclassical economics, but they cannot explain "how employees are induced to work more than minimally, and perhaps even with initiative and enthusiasm" (Simon, 1991, p. 26): "this internalization requires ... a reference to the plane of transcendent motives, as that is the plane on which there operates the 'invisible hand' that makes what the organization wants (to satisfy human needs) coincide with what a person must want in order to develop as a person (to help satisfy the needs of other people, acting out of transcendent motives)" (Pérez-López, 1993, p. 103).

This also implies that the firm must take the motivations of its employees into account in order to satisfy at least minimally their extrinsic and intrinsic motivations and foster their transcendent motivations. In other words, the firm must create *a climate of trust* in which each agent can be confident that the others will not act opportunistically, seeking their own benefit at the cost of harming each other. If everyone in the firm acts only out of extrinsic motives, trust is pointless, as no one will want to act in a way that might benefit another (Pérez-López, 1993, pp. 156–7). Opportunism is not only a problem of economic incentives or of controls, rewards and punishments.

The entrepreneur and the firm

In neoclassical theory, the profit opportunities are available and known, so there is no need for an entrepreneur to discover and judge them.[27] The Austrian theories, in contrast, highlight the figure of the entrepreneur and try to incorporate it in the theory of the firm (Langlois and Robertson, 1995; Casson 2000).

What does the theory of the entrepreneur add to the action theory? In principle, an entrepreneur will act out of any of the three motivations we have mentioned. Depending on the circumstances, there will be a predominance of one type or the other, be it extrinsic (making a profit) (Kirzner 1973; Ioannides, 2003), intrinsic (doing something the entrepreneur enjoys, learning, giving expression to his/her creative ability) or transcendent (meeting the needs of potential customers and other members of the company), or a combination of all three, which also may change over time (what started as an act of self-affirmation, for example, may later become primarily a pursuit of profit or primarily a commitment to serve). This does not, however, change the role of the entrepreneur; if anything, it accentuates the entrepreneur's intent to put into practice what only he or she knows how to do – that is, to discover and judge opportunities.

The prevailing theories, especially the Austrian theory, pay special attention to the cognitive dimension of the entrepreneur, that is, the dimension that makes the entrepreneur capable of recognizing and identifying opportunities (for profit, for self-realization, for learning, or for service, depending on motivations). This brings to the fore the problem of the *coordination of knowledge* in the firm (Dulbecco and Garrouste, 2000; Langlois and Foss, 2009; Loasby, 2009) – not in the neoclassical theory,[28] but certainly in the Austrian theory and others related to it, such as the theory of capabilities.

In none of these theories, however, is there a problem of coordination of motivations, as the anthropologies underlying them assume that the agent's response to knowledge is immediate: no sooner does the agent become aware of what motivates him or her than he/she acts on it (Argandoña, 2005). If he or she fails to do so, it may be a result of ignorance or to there being insufficient motivation (the costs of action are greater than the extrinsic rewards for the agent), which will have to be corrected by providing stronger incentives (extrinsic motivation). In fact, the neoclassical theory is more properly a theory of alignment of incentives (through contracts, hierarchies or reputation) than a theory of coordination of actions.

The introduction of intrinsic motives calls this assumption into question. In effect, the simultaneous operation of intrinsic and extrinsic motivations may lead to at least partial crowding out of intrinsic motivations (Frey, 1997; Bénabou and Tirole, 2003).[29] The existence of transcendent motivation further complicates the analysis, as this motivation may inhibit the other two types – for example, in situations where the agent acts without expecting either extrinsic (monetary reward) or intrinsic (personal satisfaction) effects, but simply for the good of others.

This means that, as well as the problem of the coordination of knowledge, there may also be a problem of coordination of motivation, which concerns not only knowledge but also the will:[30] the problem of how to get the people who work together in the firm, using their resources (physical capital, human capital and technology) and moved by different motivations, to act in a coordinated way to achieve an outcome in which they all have an interest, albeit for different reasons (Pérez-López, 1993).

A broad theory of organizations

One of the advantages of founding the theory of the firm on a broad action theory would be to have room in it for different types of organizations, including associations, nonprofit entities, cooperatives, foundations and others of a similar nature.[31] What would differentiate the theory of the firm would probably be the greater relative importance of extrinsic motivation – in the firm's object (the sale of goods or services in the market for a price), in the involvement of the firm's members (the owners seek mainly profit, and the employees a salary) and in market conditions (for example, competition, which demands that firms be highly effective). This does not exclude the other motivations, however, either in the firm's object (which must be to serve its customers) or in relations with its members (who require satisfaction, as well as operational and evaluative learning).[32]

In non-business organizations, the importance of some of these factors will be different, but the three state variables will still be relevant. A nonprofit organization, for example, must pay a salary to its employees, provide work that is attractive to its volunteers, satisfy the motivations of its donors and providers of funds, and make a profit on its operations, which in this case will not be defined by the difference between sales revenue and the cost of goods sold, but will include other revenue (donations, for example) and other costs (although the opportunity cost of its volunteers will not be the market wage they could earn elsewhere, as they have renounced that option). In any case, just like a business firm, it must be capable of creating a "fund of incentives" to satisfy its employees' extrinsic motivations.

And finally, our action theory could be a good foundation for the role of ethics in the theory of the firm. For years, the relationship between economics and ethics has been governed by the principle of separation, which treats the two as being absolutely disconnected realities. Under these conditions, ethics can only ever be a more or less arbitrary constraint that limits the economic efficiency of decisions in the firm.

If agents act out of a variety of motivations, however, including transcendent motivation, they must then consider the effects their actions have on others: customers, owners, managers, employees, suppliers and society at large. And this not for exogenous reasons, but as part of the state variables that must be considered when making decisions. This means that there is a place for ethics in the theory of the firm (Argandoña, 2008a, 2008c).

Conclusions

It is now generally accepted that Coase (1937) is the origin of modern theories of the firm. Based on Coase's article, various theories have been developed that have contributed to the expansion of our knowledge about why the institutions we call firms exist, what their boundaries are, and how they are organized internally. Naturally enough, there are criticisms of these theories, and alternative views, largely replicating what happens in other branches of economics. And many of these criticisms reach back to the basic assumptions on which these theories are built.

This chapter is not intended to be yet another critique of what we have called neoclassical institutional theories. Its goal is more modest, though perhaps still overambitious. We have taken a step back to reconsider a theory of human action that enriches the range of motivations of action; a theory that, above all, establishes some simple laws about the relations between motivations and declares certain state variables that human organizations must observe in order to achieve not just short-term results but, above all, their conditions of dynamic equilibrium in the long run. As a result, many human actions in the market and in the firm, as studied by conventional economics, become particular cases of this more general theory.

In this chapter we have outlined this broader action theory and have suggested some points where this approach may help those involved in firms to understand what the institutional theories of the firm contribute, to broaden their point of view and to correct some of their shortcomings. This may serve to improve our knowledge of the firm by linking it to other aspects of human and organizational action. The cost, however, seems high, in that the chances of formally establishing a more general theory seem slight. That is nothing new, though. It is the age-old conflict between rigor and relevance, familiar from academic debates in business schools.

NOTES

1 This study is part of the research of the "la Caixa" Chair of Corporate Social Responsibility and Corporate Governance, IESE Business School. The views expressed in this chapter are the sole responsibility of the author and do not necessarily reflect in any way the views of Caja de Ahorros y Pensiones de Barcelona "la Caixa" or of IESE and its faculty.

2 What I call here institutional theories of the firm are a set of theories that are partly complementary and partly substitute. They originate from Coase (1937) and have developed in various branches: the transaction costs branch (Williamson, 1971, 1975, 1985), the nexus of contracts or property rights branch (Alchian and Demsetz, 1972; Grossman and Hart, 1986), the agency theory branch (Ross, 1973), and others, all of which are subdivided and interwoven. Strictly speaking, not all are theories of the firm. Agency theory, for example, does not explain the boundaries of the firm, in terms of ownership of assets. We shall not go into these distinctions here, however.

3 The term is from Martínez-Echevarría (2000); see also Martínez-Echevarría (2005).

4 Despite frequent claims that there is no Austrian theory of the firm (O'Driscoll and Rizzo, 1985; Langlois, 1991), "many of the analytical components that are necessary to tell a coherent story about why there should be firms in a market economy were present in Austrian theorizing long before they became standard fare in neoclassical economics" (Foss, 1994, p. 32).

5 If the firm is simply a nexus of contracts, as Fama (1980) and Cheung (1983) maintain, there is no place for authority within it.

6 For example, behavioral (March and Simon, 1958; Cyert and March, 1963), knowledge-based organizations (Kogut and Zander, 1992; Nonaka and Takeuchi, 1995), evolutionary (Nelson and Winter, 1982; Henderson and Clark, 1990), resource-based (Penrose, 1959; Wernerfelt, 1984) and competencies or capabilities (Richardson, 1972; Langlois, 1992). Not all of these theories are theories of the firm, properly speaking, in so far as they do not try to explain why firms exist, nor the boundaries of firms.

7 In this section I draw heavily on the ideas of Pérez-López (1991, 1993, 1998); see also Argandoña (2007, 2008a, 2008b, 2008c).

8 They are called transcendent because their effects go beyond – "transcend" – the active agent.

9 Note that we are using the terms effectiveness and efficiency in a different sense from the ones in which they are generally used in economics (Grandori, 2001).

10 An extreme example would be a decision to cut off a branch of a tree in order to reach the fruit on it: the action is effective but totally inconsistent. Another example would be a manager who abuses an employee's trust and so makes it more difficult to get the employee to collaborate in the future.

11 That such learning can lead to a reconstruction of preferences during the actual decision-making process is well known (Kahneman and Tversky, 2000), but the possibility of negative learning is not usually taken into account in economics.

12 The organization theory outlined here is perhaps overdependent on the theory of individual action from which it springs. To keep our explanation simple we have not considered elements that go beyond the mere aggregation of personal actions, such as a firm's culture or history (which gives rise to phenomena such as path-dependence).

13 March and Simon (1958) also stress the coordination of actions and the variety of motivations when they define the organization as "a system of coordinated action among individuals who differ in the dimensions of interests, preferences and knowledge". The "diversity of knowledge" component, which is not mentioned explicitly in Pérez-López (1993), occupies a very important place in the theory of the firm, especially in the Austrian and capabilities schools (Foss and Klein, 2009).

14 This means that subordinates' decisions have an impact on the effectiveness, efficiency and consistency of the decisions of their superiors, and therefore of the organization as a whole.

15 The effectiveness we are talking about here will coincide with return on capital if all resources other than capital receive a remuneration that is fixed in advance in a contract (extrinsic motivation), but only if all the other motivations of the owners of those other resources remain unchanged – which, as a rule, will not be the case.

16 Only up to a point, however, as the trade-off has limits. If the employee has material needs, the firm will have to pay him or her a wage even if the work is very pleasant and satisfying. And if the work is very unpleasant, simply paying a higher wage will soon offer diminishing returns.

17 Maximizing profits in the short term, as if there were no learning and the other variables were constant, will not work, because evaluative learning will obviously occur, in which case the conditions for maximum effectiveness will no longer be met. And maximizing profits in the long term, anticipating all the learning that will take place, is equally impossible because, though we know that the agents will learn, we do not know what or when they will do so. In the language of neoclassical economics, the three dimensions (profitability, attractiveness and consistency) cannot be integrated, on the personal level, in a single preference or utility function, or on the organizational level in a single objective function (such as maximizing the value of the shares).

18 What happens outside the market and outside the firm may shed light on the actions we are concerned with here. Altruism and prosocial behavior, for example, cannot be taken as exceptions to "rational" individualistic behavior. They are simply the behavior of an agent who acts out of transcendent motives (without excluding the possibility that he or she also acts out of other motivations).

19 The distinction between extrinsic motives (a satisfaction provided by the environment) and intrinsic motives (a satisfaction internal to the agent) has long been a part of social psychology (Deci, 1975), sociology and economics (Osterloh and Frey, 1997; Fehr and Schmidt, 1999; Frey, 1999; Bolton and Ockenfels, 2000). We could also include here "acting appropriately to the situation" (March, 1994).

20 See, for example, Schelling (1978), Stark (1995), Frey and Meier (2002), Frey (2003).

21 This dynamic dimension has occasionally been dealt with in game theory, but usually under very simple assumptions. Game theory would probably gain from a closer connection with the action theory – though very likely at the expense of formal elegance.

22 So far our analysis of learning has been confined to people, but it can be extended to the organization. In so far as we can talk about the firm as an entity that

learns, other changes will take place: the nature and amount of transaction costs and the borders of the firm, for example, will vary over time.

23   This does not mean that the theory of the firm must be based on the existence of multiple principals and multiple agents, because the identity of the person who exercises power is relevant (Khalil, 1998). But the one who gives orders must not forget the variety of motivations of the one who obeys, the likelihood that those motivations will change over time, and therefore the impact such changes will eventually have on the profitability, attractiveness and consistency of the organization.

24   Another approach to coordination problems emphasizes routines, rules, procedures, recipes or conventions in the firm (Nelson and Winter, 1982; Kogut and Zander, 1996).

25   Rosanas (2001) points to another aspect of this coordination of actions: the two agents have a limited and incomplete knowledge of what is best for them, and it is the manager's job to "guess" what the employee needs, so as not to create even more serious imbalances.

26   The identification is both cognitive ("members are surrounded by information, conceptions and frames of reference quite different from those of other people outside the organization or in a different organization": Simon, 1996, p. 44) and motivational (which entails "the attachment to group goals and a willingness to work for them even at some sacrifice of personal goals": Simon, 1996. 43–4).

27   There is no generally accepted definition of what is an entrepreneur, or what an entrepreneur does. Foss and Klein (2005, 2008) mention various alternative conceptions of entrepreneurial activity – notably, for the purpose of our analysis, those that define it as innovation (Schumpeter, 1934), discovery of opportunities (Kirzner, 1973) and judgment under uncertainty (Knight, 1921).

28   The neoclassical theories usually start from very restrictive assumptions about the agents' cognitive capabilities. This is the basis of Simon's (1955) criticism of unbounded rationality. The fact that in the neoclassical theories all the agents have the same model of the environment and that this model is correct obviates the need to coordinate their knowledge; the problem is thus reduced to designing and implementing the right incentives (Cremer, 1990). Note that the problem of knowledge in the Austrian theories is not of the same nature as the problem of bounded rationality. Under bounded rationality the difficulty lies in processing a large volume of existing information, whereas in the Austrian theories the problem lies principally in discovering what knowledge is relevant.

29   As Frey (2010) points out, it is not enough just to add a supposed intrinsic motivation from outside, because intrinsic motivation interacts with extrinsic motivation and changes the agents' decision rules.

30   And not only the will, as motivations are based on knowledge (Pérez-López, 1991): "what a person wants and likes influences what he sees; what he sees influences what he wants and likes" (March and Simon, 1958, p. 158).

31 And unions, political parties, churches, and the organizations studied in Posner (2010), oriented toward national security, and the judiciary.

32 Consistency or "organizational unity depends on two circumstances, both of which must be given and both of which are therefore necessary conditions for the organization to exist: 1) The organization must measure the effectiveness of actions according to how well they satisfy people's real needs ... [and] 2) People must be capable of acting out of transcendent motives" (Pérez López, 1993, p. 109).

REFERENCES

Alchian A. and Demsetz, H. 1972. "Production, Information Cost, and Economic Organization". *American Economic* Review 62:777–95.

Argandoña, A. 2005. "La teoría de la acción y la teoría económica". In R. Rubio de Urquía, E. M. Ureña and F. Muñoz Pérez eds. *Estudios de Teoría Económica y Antropología*. Madrid: Unión Editorial. 615–46.

Argandoña, A. 2007. "Economics, Ethics and Anthropology". In M. L. Djelic and R. Vranceanu, eds. *Moral Foundations of Management Knowledge*. Cheltenham, UK: Edward Elgar. 67—84.

Argandoña, A. 2008a. "Integrating Ethics into Action Theory and Organizational Theory". *Journal of Business Ethics* 78:435–46.

Argandoña, A. 2008b. "Anthropological and Ethical Foundations of Organization Theory". In S. Gregg and J. R. Stoner, Jr. eds. *Rethinking Business Management. Examining the Foundations of Business Education*. Princeton, NJ: The Witherspoon Institute. 38–49.

Argandoña, A. 2008c. "Consistency in Decision Making in Companies" Paper presented to the Workshop "Humanizing the Firm and the Management Profession". IESE, 30 June–2 July.

Bénabou, R. and Tirole, J. 2003. "Intrinsic and Extrinsic Motivation". *Review of Economics Studies* 70:489–520.

Bolton, G. and Ockenfels, A. 2000. "ERC – a Theory of Equity, Reciprocity, and Competition". *American Economic Review* 90:166–93.

Casson, M. 2000. "An Entrepreneurial Theory of the Firm" In N. J. Foss and V. Mahnke, eds. *Competence, Governance and Entrepreneurship: Advances in Economic Strategy Research*. New York: Oxford University Press. 116–45.

Cheung, S. N. S. 1983. "The Contractual Nature of the Firm". *Journal of Law and Economics* 26:1–22.

Coase, R. H. 1937. "The Nature of the Firm". *Economica*, NS, 4:386–405.

Cremer, J. 1990. "Common Knowledge and the Coordination of Economic Activities". In M. Aoki, O. E. Williamson and B. Gustafsson, eds. *The Firm as a Nexus of Treaties*. London: Sage. 53–76.

Cyert, R. M. and March, J. G. 1963. *A Behavioral Theory of the Firm*. Englewood Cliffs, NJ: Prentice Hall.

Deci, E. L. 1975. *Intrinsic Motivation*. New York: Plenum Press.

Donaldson, L. 2002. "Damned By Our Own Theories: Contradictions Between Theories and Management Education". *Academy of Management Learning and Education* 1:96–106.

Dulbecco, P. and Garrouste, P. 1999. "Towards an Austrian Theory of the Firm". *Review of Austrian Economics* 12:43–64.

Dulbecco, P. and Garrouste, P. 2000. "Structure de la production et structure de la connaissance: éléments pour une théorie autrichienne de la firme". *Revue Économique* 51: 75–101.

Fama, E. 1980. "Agency Problems and the Theory of the Firm". *Journal of Political Economy* 26:288–307.

Fehr, E. and Schmidt, K. 1999. "A Theory of Fairness, Competition and Cooperation". *Quarterly Journal of Economics* 114:817–68.

Ferraro, F., Pfeffer, J. and Sutton, R. I. 2005. "Economics Language and Assumptions: How Theories Can Become Self-Fulfilling". *Academy of Management Review* 30:8–24.

Finnis, J. 1998. *Aquinas: Moral, Political, and Legal Theory*.Oxford: Oxford University Press.

Foss, N. J. 1994. "The Theory of the Firm: The Austrians as Precursors and Critics of Contemporary Theory". *Review of Austrian Economics* 7:31–65.

Foss, N. J. 2007. "The Knowledge Governance Approach". *Organization* 14:29–52.

Foss, N. J. and Klein, P. G. 2005. "Entrepreneurship and the Theory of the Firm: Any Gains From Trade?". In R. Agarwal, S. A. Alvarez and O. Sorenson, eds. *Handbook of Entrepreneurship: Disciplinary Perspectives*. Berlin: Springer. 55–80.

Foss, N. J. and Klein, P. G. 2006. "The Emergence of the Modern Theory of the Firm". Working Paper No. 1/2006. Center for Strategic Management and Globalization, Copenhagen Business School, Denmark.

Foss, N.J. and Klein, P. G. 2008. "The Theory of the Firm and Its Critics: A Stocktaking and Assessment". In E. Brousseau and J.-M. Glachant, eds. *Handbook of New Institutional Economics*. Cambridge: Cambridge University Press. 425–42.

Foss, N. J. and Klein, P. G. 2009. "Organizational Governance". In R. Wittek, T. Snijders and V. Nee, eds. *Handbook of Rational Choice Theory*. New York: Russell Sage Foundation.

Fransman, M. 1994. "Information, Knowledge, Vision and Theories of the Firm". *Industrial and Corporate Change* 3:713–57.

Frey, B. S. 1997. *Not Just for the Money: An Economic Theory of Personal Motivation*. Aldershot, UK: Edward Elgar.

Frey, B. S. 1999. *Economics as a Science of Human Behaviour. Towards a New Social Science Paradigm*, 2nd edn. Dordrecht: Kluwer.

Frey, B. S. 2003. "Corporate Governance: What Can We Learn From Public Governance?". Working paper. Institute for Empirical Economic Research, University of Zurich.

Frey, B. S. 2010. "Superb Posner – But Can We Go Further?". *Journal of Institutional Economics* 6:65–9.

Frey, B. S. and Meier, S. 2002. "Pro-social Behavior, Reciprocity, or Both?". Working paper No. 750. Munich: CESIFO.

Ghoshal, S. and Moran, P. 1996. "Bad for Practice: A Critique of Transaction Cost Theory". *Academy of Management* Review 21:13–47.

Grandori, A. 2001. *Organization and Economics Behavior*. London: Routledge.

Grossman, S. and Hart, O. 1986. "The Costs and Benefits of Ownership: A Theory of Vertical Integration". *Journal of Political Economy* 94, 691–719.

Henderson, R. M. and Clark, K. B. 1990. "Architectural Innovation: The Reconfiguration of Existing Product Technologies and the Failure of Established Firms". *Administrative Science Quarterly* 35:9–30.

Holmström, B. and Tirole, J. 1989. "The Theory of the Firm" In R. Schmalensee and R. D. Willig, eds. *Handbook of Industrial Organization*, Vol. I. Amsterdam: North-Holland. 61–133.

Ioannides, S. 1999. "Towards an Austrian Perspective of the Firm". *Review of Austrian Economics* 11:77–97.

Ioannides, S. 2003. "Orders and Organizations: Hayekian Insights for a Theory of Economic Organization". American Journal of Economics and Sociology 62:533–66.

Jensen, M. C. and Meckling, W. 1976. "The Theory of the Firm: Managerial Behavior, Agency Costs and Organizational Structure". *Journal of Financial Economics* 3:305–60.

Kahneman, D. and Tversky, A. 2000. *Choices, Values, and Frames*. Cambridge: Cambridge University Press.

Khalil, E. 1998. "The Janus Hypothesis". *Journal of Post Keynesian Economics* 21: 315–42.

Kirzner, I. M. 1973. *Competition and Entrepreneurship*. Chicago, IL: University of Chicago Press.

Knight, F. H. 1921[1965]. *Risk, Uncertainty, and Profit* (Boston, MA: Houghton Mifflin).

Kogut, B. and Zander, U. 1992. "Knowledge of the Firm, Combinative Capabilities, and the Replication of Technology". *Organization Science* 3:383–397.

Kogut, B. and Zander, U. 1996. "What Firms Do? Coordination, Identity and Learning". *Organization Science* 7:502–18.

Langlois, R. N. 1991. "Transaction Cost Economics in Real Time". *Industrial and Corporate Change* 1:99–127.

Langlois, R. N. 1992. "Orders and Organizations: Toward and Austrian Theory of Social Institutions" In B. J. Caldwell and S. Boehm, eds. *Austrian Economics: Tensions and New Directions*. Boston, MA: Kluwer. 175–98.

Langlois, R. N. and Foss, N. J. 2009. "Capabilities and Governance: The Rebirth of Production in the Theory of Economic Organization". *Kyklos* 52:201–18.

Langlois, R. N. and Robertson, P. L. 1995. *Firms, Markets and Economic Change: A Dynamic Theory of Business Institutions*. London,: Routledge.

Lewin, P. and Phelan, S. E. 2000. "An Austrian Theory of the Firm". *Review of Austrian Economics* 13:59–79.

Loasby, B. J. 2009. "Knowledge, Coordination and the Firm: Historical Perspectives". *European Journal of the History of Economic Thought*. 16:539–58.

March, J. G. 1994. *A Primer on Decision Making: How Decisions Happen*. New York: Macmillan).

March, J. G. and Simon, H. A. 1958. *Organizations*. New York: John Wiley & Sons.

Martínez-Echevarría, M. A. 2000. "Hacia una nueva teoría de la empresa". *Cuadernos Empresa y Humanismo*, No. 79. University of Navarra, Spain.

Martínez-Echevarría, M. A. 2005. *Dirigir empresas: De la teoría a la realidad.*Madrid: Ediciones Internacionales Universitarias.

Nelson, R. R. and Winter, S. G. 1982. *An Evolutionary Theory of Economic Change*. Cambridge, MA: Harvard University Press.

Nonaka, I. and Takeuchi, H. 1995. *The Knowledge-Creating Company*. New York: Oxford University Press.

O'Driscoll, G. P. and Rizzo, M. J. 1985. *The Economics of Time and Ignorance*. Oxford: Basil Blackwell.

Osterloh, M. and Frey, B. S. 1997. "Managing Motivation: Crowding Effects in the Theory of the Firm." Working Paper No. 31. Institut für betriebswirtschaftliche Forschung, Zürich.

Penrose, E. T. 1959[1995]. *The Theory of the Growth of the Firm.* Oxford: Oxford University Press).

Pérez López, J. A. 1981. "Dimensiones de la responsabilidad social en la empresa." Research paper No. 49. IESE, January.

Pérez López, J. A. 1990. "I am the Boss. Why Should I Be Ethical?." In G. Enderle, B. Almond and A. Argandoña, eds. *People in Corporations. Ethical Responsibilities and Corporate Effectiveness.* Dordrecht: Kluwer.

Pérez López, J. A. 1991. *Teoría de la acción humana en las organizaciones. La acción personal.* Madrid: Rialp.

Pérez-López, J. A. 1993. *Fundamentos de la dirección de empresas.* Madrid: Rialp.

Pérez-López, J. A. 1998. *Liderazgo y ética en la dirección de empresas.* Bilbao: Deusto.

Posner, R. A. 2010. "From the New Institutional Economics to Organization Economics: With Applications to Corporate Governance, Government Agencies, and Legal Institutions." *Journal of Institutional Economics* 6:1–37.

Richardson, G. B. 1972. "The Organisation of Industry." *Economic Journal* 82:883–96.

Robbins, L. C. 1932. *An Essay on the Nature and Significance of Economic Science.* London: Macmillan.

Rosanas, J. M. 2001. 'Herbert Simon (1916–2001) y Juan Antonio Pérez López (1934–1996), "In Memoriam"'. *Revista Empresa y Humanismo* 4:317–31.

Rosanas, J. M. 2008. "Beyond Economic Criteria: A Humanistic Approach to Organizational Survival." *Journal of Business Ethics* 78:447–62.

Ross, S. 1973. "The Economic Theory of Agency: The Principal's Problem." *American Economic Review* 63:134–9.

Schelling, T. 1978. "Egonomics or the Art of Self-Management." *American Economic Review* 68:290–4.

Schumpeter, J. A. 1934. *The Theory of Economic Development: An Inquiry into Profits, Capital, Credit, Interest, and the Business Cycle.* Cambridge, MA: Harvard University Press.

Simon, H. A. 1955. "A Behavioral Model of Rational Choice." *Quarterly Journal of Economics* 69:99–118.

Simon, H. A. 1991. "Organizations and Markets." *Journal of Economic Perspectives* 5:25–44.

Simon, H. A. 1996. *The Sciences of the Artificial*, 3rd edn 2001. Cambridge, MA: MIT Press.

Stark, O. 1995. *Altruism and Beyond. An Economic Analysis of Transfers and Exchanges within Families and Groups*. Cambridge: Cambridge University Press.

Wernerfelt, B. 1984. "A Resource-based View of the Firm". *Strategy Management Journal* 5:171–80.

Williamson, O. E. 1971. "The Vertical Integration of Production: Market Failure Considerations". *American Economic Review* 61:112–23.

Williamson, O. E. 1975. *Markets and Hierarchies: Analysis and Antitrust Implications*. New York: The Free Press.

Williamson, O. E. 1985. *The Economic Institutions of Capitalism*. New York: The Free Press.

Yu, T. F. 1999. "Toward a Praxeological Theory of the Firm". *Review of Austrian Economics* 12:25–41.

A Humanistic Approach to Organizations and Organizational Decision-making

JOSEP M. ROSANAS, Credit Andorra Professor of Markets, Organizations and Management, IESE Business School, University of Navarra

Changes in business schools

Research in management has changed greatly since the 1950s. At the same time, business schools and what they teach have also changed, though whether business schools have changed because the research agenda has changed or vice versa is open to question. What sparked the change, namely the Ford Foundation and Carnegie Foundation reports, how these reports changed the spirit of business schools, and how this change has led to the current situation has been well documented by Khurana (2007).

One dimension of the change has been the explosion in the number of publications. In 1960, in my own original field of accounting, there was one academic journal (*The Accounting Review*); now, there are well over fifty, of different degrees of quality, including five or six top journals. Much the same can be said, I believe, of all the other fields of management. The EBSCO database contains over a thousand journals related to management.

The change in quantity has been accompanied by qualitative changes, essentially in three directions: (i) the increasing importance of the basic disciplines (economics, sociology, psychology) in the research conducted in business schools; (ii) the emphasis on empirical methods, particularly those based on statistical techniques, often considered to be (implicitly perhaps) the only source of scientific validity; and (iii) a much higher degree of specialization in the research being done. If we had taken one article at random from any of the journals that existed in 1960 and read the title to the average management professor of that time, the professor would probably have known more or less what the article was about. Today, it would be pure chance if an average management professor could guess the content of an article outside his or her (possibly narrow) field of specialization, just by its title. Even within a functional area (finance, say) the title might not be enough for some finance faculty member to guess the article's content.

To some extent the same has happened in many other disciplines, including the hard sciences. In management, however, which has important interdisciplinary elements, the change has perhaps had greater consequences and has raised concerns about the way human beings are considered and treated, both in theoretical analysis and in practice. Gary Hamel proposes "reinventing management", making firms "more resilient", "as nimble as they are efficient", and "more uplifting and a lot less dispiriting" (Hamel, 2007). Donaldson (2005) proposes a "Positive Management Theory", with a "positive" view of managers in particular, and of human beings in general, as opposed to the "anti-management theories" so popular nowadays (Donaldson, 2002). Davis *et al.* (1997) advance "stewardship theory" in the same spirit of "positive" human beings and a "human" organization. Ghoshal and Moran (1996) argued that "opportunism", one of the bases of transaction cost economics, may be a self-fulfilling prophecy; in his often cited posthumous article, Ghoshal raised important issues as to the basic ("pessimistic") assumptions about human beings on which the economics models are built (Ghoshal, 2005). Ferraro *et al.* (2005) argue, more generally, that the language and assumptions of economics make theories self-fulfilling.

According to these views, a different approach to the analysis of organizations is needed, one that brings a more humanistic and realistic spirit to the task. The main aim of this chapter is to provide some bases for an alternative way of looking at organizations – one that: (i) departs from the current assumptions and has a more "human face"; (ii) has a logically consistent, rational basis that retains the good, rigorous properties of the economic models and can be tied in with the economics framework; and (iii) is at the same time more operational than the usual economic approaches.

The influence of economics

The basic discipline that has had by far the most influence on business school teaching and research is neoclassical economics (Gintis and Khurana, 2008). As a result, variables that are crucial for decision-making are simply assumed away, while management risks losing its essence, as we shall try to show below.

On the other hand, economics has the advantage of being a well-structured theory, with a well-developed formal apparatus, a theory that attempts to be comprehensive, and in which every issue can find its place and context.

Economics has strongly influenced the strategy field, for example, through industrial economics, which analyzes individual industries to see whether and how in a given context a particular firm may have a competitive advantage. This is no doubt an interesting approach that has shed some light on real-world phenomena, but it neglects cooperation in favor of rivalry and mistrust. More important, it overlooks each firm's distinctive competence and specific strengths. One of the basic assumptions of economic theory, namely the primacy of self-interest, is certainly one of the reasons for that omission.

The influence of economics is by no means confined to strategy, however. Other areas of management, including finance and accounting, are so heavily influenced by economics or econometrics as to be almost enslaved to them. Perhaps unwillingly, even marketing and organizational behavior often fall under the sway of economic concepts and methods of analysis, such as shareholder value, self-interest or an instrumental, even mechanistic, view of human beings.

Three basic assumptions of economic theory are particularly important. Two of them are quite explicit: self-interest and unbounded rationality. The other is only implicit: a static view of individuals which assumes that individuals do not learn – that is, that they do not change their preferences, abilities or attitudes over time. When applied to the analysis of organizations, these assumptions result in a model of the firm that is not too different from the idealized market of economic theory: relationships between people are impersonal, guided only by self-interest and based on perfect knowledge of action alternatives, their possible consequences and each individual's own preferences. Yet firms and markets are supposed to be alternative means of coordinating human activity, so presumably they should also be different in nature and should therefore be analyzed on different bases.

In economic analysis, "real people" have been replaced by abstract, mechanistic utility functions. The arguments of the utility function are typically restricted to "commodities", which means that the economic approach to organizations assumes an exclusively selfish attitude in human beings and ignores the possibility of their being interested in each other's welfare or in cooperation. It also ignores certain crucial variables such as individuals' "abilities" or their "attitudes" toward each other and toward "firms".

An economics-based model of the firm

Neoclassical economic models start from the assumption that firms maximize their profit and show how that is what firms should do. The foundations of this idea are to be found in general equilibrium theory: competitive equilibria based on consumers maximizing their utility and firms maximizing their profits are Pareto-efficient; and any Pareto-efficient outcome can be produced by a competitive equilibrium.

Expressed in its simplest form and in modern terms, including a multi-period analysis, the argument can be found in Jensen (2000): managerial decisions should maximize the firm's value. This conclusion has gained wide acceptance, first in theory and then (purportedly, at least) in practice. On paper, this rule takes into account long-run considerations. All cash flows, no matter how far into the future, should be included and properly discounted. In practice, however, the value of a firm is often decided without taking much of this into account. Very often, actual stock market valuations are based more on quarterly earnings than is generally recognized, through the opinions of investment bank officials and financial analysts. In many of the recent scandals, financial analysts continued to overvalue companies' shares until a few months, or even weeks, before the scandal broke, despite there being, in some of the best-known cases such as Enron, grounds for suspicion well before the failure was announced. The practical application of the value maximization rule is therefore more short-sighted than might be expected from models that claim to take the long run into account.

If one accepts that the socially optimum goal for a firm is to maximize its value, then the firm can be viewed as a principal–agent problem in a multiple version. The "principals" would be the shareholders, while everybody else in the firm should do whatever is necessary to maximize the firm value, of which they are the residual claimants. All agents are assumed to be selfish in the sense that they maximize their own utility function (Ghoshal, 2005; Gintis and Khurana, 2008; Khurana, 2007). The only way to ensure that they do what the shareholders would like them to do, therefore, is by using an incentive system, typically involving shares or stock options.

Ghoshal (2005) has argued that this presupposes an unjustifiably pessimistic view of humankind, and that this pessimistic view can become a self-fulfilling prophecy, making human beings selfish and opportunistic, when at the beginning they were not. A mechanical system of incentives

based on measurable variables and applied automatically may well acceler-
ate the process and is diametrically opposed to the "humanistic" approach to
management that, as we have seen, many researchers advocate.

Operational problems of the economic models

Consider a downsizing decision by a business firm. Seemingly, such a decision should increase profits, since it decreases an expense. Indeed, that is often
the reason why the downsizing decision is made. In many cases, however, the
overall impact of downsizing on the income statement is negative (Cameron,
1991, 1993; Freeman and Cameron, 1993; Pfeffer, 1999). Conceptually,
analyzing a downsizing decision based only on its immediate effects on the
income statement would be the equivalent, in mathematics, of counting only
the partial derivative to calculate the change in the value of a function when
one of the independent variables changes. The correct procedure would be to
consider the total derivative, which in the case of a downsizing decision means
including *all* the effects of the decision. The analysis should therefore take into
account the possibility of a reduction of revenues in the future because of loss
of morale among the workforce, lack of sufficiently qualified people, loss of
credibility of management and many other reasons. Unlike the situation in
well-structured economic models, where all the relevant variables are known
(though there may be uncertainty as to their value), one of the basic difficulties of making decisions in real life is that some of the variables that should be
considered are not known beforehand. Most of these variables are essentially
qualitative and some of them unforeseeable and therefore very difficult to estimate objectively in the short run; indeed, some may be impossible to estimate.
Eventually, of course, the feedback loop will close and the positive and negative
effects will become known; but even then the decision-makers may not immediately associate the cause (which occurred many months or even years before)
with the effects (which have occurred at different points in time). So there is
no guarantee that what the decision-makers learn will be in any sense "right".

This analysis is not exclusive to downsizing decisions, of course. It can
easily be extended to other areas. For example, what if a firm puts heavy
pressure on its suppliers to lower their prices? On the one hand, this might
improve the firm's profits; but on the other, it is bound to elicit negative reac-
tions from suppliers, possibly leading to lower quality, late delivery, poor
service and, in extreme cases, supplier bankruptcy. Or what if a firm treats its

employees in a "dehumanized" way – that is, not listening to their proposals, ignoring their personal needs and so on? Again, the firm may save money in the short run, but eventually the more competent people may leave and those who stay may perform poorly. Or what about environmental damage? For the sake of short-run profit, the firm may create a hostile environment in which government places even stricter limits on companies' freedom.

In such cases, management may make the wrong decision for the sake of immediate gains that are more than offset by subsequent losses, or because it overlooks important variables that should have been considered. Conventional economic models do not inquire into the decision-making process, so the problem may be considered solved by a sort of Darwinian argument whereby firms that make the right decisions survive, while those that do not make the right decisions disappear. This does not help decision-makers, however, who are the ones that matter in management. The inability to help decision-makers is neutering management. Decision-makers need specific rules or criteria to be able to make decisions operationally, and the threat of extinction does not make things any better from a cognitive point of view. If anything, it puts pressure on management to use unorthodox methods that harm the firm more than anything else. In fact, many of the recent scandals (for example, Enron, or most financial institutions involved in the disaster of the subprimes) originated in pressure for short-term results (quarterly earnings, growth objectives, or any kind of short-term, quantitative goals), which were supposed to enhance long-term performance. As Jensen (2002) argued, telling the truth to Wall Street, at the risk of provoking an adverse reaction, might have lowered Enron's market value to some extent, but not to the levels (practically zero) that it reached a few months later when the forgeries were discovered. Therefore, while profit or value maximization may be the "best" possible guide to decision-making in theory, it may not be a good guide in the short run because it is too difficult to put into practice. As Senge (2000) has suggested, when you insist on firm value maximization as a criterion for decision-making, "it will almost always become, by default, short-term profit maximization ... Given a short enough time horizon, many of (the complex) feedbacks can be ignored. This is why manipulating profits over the short term is much easier than building wealth over the long term".

The fundamental assumptions

As stated earlier, some of the shortcomings of the economic approach to organizations come from the assumptions on which it is based. Three of these assumptions are crucial: unbounded rationality, self-interest, and absence of learning. Two others are complementary: competitive markets and production efficiency. We shall examine them in turn.

Unbounded rationality

The assumption of unbounded rationality is indeed crucial in the above examples of decision-making. Given unbounded rationality, any decision-maker could immediately measure the costs and benefits of any kind of decision on downsizing, procurement, human resource management or any other subject. Even in the presence of uncertainty, an unboundedly rational decision-maker could adequately weigh the costs and benefits of the decision and face uncertainty in a perfectly rational way, consistent with his/her attitudes to risk. For this to be true there have to be "complete markets"; that is, markets for commodities contingent on any conceivable event. Uncertainty is therefore not incompatible with unbounded rationality: bounded rationality means inability to foresee all possible contingencies, lack of knowledge of one's own preferences – even inconsistencies in those preferences, but it does not mean lack of the perfect knowledge of the future implied by certainty. In our previous example, many of the long-run effects of a downsizing decision cannot be foreseen, let alone quantified or have contracts established on them.

The longer the time period, the greater the impact that bounded rationality has on decision-making, as the number of unforeseeable contingencies increases substantially. Technology is a good example. If we think that the future development of technology can be guessed from today's situation, past developments and current research efforts, we have only to watch a science-fiction movie produced in the 1950s to realize how, in many respects, we have gone well beyond what anyone could have imagined at that time, while some of the inventions in the movie are, we now know, simply impossible.[1]

Furthermore, our knowledge about our own future preferences decreases the further we go into the future. Bounded rationality therefore makes it as good as impossible to use the maximization of firm value, long-run profit or any other quantitative variable as an operational objective.

Self-interest

Value maximization naturally has a lot to do with the hypothesis of self-interest, which is one of the bases on which much of neoclassical economic theory stands. The "narrow" version of self-interest consists of individuals having their own utility functions and attempting to maximize them with absolute disregard for other people's interests and welfare. As was suggested above, while this may be a useful hypothesis for analyzing the economic system as a whole, it is not a good guide to individual behavior.

For one thing, the hypothesis of narrow self-interest is descriptively false. As Ghoshal (2005) has observed, not only do mothers care for their children, or people volunteer to work in impoverished countries or regions, and so on, but also the limitations of the self-interest model "become manifest even in careful experiments devised by economists to test their theories under controlled conditions in which 'aberrations' such as altruism or love are strictly excluded".

It should not, then, be too surprising to find people in the world of business who are willing to sacrifice part of their own welfare for the welfare of others, thus developing what might be called "transitive" motives,[2] –that is, motives that take into account the needs of other people within the organization and in the marketplace. Sen (1977) made a subtle but important distinction about taking the interest of others into account. He distinguished between "sympathy" and "commitment". "Sympathy" is in fact a form of self-interest: if you see a child being tortured (to use Sen's example) and this distresses you so much that you want to stop it, then this is "sympathy". If the same fact does not affect you personally but you believe that it should not happen and are willing to commit some of your own resources to stop it, that is "commitment". Transitive motives, in the sense that I use the word here, are related mainly to commitment and, more specifically, commitment to specific people.

"Enlightened" self-interest is not much better than plain, narrow self-interest. "Enlightened self-interest" is an expression originally used by Alexis de Tocqueville (1981, pt II, ch. VIII).[3] He thought that "enlightened self interest" was common in the USA, producing results that were probably mediocre from the point of view of developing virtues but could be considered necessary for the benefit of society in general. According to Tocqueville, Americans thought that narrow, egoistic attitudes were self-defeating and therefore often thought in terms of "enlightened self-interest" as a second best. He was critical of that position because he thought that the important thing was to develop virtue in individuals, so that all individuals were truly "committed" to doing the right thing. In his analysis, however, as commitment can be difficult to obtain, one might opt for "enlightened self-interest" and mediocre results in preference to the results that would be obtained if everyone was narrowly selfish.

As we shall see, commitment is essential in business firms if they are to serve their customers' interests. Enlightened self-interest is insufficient to develop a sense of "mission" to solve customers' needs and at the same time develop a strong sense of unity within the organization.

Absence of learning

The third critical element (missing, in fact) in neoclassical economic analysis is learning. Certainly, there is a branch of game theory in which some type of learning is taken into account. But it is a very narrow concept of learning, essentially related to Bayesian updating of probabilities about uncertain variables. The kind of learning we are talking about here includes this, but also goes well beyond it. It is related to knowledge, of course, but also to abilities, on the one hand, and attitudes, wants and preferences on the other.

Whenever an interaction between two people takes place, three kinds of results are always present (Rosanas, 2008). First, the explicit results of the interaction, which are related, of course, to what the two individuals intended. An action can be said to be *effective* if the results are those the individual who started the interaction expected, and *ineffective* if they are not. But the interaction also has effects on the individuals themselves, in that afterwards: (i) they know better to what extent the explicit results satisfied their expectations; and (ii) how good the experience was with the other person participating in the interaction, and therefore whether the individual wants to interact with this other person again in the future. In other words, they learn. From the point of view of each of the participants in the interaction, therefore, as well as the explicit results of the interaction, there are always two other kinds of results: what the individual who started the interaction learns, and what the other person learns. What these two individuals learn will condition the future of their interactions, and thus also of the organization.

Competitive markets and efficiency in production

In addition to the above three crucial assumptions (which are complementary for some purposes, mainly that of analyzing the markets that surround organizations, and to some extent may be considered more technical, though they have considerable implications), economic approaches typically assume: (i) that the output to be obtained from the inputs is determined by a production function; and (ii) that all transactions between firms and consumers go through competitive markets.

If the production function entirely determines the output from a given mix of inputs, then production is "efficient" (that is, it is impossible to produce more output from the same inputs, or the same output with fewer inputs). This is what Leibenstein (2002) calls X-efficiency, to distinguish it from other concepts of efficiency (for example, Pareto efficiency, in the sense used above). Needless to say, this hypothesis is at odds with learning because, in practice, learning means expanding the efficient frontier. The hypothesis also excludes bounded rationality, because efficiency means that the firm knows all the possibilities and is able to choose the best one. Self-interest, then, leads to profit (or value) maximization.

Markets are perfectly competitive when a single producer can sell as much of the product as it produces, and a single consumer or firm can buy as much of it as it wants, without affecting the price in either case. Again, this is incompatible with learning, because if you accept the competitive hypothesis, all firms are at the efficient frontier.

Suppose the two hypotheses hold, that is:

1. The firm can find a supply of the kind of labor it needs at a known price in a competitive market and the same applies to raw materials and intermediate products, financial inputs, and so on. Also, the firm can sell as much as it wishes of an undifferentiated product at prevailing market prices.

2. Production is X-efficient: that is, the production function completely determines the output given the inputs.

If these two hypotheses hold, together with unbounded rationality, then the classical argument of profit maximization (or value maximization, in more modern terms) is unassailable. A "dollar taken out of the economy", to use Jensen's (2000) expression, is perfectly well defined and the amount of product to be obtained is also known, so that the comparison between the value of the product and the value of the input can readily be made.

These hypotheses do not hold in practice, however. One crucial factor is labor. With the possible exception of unskilled workers, by definition there cannot be a competitive market for labor. In today's economy, where an employee's specific knowledge is crucial and part of that knowledge is implicit, embedded and useful only to a specific firm, it is impossible to find that kind of knowledge readily available in the market (Polanyi, 1958; Nonaka, 1994; Andreu, 2009). Therefore, the meaning of "a dollar taken out of the economy" is ill-defined. And of course, the more differentiated the product and the more specific the knowledge required, the more ill-defined that dollar becomes.

To the extent, therefore, that the firm has a differentiated product and needs specific raw materials or supplies, the same is bound to be true of most suppliers. The same can be argued, of course, for all other stakeholders.

The efficiency assumption is quite a strong one too. From the point of view of the whole economy, again the Darwinian hypothesis is right. Given equal technology, a firm that is not X-efficient will disappear because efficient competitors (which always abound in competitive situations) will take the whole market. This does not solve the problem of a specific firm, however. For a specific firm, achieving efficiency is one of the basic goals. X-efficiency is therefore endogenous, just one of the variables that will determine a firm's success or failure.

Hence, if "a dollar taken out of the economy" is likely not to be well defined, the amount of product obtained may not be well defined either, and still less what can be obtained in an imperfect market for a unit of product. Therefore, the value maximization rule may not be applicable. What in fact happens is that in every interaction between "the firm" and another party a relationship is created that may be either satisfactory for both, unsatisfactory for one and satisfactory for the other, or unsatisfactory for both. In practice, "the firm" means any person who belongs to the firm; and "another party" means any person that represents that other party.

An alternative framework for analysis of managerial action: basic assumptions

An alternative formulation must depart from some of the assumptions on which the economics model is based. It would include: (i) bounded rationality; (ii) "satisficing" behavior; (iii) qualitative, non-measurable organizational goals – limitations of formal evaluation and control systems;

(iv) long-run and institutional identity; (v) wider individual objectives and motives; (vi) competitive advantage through knowledge; and (vii) organizations as communities – loyalties and identification. We shall discuss these in turn.

Bounded rationality

Individuals are boundedly rational. They cannot choose the optimal course of action because they do not know of all the possible courses of action. They cannot make the computations and inferences to analyze the actions they know thoroughly and they are not certain as to what level of satisfaction they will achieve through the results of their actions. This is one aspect of bounded rationality which, though stated in Simon's (1957) original formulation of the concept ("It is a commonplace experience that an anticipated pleasure may be a very different sort of thing from a realized pleasure" –p. 95), is often overlooked nowadays, perhaps on the assumption that it is already included in value maximization. If we analyze the firm in more depth, however, we shall see how it is crucial to think of bounded rationality with respect to both consumers and employees: we contend that management (or, more abstractly, "firms") should attempt to satisfy the real needs of both groups, so as to leave them genuinely satisfied after the event, not merely in terms of what they thought was attractive or desirable before the event.

The first aspect of bounded rationality mentioned above is also often overlooked: that is, that action alternatives are not freely available for the decision-maker to pick the one he or she prefers. Instead, they have to be generated at a cost. This cost would include at least the opportunity cost of the decision-maker's time; more often, however, other explicit costs also have to be included. In fact, whether it is worth spending time and money on looking for alternatives is part of the problem. Often it is not a just matter of choosing among different, already available alternatives, but of accepting one that has been found to meet sufficiently well all the criteria the organization considers relevant.

Finally, of course, bounded rationality implies the inability to calculate precisely the results of any alternative. This is the criterion most often used in recent times and was used at the beginning of this chapter in the context of a downsizing decision.

"Satisficing" behavior

Simon's (1957) concept of "satisficing behavior" is the ideal complement to bounded rationality, and it is a crucial concept when several criteria have to be met. It is impossible to maximize two (or more) variables at the same time, unless the variables are all monotonic transformations of each other (Jensen, 2000); and having a multiplicity of variables often leads to poor decision-making, resulting in a "performance freeze" (Ethiraj and Levinthal, 2009).

Thus, when we say that several criteria have to be met, either we are saying that we are aiming for a satisficing level of all the variables and will not even attempt to maximize anything; or else we must maximize only one variable, which has priority over all the others, which act as constraints. In a classical paper, Simon (1964, pp. 1–22) expressed this idea very clearly:

> In decision-making situations of real life, a course of action, to be accept-able, must satisfy a whole set of requirements, or constraints. Sometimes one of these requirements is singled out and referred to as the goal of the action. But the choice of one of the constraints, from many, is to a large extent arbitrary. For many purposes it is more meaningful to refer to the whole set of requirements as the (complex) goal of the action. This conclusion applies both to individual and organizational decision-making.

This analysis has important implications. A certain minimum of each vari-able must be obtained to reach a satisfactory solution. Below that minimum for each variable there are no trade-offs one can think of, so conventional analysis based on continuous utility functions and differential calculus is not applicable. If one solution does not satisfy the minimum satisficing levels for all variables, the decision-maker has no alternative but to keep generating better alternatives. Under bounded rationality, one would expect this to occur quite frequently. In fact, success in business may have more to do with finding good alternatives than with choosing between those that are readily available.

Occasionally, there may be more than one of the generated alternatives that meet all the criteria. In this case, one could choose "freely"(at random) from these alternatives, though it would seem logical to choose on the basis of maximizing one of the criteria.

Qualitative, unmeasurable organizational goals – limitations of formal evaluation and control systems

It follows from the analysis above that: (i) many of the important variables in organizations are impossible to measure with any degree of accuracy; and (ii) there are several dimensions to the goals of any company. Under these conditions, it is impossible for formal evaluation and reward systems to push people in the right direction (Holmstrom and Milgrom, 1991; Baker, 1992; Gibbons, 1998). The basic idea in these analyses is that if there is an underlying variable (profit, firm's value, or any other) that the firm should maximize, this variable is measurable only imperfectly, so any explicit variables being measured will only be imperfectly correlated with the underlying variable.

The phenomena analyzed in the previously cited papers of Baker (1992) and Gibbons (1998) largely explain the recent scandals. Specifically, suppose that the underlying variable the firm wants to increase (say, long-run firm value) is not perfectly measurable today, and that the performance variable measured is only imperfectly correlated with that underlying variable. Then, when considering two specific courses of action, $a1$ and $a2$, it may well be that $a1$ is better than $a2$ from the point of view of the performance measure but is worse from the point of view of the underlying value. Suppose now that the firm has an incentive system that rewards measured performance – for example, a linear compensation system where employees are paid a fixed amount independent of performance, plus an amount for each unit of measured performance. For the firm as a whole, $a2$ is better than $a1$, but the opposite is true for the decision-maker. Hence, the decision-maker is quite likely to choose $a1$. In the extreme case, an agent could earn higher incentive pay by manipulating performance measurements, lying or cheating.

Therefore, a system that was supposed to align the interests of the professional managers perfectly with the long-run interests of the stockholders has in fact achieved the opposite.[4]

Long-run and institutional identity

There is another sense in which short-run maximization of any variable may not be desirable. Often, when we speak of the long run, we do not refer so much to the time horizon itself as to other variables related to the institution's values. Selznick made this point in the 1950s:

> To take advantage of opportunities is to show that one is alive, but institutions no less than persons must look to the long-run effects of present advantage. In speaking of the "long run" we have in mind not time as such but how change affects personal or institutional identity. Such effects are not usually immediately apparent, and therefore we emphasize the lapse of time. But changes in character or identity may occur quite rapidly.

> Leadership is irresponsible when it fails to set goals and therefore lets the institution drift. The absence of controlling aims forces decisions to be made in response to immediate pressures. (Selznick, 1957, p. 143)

This last paragraph is particularly important. The only way for an organization to avoid the long-run consequences that would make it drift is to have "controlling aims". Those "controlling aims" have to be well-established decision-making criteria aimed at ensuring that the organization preserves its identity. This, in turn, implies a multiple-criteria decision-making process. Profit, value or some such financial variable is certainly one criterion; but we shall need more criteria if we want to preserve the organization's personality. This is much more difficult to put into practice than a single-criterion decision-making process, but it is indispensable. Later I shall attempt to show how this can be done.

Wider individual objectives

There is something else missing from the conventional economic approaches to organization. Everyone (including shareholders) actually have wider objectives: besides wealth or economic value they also want something else. This something else should include the interests of other people affected by the firm or its actions: first and foremost, the firm's employees, suppliers and customers. The concern for other affected people or institutions is what gave birth to the so-called "stakeholder theory of the firm" (Freeman, 1984). Jensen (2000) objects that when there is no single maximand, the firm does not know what to do; but he recognizes that narrow firm value maximization may lead to mistakes in the short run. Therefore, he advocates an "enlightened stakeholder theory" and argues that it is practically equivalent to "enlightened value maximization": respecting the interests of all stakeholders, but adding "the simple specification that the objective function of the firm is to maximize total long-term firm market value". This is, of course, well-intentioned, but it is difficult to ascertain whether it can be true because, unlike shareholder theory, stakeholder theory is not a clear and well-defined theory connected with a more general theory of resource allocation. All the same, it represents a substantial departure from the doctrine of narrow self-interest that has been so popular in recent years, in both theory and practice.

Motives of individuals

A person's motives clearly exceed the economic variables that affect only the person him/herself. That there are other motives in addition to compensation and monetary incentives ("extrinsic motives") has been recognized in the behavioral literature for some time (see, for example, Maslow, 1954; McGregor, 1960; Porter and Lawler, 1968). "Intrinsic" motives – that is, motives related to the job itself, the satisfaction of working with other people, doing something for others and so on, have also been recognized in the economics literature in recent years (see, for example, Kreps, 1997). Osterloh and Frey (2003) state:

> Extensive research accumulated over recent decades has established the importance of a very different kind of motivation in the firm, namely intrinsic motivation. In this case, an activity is valued for its own sake and is self-sustained. The work content itself provides satisfaction or utility.
>
> Intrinsic motivation is indispensable when external incentives cannot solve the problems of social dilemmas, either because behavior is not observable, or because the outcomes are not attributable to individuals. If there is an intrinsic motivation to work and to cooperate, contributing to the common good ceases to become a social dilemma.

Intrinsic motivation, thus defined, is indispensable in situations where there are severe limitations in the measures of the output and results of the firm, as suggested in the previous section. Often, however, "intrinsic motivation" is a composite of different factors. In Osterloh and Frey, for example, intrinsic motives include what, following Frey (1997), they call "obligation-based" or "pro-social motives", which are clearly different from enjoying an activity for its own sake, irrespective of the other people involved.

Here I prefer to reserve the expression "intrinsic motivation" to denote the pleasure (or displeasure, if it requires effort) of simply doing a good job, while I have already used the expression "transitive" motivation to refer to motives targeted at other people's well-being. Transitive motives are related to an individual's wish to satisfy someone else's needs, which is crucial when it comes to defining the mission of an organization. They are different from "pro-social" or "altruistic" motives in that such motives are to some extent abstract, aimed at society as a whole, perhaps more related to "sympathy", whereas transitive motives are related to specific people (customers, employees, other stakeholders), whose needs one may attempt to satisfy, and thus related to "commitment".

Competitive advantage on through knowledge

The competitive advantage of a firm rests heavily on a type of knowledge that is produced internally, is somewhat implicit (as opposed to explicit) and can be used only within the firm itself, it being impossible to sell it as a market good (Nonaka, 1994; Andreu, 2009). In 1945 Hayek expressed the idea that "practically every individual has some advantage over all others because he possesses unique information of which beneficial use can be made only if the decisions depending on it are left to him or are made with his active cooperation". Today, this is truer than ever: knowledge has become crucial in all sectors of economic activity.

This has an important implication. If it is impossible to have a perfect evaluation and incentive system (except perhaps in marginal, mechanical, trivial jobs), then we cannot rely on extrinsic motives to make individuals do what is good for the organization. For individuals to cooperate effectively in an organizational context, therefore, they must have intrinsic or transitive motives.

Organizations as communities: loyalties and identification

A "good climate", "good team work" or, more succinctly, "union" between members of an organization has always been considered crucial for an organization to function. However, the individualism implicit in most economic theories seems to have obliterated this crucial fact recently. Pfeffer (2005) argues strongly in favor of the idea of organizations as communities:

> Organizations that are more communal have arrangements for helping employees in need, offer more generous employee benefits and assistance,

eschew anti-nepotism policies, have more company-sponsored social events, are better at resolving work–family issues, and foster long-term employment relations ... The logic linking the less communal aspect of companies and the rise of distrust, disengagement, and diminished satisfaction, although not extensively empirically demonstrated, seems clear. Trust is enhanced through longer-term interactions and by believing that the other party is taking your interests into account.

Individuals' identification with or loyalty to organizational objectives, which classical writers such as Barnard (1938) or Simon (1957) considered to be the basis of organizational efforts, has lost ground to the individualism implicit in today's economics-based analyses. In Barnard's words (1938, ch. 7):

> to me, at least, it appears utterly contrary to the nature of man to be sufficiently induced by material or monetary considerations to contribute enough effort to a cooperative system to enable it to be productively efficient to the degree necessary for persistence over an extended period. If these things are true, then even in purely economic enterprises efficiency in the offering of non-economic inducements may be as vital as productive efficiency.

Simon (1957, ch. VI) expresses a complementary point of view:

> Individuals are willing to accept organization membership when their activity in the organization contributes, directly or indirectly, to their own personal goals. The contribution is direct if the goals set for the organization have direct personal value for the individual – church membership is a typical example of this. The contribution is indirect if the organization offers personal rewards – monetary or other – to the individual in return for his willingness to contribute his activity to the organization. Employment in a business concern is a typical example of this ... The phrase 'personal goals' which is used here should be understood in a broad sense. It is by no means restricted to egoistic goals, much less to economic goals. "World peace" or "aid to the starving Chinese" may be just as much a personal goal for a particular individual as another dollar in his pay envelope. The fact that economic incentives frequently predominate in business and governmental organizations should not obscure the importance of other types of inducements.

Both Barnard and Simon thus attach a great weight to nonmonetary motives and think that firms should take care of the motives of the individuals (the famous concept of "efficiency" in Barnard), so that individuals can identify with the firm.

An alternative view of organizations[5]

This set of assumptions has strong implications for how we view organizations. For one thing, maximizing value cannot be the firm's goal: maximization is not possible because of the hypotheses of bounded rationality and satisficing behavior; and value maximization might not even be desirable if it is done at the expense of long-run qualitative variables. In fact, the basic goal of the firm has to be to adequately and simultaneously satisfy the needs of all stakeholders.

In fact, if any one group of people is to be singled out as the main beneficiaries of the organizational goal it is customers. This was already seen by Simon (1957, ch. VI). Specifically and operationally, customers define the basic purpose of organizational action: the goal is precisely to deliver a product or service that solves their needs.

Mission

This basic purpose is what is sometimes called the "mission" of the firm. It may have been Selznick (1957) who first used this (originally military) term in a management context. In Selznick's original formulation, the mission is a guide to what has to be done, the general purpose that gives meaning to all particular actions that have to be undertaken, and it is in this sense that we use the word here. It is very unfortunate that nowadays the "mission" of a firm is often equated with a set of high-sounding phrases void of content. Most "mission statements" in published annual reports are meaningless, fine words saying how much the firm wants to be the best in everything it does and how much it cares about shareholders, customers, the environment and everybody else in the world, usually without explaining how it sets priorities, how or to what extent it guides employees' actions, or to what extent it sacrifices short-run success for long-run advantage.[6]

Here, "mission" means what kind of customer needs the firm will try to satisfy. For example, the firm may say that its mission is to help to keep the inhabitants of a particular geographical area warm in winter. It can do that with electricity, fuel oil, coal, insulation or other means, possibly including some that have not yet been invented. But what the firm wants to do and considers to be its mission is to solve the heating needs of a specified population group.

In order to be interested in the organizational goal as it has just been defined, the organization's employees need to have what we have called transitive motives; that is, they have to want to solve the customers' problem (that is, to keep them warm). If the employees have only extrinsic motives, they will just want to do whatever they are rewarded for doing. What's more, there cannot be an "objective" reward for satisfying customer needs, because such satisfaction is subjective by its very nature; not to mention the fact that whether customers are really satisfied or not may not be known until years after the sale is completed. If employees have only intrinsic motives, they may produce a product that is technically perfect and that they enjoy producing, but that is unfit or impractical for customers. In either case, consumers are obviously not going to be satisfied, there will be no repeat business, and stockholders will also be unsatisfied.

It is interesting at this point to recall Hayek's argument that employees' active cooperation is needed to make full use of the personal, relevant information they have (Hayek, 1945). If the firm does not obtain such active cooperation, decisions are likely to be mediocre and the firm will not be competitive. If a firm wants to limit itself to producing a product that is as good as possible from a technical point of view, then it may be solving the wrong problem for the customer. In contrast, if the firm actually tries to solve the consumer's problem, it may have a competitive advantage and be highly profitable. In order to do that, however, the firm needs to develop transitive motives in its employees. Unless its employees have transitive motives, they are not going to be interested in solving customers' problems. Trying to obtain as much money as possible for stockholders may just be putting the cart before the horse.

Distinctive competence

To fulfill its mission and develop a competitive advantage, a firm needs to have a "distinctive competence" that defines its character and identity. Distinctive competence is the opposite of opportunism (seizing every opportunity to make an immediate gain) because it is developed in precisely the opposite way; that is, by specializing in satisfying a particular kind of need and developing the products to do so most effectively. Distinctive competence is created on the basis of an organizational mission. Identifying individuals with the targeted need is what creates the organization's ability to meet that need and may give the organization an advantage over competitors that have neither the sense of mission nor the knowledge to do so.

Knowledge is a crucial resource, especially in today's "knowledge economy". Part of this knowledge, as we have said, is: (i) specific to the individual firm in the context of its strategy and mission; and (ii) implicit, in that people may not be aware that they know what they know (Polanyi, 1958). Developing a distinctive competence has to do with these kinds of knowledge. Knowledge that is standard and explicit can be acquired in the market, either in the form of literature and technology or in the form of a person who possesses the knowledge. Precisely for that reason, however, distinctive competence cannot be based on such knowledge. Instead, it has to be based on knowledge that is specific not only to a particular job, but also to the person and the firm. Firms in the same industry but with a different sense of mission and a different strategy will develop specific knowledge that has very little in common.

The core issue here is how a sense of mission and identification can lead to the development of implicit, specific knowledge. If specific knowledge is tied to a particular firm's mission and strategy, it is by definition useful only to that firm, not to any other. Extrinsic motives can therefore never be sufficient to induce people to invest in this type of knowledge. Why would anyone develop it if they do not identify with their particular firm and its mission? It is the kind of knowledge that has no market value and equally adds no market value to the person acquiring it, since by definition it can be used only in the firm in which it originated. To invest in it, therefore, a person must expect to stay in the firm, which is unlikely to happen unless the individual identifies with the firm; otherwise, he or she will be looking for another job somewhere else.

The two concepts are therefore interrelated: a firm cannot develop a distinctive competence unless its employees identify with it; and employees cannot identify with a firm unless the firm is doing something different – that is, has a personality, a character or a distinctive competence.

The impact of any decision on an organization's distinctive competence is therefore crucial for the organization's future, but mainly in a negative sense.

In other words, if a given action alternative simply takes advantage of an opportunity, the chances are that it will contribute to destroying the firm's distinctive competence and, with it, the employees' identification with the firm. Selznick (1957) saw most of these points many years ago, but we seem to have forgotten a number of them recently in favor of quantitative goals:

> To take advantage of opportunities is to show that one is alive, but institutions no less than persons must look to the long-run effects of present advantage. In speaking of the 'long run' we have in mind not time as such but how change affects personal or institutional identity ... Leadership is irresponsible when it fails to set goals and therefore lets the institution drift. The absence of controlling aims forces decisions to be made in response to immediate pressures. (Selznick, 1957, p. 143)
>
> In studying character we are interested in the distinctive competence or inadequacy that an organization has acquired. In doing so, we look beyond the formal aspects to examine the commitments that have been accepted in the course of adaptation to internal and external pressures ... we come back to the problem of maintaining institutional integrity. The ultimate cost of opportunistic adaptation goes beyond capitulation on specific issues. A more serious result is that outside elements may enter the organization and dominate parts of it ... The avoidance of opportunism is not the avoidance of all compromise; it is the avoidance of compromise that undermines institutional integrity ... To act as if only a set of impersonal transactions were involved, with no responsibility beyond the strict terms of a contract, creates anxiety in the buyer, threatens to damage his reputation for dependability, and in the end weakens both parties. (Selznick, 1957, pp. 42–4)

Distinctive competence is related to intrinsic motives on the part of individuals; that is, the desire to do a good job, practice one's abilities, enjoy a job well done, and so on. In the previous section, we saw that identification with the organizational mission is related to transitive motives. Thus intrinsic and transitive motives play a key role in the development of an organization.

"Internal" mission and identification with organizational goals

As stated earlier, we need employees to identify with the organizational goal (defined in terms of consumers' needs). But we also need them to identify with one another. In a world in which there is very little a person can do on his or her own, team spirit is essential in any organization, no matter how small. In other words, we need organizational "unity", where all employees identify with the organizational mission and, at the same time, with each other, and where each cooperates with the rest of the organization in doing whatever has to be done in order to achieve the goal. This is what Pérez López (1993) calls the "internal mission" – that is, the ("external") mission as internalized by individual employees. Unity thus becomes crucial to firms' long-run survival and competitive advantage.

Transitive motives come into the picture here again. Unity will only be achieved if employees have transitive motives towards each other; otherwise, they can be expected to behave bureaucratically or even do a technically perfect job, but without actively cooperating with the rest of the people in the organization in solving customers' real problems. Employee development is possibly the most important means of building unity, competitive advantage and profitability at the same time; and it has to be done in all three dimensions of extrinsic, intrinsic and transitive motives.

Every individual has extrinsic motives, because every individual has physical needs that must be satisfied (food, shelter, and so on). Also, every individual has intrinsic motives (the need to learn and do a good job). Transitive motives are to some extent spontaneous, but also need to be developed. This is one of the key tasks of management: to help individuals develop the intrinsic and transitive motives they need in order to achieve organizational goals. It is not an easy task, though, and cannot be done directly. It is easy to create or develop extrinsic motives through an incentive system, to the extent of displacing or even destroying intrinsic and transitive motives (Frey and Jegen, 2001), but it is impossible to create and develop intrinsic and transitive motives in the same way. Possibly, the only way to do it is by creating a culture in which everybody in the organization promotes, respects and praises transitive motives. Transitive motives may help to develop intrinsic motives, but in contrast, developing extrinsic motives may kill both intrinsic and transitive ones.

To sum up, organizations can be viewed as having a mission, which is related to satisfying their customers' real needs, as opposed to short-run perceived needs or wishes. In order to induce employees to cooperate in doing this, firms need employees to have both intrinsic and transitive motives. Transitive motives will make employees try hard to solve customers' problems, while intrinsic motives will help to solve the problem in a technically correct way. For employees to cooperate with each other and invest in specific knowledge, which is the key to distinctive competence and therefore to competitive advantage, it is crucial that they integrate and identify with the firm. This will naturally result in greater profitability: if a firm solves its customers' real needs, the customers will purchase its products and the firm will survive indefinitely. Profitability is therefore an outcome of the firm's actions, not the starting point; the scorecard rather than the compass.[7]

Implications for managerial decision-making

Under the assumption of competitive markets for the company's products, as well as raw materials, labor and all other inputs, managerial decisions have only an economic component and can be made almost mechanically. The criterion on which they have to be based is, of course, the maximization of firm value.

We have shown that this is generally unrealistic, though for some simple decisions it may not be too unrealistic. A decision of the kind taught in elementary cost accounting courses (for example, about adding or dropping a product that is similar to many others the firm already has, or about accepting a special order at a special price, and so on) can be made ("*ceteris paribus*", one might add) on the basis of contribution and profitability alone, which amounts to maximizing the firm's value. If the decision affects more than one period, present value analysis leads to maximization of the firm's profit and value.

With more complex decisions of the kind suggested above (downsizing, and so on), however, a single criterion of profit or value maximization is unrealistic and incomplete. Of course, there has to be a quantitative analysis of the financial variables, and the result of this analysis will be one of the (important) inputs to the decision process. Firms need to survive, so they must make some profit (all costs being taken into account) over an extended period.

More generally, as well as the financial variables there may be other quantitative variables where the firm either has to obtain a certain minimum or it will not survive, or variables that are indices of other important variables. Examples for certain decisions might include on-time delivery, absenteeism, statistical distribution of demand for different products and so on. All of them are related to achieving specific, preestablished, quantitative goals. The degree to which these goals are achieved is usually expressed in terms of effectiveness. Effectiveness is important, of course, but it follows from the previous analysis that it is not nearly enough. We can probably see this better through an example.

An illustrative example

Rigorously, in order to illustrate properly the concepts we have defined, we would need a detailed specific case; but this would clearly exceed the limits of this chapter. At the risk, then, of not going in enough depth into the subject, we shall have to settle for an illustration relying on the intuitive ideas that the reader may have about the way a professional firm might work; for example, a consulting company.

To begin, notice that there are substantially different types of consulting companies, with different aspirations, different specializations and different strategies. But in any case, they all have in common that they consist of a set of high-level professionals, with direct contact with the client, for whom they have to carry out a specific assignment. This specific assignment has to be adapted to the client's concrete characteristics and circumstances. This requires a deep knowledge of these characteristics and circumstances, which in turn requires direct contact with the firm.

A consulting company has to meet the effectiveness criterion – that is, must be able to obtain a value added that is enough to compensate its employees and shareholders. The effectiveness criterion may include other quantifiable variables, some of the financial type (income, revenues), some of any other type (percentage of clients brought in by other clients, for example). In fact, which indices the firm uses to measure effectiveness determines (partially, at least) the distinctive character and personality of the firm.

Suppose, then, that at some point in time a firm receives a request for an assignment from a potentially important client. Obviously, the first question the firm should ask itself is related to the effectiveness principle: how would the assignment improve the value added and the other quantitative variables that the firm considers important?

This question can be answered categorically only by exception. While some assignments are so good (and some others so bad) that they do not require any deep analysis, in most cases, such an analysis is necessary. In the consulting industry, an important percentage of the costs are fixed, which means that even very small revenues will bring in a positive contribution. But what contribution can be considered to be sufficient? Any positive contribution? What price is the potential client willing to accept? Will the potential client accept the contribution we customarily charge according to our pricing policies? Can the firm offer a lower price to obtain an important client? These, and other similar questions, have to be answered to be able to solve the effectiveness problem.

The second criterion is that of attractiveness. Has the possible job any good quality in terms of learning, or is simply a repetition of what has been made dozens of times? Is it something that contributes to the personal development of those involved, or something that will make them deviate from the professional path they are following? It is something that will strengthen the knowledge and skills they already have, or something that will make their knowledge and skills appear trivial?

None of these questions has an easy answer. And whatever the answer might be, it will seldom be an "objective" one, because subjectivity is always an element of managerial decision-making. Obviously, one should try to make the answers as "objective" as possible, but one should never forget that the conceptual basis of a market economy is precisely the decentralized decision-making process, where firms make the decisions they want, according to their information and beliefs; and the ones that do "better" survive and are successful. Perhaps the key question, then, to evaluate an alternative in terms of its attractiveness (or in terms of unity, as we shall see next) is what would happen to the company if a course of action such as the one we are considering were to be repeated many times? Would following that course of action improve the firm's competitive position given the strategy it wants to pursue? Or would it lead the company in a direction that management does not want to go?

Let us emphasize again that there are no simple, clear answers to questions of this kind and that, furthermore, strategy is essential as the context in which they have to be answered. A consulting company can employ the strategy, for example, of having a standard product for sale in a "standard package", which can then be used in many different companies; then, a repeat version can be helpful to further redesign this "package" (by trial and error if you like), provided it has the right personnel to do this satisfactorily. Another company, in contrast, can have a strategy consisting of a differentiated product, tailor-made for the customer, that has a much higher cost, needs first-rate professionals and is much more satisfactory for them as professionals.

Simplifying things a bit, one could say that there are two types of consulting companies, and that either of the strategies might be valid if it is consistent with everyday practice; which means, in essence, that it should have the right people for what the company says it wants to do, and act consistently with that. Constantly changing from one approach to another will not help to establish a "character" for the company, or to push a strategy. If the staff is only of an average quality, the logical thing to do is to try the "repetitive" strategy; while if staff is of very high quality, asking them to do "repetitive" work will be a waste of very valuable resources. Obviously, the attractiveness for this type of staff of routine production is close to zero, or even negative.

Finally, the principle of unity requires asking explicitly the question of whether the order being considered will or will not promote trust among participants and their identification with the organization. Again, these are not easy questions to answer, of course. But the first thing a manager should consider is whether the assignments people are asked to do will develop them personally and professionally. If not, unity will decrease, whether in the short or the long run. There will be less identification among them and between them and the objectives of the organization; and this will inevitably reduce trust.

Possibly the best way to begin thinking about it is by looking at the customer: if what we are doing is worthwhile to the customer, then people that are part of the organization can feel identified with it. In fact, this would not have any importance if we believe that employees only have extrinsic motives; but if their motives are transitive, then it will be crucial. If we want to promote identification, we have to make them see to what extent their work meets the real needs of the customers; and therefore the extent to which it can satisfy their transitive motives. If their motives are purely extrinsic, is not possible to identify them with anything other than money.

In a product as intangible as that of the consulting business, the difference between meeting the *real* needs of a customer and meeting the *perceived* needs of that customer can be substantial. A company can sell a "miracle" product knowing that it will not work (or at least that it will not provide the promised miracles) or can sell a product that actually solves a real problem. To promise a lot may be intended to be a marketing trick to sell more, but if then the product does not solve the real problems of the affected organizations, it is doubtful that this company can remain in business indefinitely. Typically, in most situations, you can promise only hard work, discussing issues in depth, and trying to resolve them with common sense; together, of course, with a minimum of managerial techniques. But, obviously, anyone can promise such a thing and it does not sound very attractive; it is easier to lie, promising a wonderful formula. This type of strategy may provide benefit in the short term, but if it does not solve the real problems of customers, they will notice and the company will not go far in the long run. Telling the truth may be more difficult as a strategy in the short run, but it is sustainable in the long run if the company is able to help the client solve real problems. Promising miracles as a way to lure customers in can also be feasible – but one must be sure then that the real problems of the customer are resolved.

Typically, the way to solve the real needs of the customer is not by making unrealistic promises. A consultant should act like a doctor, giving his or her diagnosis no matter what the client believes: the client may very well be wrong. Sometimes, the distinction between real problems and perceived ones is ignored and the customer is sold a supposedly wonderful product to solve the perceived problems. Sometimes, the product sold has some good qualities in other aspects, and this is good for the client company; but since it does not solve the problems as promised, the client may demand that these problems are solved, and then the consulting company can be tempted to do something purely cosmetic that does not solve anything but consumes real resources instead.

Doing one thing or another has a strong impact on the attractiveness and unity of the organization. Doing something that does not solve any real problem is neither attractive nor identifies anyone with the organization or the product. The two criteria, then, are crucial for the future of the organization: attractiveness can be achieved only by producing and selling a product that represents a professional challenge for employees, and unity can be achieved only by solving real customer problems.

Summary: three criteria for decision-making

Let us now summarize and restate the essential concepts. To begin, effectiveness is the always the first criterion to be taken into account for decision-making, and it may have many subcriteria consisting of different quantitative variables, where the financial ones occupy the place of honor.

Next, we have to evaluate in second place the firm's distinctive competence or, rather, the extent to which distinctive competence is affected by the
decision. This means answering the following types of question: Is the action
alternative we are contemplating going to teach the company something that
is congruent with the direction set by the company's mission? Will it help
to make the company progress in that direction? Or is it an alternative that
does not contribute to the development of distinctive competence but simply
provides a high financial contribution and so merely increases effectiveness? If
that is the case, it is what Selznick called "opportunistic adaptation", which he
considered a serious threat to distinctive competence (Selznick, 1957).

Assessing the impact on distinctive competence is crucial, but by its very
nature qualitative. The decision-maker has no alternative but to make a subjective assessment of whether the alternative of the action being considered is
"satisficing". Any attempt to quantify certain dimensions of distinctive competence will not exhaust the concept. In other words, if the decision-maker
attempts to use quantitative indices to assess the impact, there will always be
a residual that is omitted, possibly a very important residual that cannot be
measured. Indices may be useful for assessing distinctive competence, but
once they have been quantified they become part of effectiveness, the first
criterion evaluated. If one believes that "there is more to it" than the value of
the index – that is, that there is a qualitative component that is important and
cannot be measured – then this assessment is not only necessary but at least
as important as a quantitative measurement of effectiveness.

Finally, we have to consider the effects of the proposed course of action
on unity and identification. To what extent does the decision encourage
employees to identify with one another and with the organization's mission?
Here, too, there is a minimum ("satisficing"), non-quantifiable level that must
be met.

There may be trade-offs between the three variables, but they are extremely
difficult to handle, partly because a ("satisficing") minimum of the three
variables is needed, so no amount of effectiveness will compensate for a
destruction of unity or opportunistic adaptation. Bounded rationality, on the
other hand, means that only a few action alternatives will be explicitly considered. Therefore, when an alternative is found that does not satisfy the three
minimum levels of aspiration, new alternatives must be generated until one is
found that does.

Maximizing variables of this nature is typically impossible; thus we should aim for a satisficing level. If in some cases one has to choose between two alternatives that meet the minimum levels of the three variables, the one that has the most favorable impact on unity should be chosen, because unity and identification are the "engines" of the whole process; distinctive competence is one consequence and effectiveness is a consequence of both. An organization whose priority is to protect its unity and distinctive competence is bound to have good results from the point of view of effectiveness in the long run, while a satisficing level of effectiveness will ensure survival in the short run. A competent manager should be able to find at least one alternative with satisficing levels of the three criteria, because human beings always find solutions to problems when they try hard enough; and they do so when they think those problems are worthwhile, because of intrinsic motives, because of transitive motives, or of both.

Acknowledgments

I am indebted, first, to Juan Antonio Pérez López, who inspired the last part of this chapter but passed away many years before it was ever written. I thank Rafael Andreu, Jordi Canals, Josep Riverola, Manuel Velilla and the participants in the IESE Conference on "Humanizing the Firm and the Management Profession" (June/July 2008) for comments, suggestions and stimulating discussions on the subject.

NOTES

1 See, for example, the interesting analysis in L. M. Krauss, *The Physics of Star Trek*, New York: Basic Books.

2 See Rosanas (2008). I am indebted to Domènec Melé for suggesting the use of this adjective.

3 The original expression in French was "l'intérêt bien entendu"; that is, literally, "self-interest well understood", which is slightly different from "enlightened self-interest".

4 For a pathetic example of this, see in YouTube what Richard Fuld, former CEO of Lehman Brothers, had to say in the Congressional Hearings about the crisis. Available at http://www.youtube.com/watch?v=—cifEkRXc4andfeature=related.

5 In this section, I draw freely on the work of Pérez López (1993).

6 Just to illustrate, I have copied this completely meaningless "mission statement" from the annual report of an international firm in the paper industry:

Our mission is to grow in the production and distribution of paper, with a commitment to quality and service that satisfies the needs of the customer, all this from criteria of economic profitability, social responsibility, and sustainability.

7 A word of caution is in order here with respect to profitability, though. One might argue that a firm can have an excellent product, but that the product cannot be produced profitably because consumers cannot pay the cost. If that is the case, the firm is not solving consumers' real needs, as that requires making a product consumers can afford.

REFERENCES

Andreu, R. 2009. *Knowledge, Learning and Competitive Advantage: Implications for the Management Profession.* Conference on "Humanizing the Firm and the Management Profession", IESE, University of Navarra.

Baker, G. 1992. "Incentive Contracts and Performance Measurement". *Journal of Political Economy* 100(3):598-614.

Barnard, Ch. 1938. *The Functions of the Executive.* Boston, MA: Harvard University Press.

Cameron, K. S. 1991. "Downsizing Can Be Hazardous to Your Future". *HR Magazine*, May.

Cameron, K. S. 1993. "Organizational Downsizing". In G. Huber and W. Glick, eds. *Organizational Change and Redesign.* New York: Oxford University Press, 19–65.

Cameron, K.S., Dutton, J. E. and Quinn, R. E., eds. 2003. *Positive Organizational Scholarship.* San Francisco: Berrett-Koehler.

Davis, J. H., Schoorman, F. D. and Donaldson, L. 1997. "Toward a Stewardship Theory of Management". *Academy of Management Review,*22: 20–47.

Donaldson, L. 2002."Damned By Our Own Theories: Contradictions Between Theories and Management Education". *Academy of Management Learning & Education* 1:96–106.

Donaldson, L. 2005. "For Positive Management Theories While Retaining Science: Reply to Ghoshal". *Academy of Management Learning & Education* 4:109–13.

Ethiraj, L. and Levinthal, D. 2009. "Hoping for A to Z While Rewarding Only A: Complex Organizations and Multiple Goals". *Organization Science* 20(1):4–21.

Ferraro, F., Pfeffer, J. and Sutton, R. 2005. "Economics Language and Assumptions: How Theories Can Become Self-Fulfilling". *Academy of Management Review* 30(1):8–24.

Freeman, R. E. 1984. *Strategic Management: A Stakeholder Approach*. Boston, MA: Pitman.

Freeman, S. J. and Cameron, K. S. 1993. "Organizational Downsizing: A Convergence and Reorientation Framework". *Organizational Science* 4:10–29.

Frey, B. 1993. "Does Monitoring Increase Work Effort? The Rivalry With Trust and Loyalty". *Economic Inquiry* 31:663–70.

Frey, B. 1997. *Not Just For the Money: An Economic Theory of Personal Motivation*. Brookfield, UK: Edward Elgar.

Frey, B. and Jegen, R. 2001. "Motivation Crowding Theory: A Survey of Empirical Evidence". *Journal of Economic Surveys* 15(5):589–611.

Friedman, M. 1953. "The Methodology of Positive Economics". In M. Friedman, *Essays in Positive Economics*. Chicago, IL: University of Chicago Press.

Ghoshal, S. 2005. "Bad Management Theories Are Destroying Good Management Practices". *Academy of Management Learning & Education* 4: 75–91.

Ghoshal, S. and Moran, P. 1996 "Bad for Practice: A Critique of the Transaction–Cost Theory". *Academy of Management Review* 21(1), 13–47.

Gibbons, R. 1998." Incentives in Organizations". *Journal of Economic Perspectives* 12(4):115–32.

Gintis, H. and Khurana, R. 2008. "Corporate Honesty and Business Education: A Behavioral Model". In Paul J. Zak, ed. *Moral Markets: The Critical Role of Valuesin the Economy*. Free Enterprise: Values in Action Conference Series. Princeton, NJ: Princeton University Press.

Hamel, G. 2007. Available at: http://discussionleader.hbsp.com/hamel/2007/10/is_it_really_possible_to_reinv.htlm

Hayek, F. A. von 1945. "The Use of Knowledge in Society". *American Economic Review* 35(4):519–30.

Jensen, M. 2000. "Value Maximization, Stakeholder Theory and the Corporate Objective Function". In M. Beer and N. Nohria, eds. *Breaking the Code of Change*. Boston, Mass.: Harvard Business School Press. Also in *Journal of Corporate Finance*, Fall 2001.

Jensen, M. 2002. *Just Say "No" to Wall Street*. NOM Working Paper No. 02-01, Harvard Business School, Boston, MA.

Khurana, R. 2007. *From Higher Aims to Hired Hands*. Princeton, NJ and Oxford, UK: Princeton University Press.

Kreps, D. 1997. "Intrinsic Motivation and Extrinsic Incentives". *American Economic Review* 87(2):359–64.

Leibenstein, H. 2002. *Beyond Economic Man*. 2nd edn. Cambridge, MA: Harvard University Press.

Maslow, A. 1954. *Motivation and Personality*. New York: Harper and Row.

McGregor, D. 1960. *The Human Side of the Enterprise*. New York: McGraw-Hill.

Munier, B., Selten, R. *et al.* (11 other authors). 2003. "Bounded Rationality Modeling". *Marketing Letters* 43:197–200.

Nonaka, I. 1994. "A Dynamic Theory of Organizational Knowledge Creation". *Organization Science*, 5(1), February.

Osterloh, M. and Frey, B. 2003. *Corporate Governance for Crooks? The Case for Corporate Virtue*. Working paper ISSN 1424-0459, Institute for Empirical Research in Economics, University of Zurich.

Pearce, J. L. 2003. "What Do We Know and How Do We Really Know It?". *Academy of Management Review* 29(2):175–9.

Pérez López, J. A. 1993. *Fundamentos de la Dirección de Empresas*. Madrid: Ediciones Rialp.

Pfeffer, J. 1999. *Labor Market Flexibility. Do Companies Really Know Best?* Research Paper 1592, Stanford University, Stanford, CA.

Pfeffer, J. 2005 *Working Alone: What Ever Happened to the Idea of Organizations as Communities?* Research Paper No. 1906, Stanford University, Stanford, CA.

Polanyi, M. 1958. *Personal Knowledge*. Chicago, IL: University of Chicago Press.

Porter, L. W. and Lawler, E. E. 1968. *Managerial Attitudes and Performance*. Homewood, IL: Richard D. Irwin.

Rosanas, J. 2008. "Beyond Economic Criteria: A Humanistic Approach to Organizational Survival". *Journal of Business Ethics*, DOI 10.1007/s10551-006-9341-9.

Selznick, P. 1957. *Leadership in Administration*. Berkeley, CA: University of California Press.

Sen, A. 1977. "Rational Fools: A Critique of the Behavioral Foundations of Economic Theory". *Philosophy and Public Affairs* 6:317–44.

Senge, P. 2000. "The Puzzles and Paradoxes of How Living Companies Create Wealth". In M. Beer and N. Nohria, eds. *Breaking the Code of Change*. Boston, MA: Harvard Business School Press, 59–81.

Simon, H. 1957. *Administrative Behavior*. 2nd edn. New York/London: The Free Press.

Simon, H. 1964. "On the Concept of Organizational Goal". *Administrative Science Quarterly* 9:1–22.

Tocqueville, A. de. 1981 (originally published 1840). *De la Démocratie en Amérique*. Paris: Garnier Flammarion.

CHAPTER 2.3

Bridging the Globalization Gap at Top Business Schools: Curricular Challenges and a Response

PANKAJ GHEMAWAT, Anselmo Rubiralta Professor of Globalization and Strategy, IESE Business School, University of Navarra

This chapter had its origins in a colloquium I organized in Fall 2007 as part of a cycle celebrating IESE Business School's 50th anniversary. The colloquium focused specifically on teaching globalization rather than researching it. The colloquium provided an opportunity to examine two very broad questions: what do top business schools *actually* do about globalization; and what *should* they do? Since then, my understanding of the issues involved has been further enriched my numerous other activities, including participating in an AACSB (Association to Advance Collegiate Schools) taskforce on the globalization of management education, and piloting a new required course on globalization in the first year of the IESE MBA program. This chapter revisits the two original questions and identifies a key globalization gap in terms of curricular content. It also proposes a specific solution to this problem, involving a platform course on globalization and the deliberate creation of interlocks with other required (functional) courses.

The next section looks, as a baseline, at what top business schools say on their websites about their globalization efforts. The analysis covers lists of the top thirty US and the top ten non-US full-time MBA programs. All forty schools emphasize globalization on their websites; nearly all cite international partnerships and provide data on international students; most also discuss student diversity; but only a minority, however, mention faculty diversity. The non-US business schools in the sample place more emphasis in absolute terms on globalization and student and faculty diversity than do the US schools, but the discourse across the two groups is broadly similar.

The following section looks at what top business schools in fact do about globalization. The data do indicate significant activity around diversity and partnerships – the latter focused mainly on student exchange programs. Top European schools average higher scores along both dimensions than their US counterparts, and within regions, measures of diversity seem positively correlated with status. But there seems to be significantly less attention paid to the globalization of course development and research.

We next look more carefully at top business schools' globalization efforts and conclude that there is a dangerous deficiency in terms of the globalization of curricular content. In this section we point out too that the development and deployment of better globalization-related content would, in addition to benefiting the schools that play a leading role in such development, also have a large social multiplier.

The next section addresses what should be done to close the globalization gap. It draws on the results of a new cross-functional survey of leading academic thinkers about the globalization-related content that business schools should put into their MBA programs. In the broadest terms, the survey recommends that such content should focus on cross-country differences and their business implications. Both empirical and logical reasons can be cited as to why this recommendation is compelling.

We then discuss some of the well-known design challenges involved in implementing such ideas and, in the spirit of stimulating more creative responses to them, present a proposal on how business schools might move forward. Specifically, it presents an outline for a globalization course, with the suggested focus on cross-country differences, designed to be inserted into the core MBA curriculum and meant to serve as a platform to launch discussions from functional and strategic perspectives about management across borders.[1] A version of this *interlock* model was piloted at the IESE Business School in 2010 and will be offered again in 2011.

What top business schools say

Based on AACSB estimates, there are (approximately) 11,767 higher education institutions worldwide that offer one or more business degree programs at undergraduate level or above. Since that is an unwieldy description, all such educational institutions will be referred to in this chapter as business schools, even though many – perhaps most – have very small business programs or offer a single business degree through another department. The number with global accreditation from the AACSB or EQUIS totals 668, according to these organizations, or less than 6 percent of the global total. Most ranking schemes focus on the top 1–2 percent, at most, of the global total, which tend to be the schools for which we have at least some systematic information. They represent an obvious starting point, though we shall come back later in the chapter to compare them with lower-ranked institutions.

What, as a baseline, do top business schools say about their globalization efforts? Schools' websites seemed a convenient, considered communications channel through which to examine this question. Since the quantitative and qualitative analysis of websites did require nonnegligible time per school, the number of schools studied was restricted to forty, taken from *BusinessWeek*'s lists of the top thirty US and the top ten non-US (European and Canadian) full-time MBA programs. A research assistant and I accessed the targeted websites in July 2009 and looked for mentions of globalization and three levers for globalization identified by previous research: student diversity, faculty diversity and international partnerships. In addition to a binary classification of websites based on whether they mentioned a particular theme or not, we rated websites based on the emphasis accorded a theme, with "0" equaling no significant mentions found on the website, "1" equaling at least one mention on the website, "2" equaling significant emphasis of at least a full webpage, and "3" equaling primary emphasis on the website. Table 3 summarizes the results at varying levels of aggregation, and the rest of this section elaborates on them.

At the most aggregated level, the websites of all forty schools mention globalization, thirty-six mention partnerships, twenty-five mention student diversity and thirteen faculty diversity. The average emphasis ratings preserve that order but widen the gap between globalization, which averages a rating of 1.8 – that is, close to a full webpage – and partnerships, which averages 1.3, or closer to just a mention.

Disaggregating (partially) by geography, the non-US top ten rate substantially higher on most of these indicators than the US schools. Partnerships provide the exception: there, the comparison depends on whether one looks at mentions in Table 3A or emphases in Table 3B – but the comparison is close either way. A plausible inference is that for the schools at this level, involvement in partnerships is more or less a given – something to be mentioned but not made too much of as a differentiating factor. The big differences between non-US and US schools involve more mention of and

Table 3: Globalization in top business schools' websites

	A Mentions				B Emphases*			
	Globalization?	Student diversity (%)	Faculty diversity (%)	Partnerships? (%)	Globalization?	Student diversity	Faculty diversity	Partnerships?
All (40)	100%	63	33	90	1.8	0.9	0.5	1.3
Non-U.S. Top 10	100%	100	80	80	2.2	1.8	1.2	1.4
US Top 10	100%	80	10	100	2.1	0.8	0.1	1.3
US Top 11–30	100%	35	20	90	1.4	0.4	0.3	1.2
US All	100%	50	17	93	1.6	0.5	0.2	1.2

*0 = Absent; 1 = Mentioned; 2 = Significant Emphasis; 3 = Primary Emphasis

Source: Based on an analysis of websites on *BusinessWeek*'s list of top MBA programs.

emphasis on student and faculty diversity among the non-US schools, and in particular versus US schools eleven to thirty, more emphasis on globalization.

The latter observation suggests further examination of how status is linked to public emphasis on globalization and related indicators within the USA, where the number of data points seems minimally adequate for further analysis. Comparisons of the US top ten with the rest of the US top thirty indicate that the top ten schools place substantially greater emphasis on globalization and student diversity. The differences are particularly striking if one recalls that one is looking *within* the top 2 percent of the business schools in the USA. So the top business schools seem to be the most vociferous about tackling globalization in their educational programs. That said, the US top ten do place a little less emphasis on faculty diversity than the US top eleven to thirty schools – a pattern revisited in the next section.

Digging deeper, the top programs almost invariably include a special section on their websites exploring how the school was addressing international/global issues. In qualitative terms, these schools target themselves in a position as global leaders serving a worldwide audience and performing cutting-edge research with global relevance. Lower-status schools also emphasize globalization, but focus more on partnerships and exchange programs, which seem to be the minimum requirements to compete at this level.

To summarize, the top ten US business schools generally place much more emphasis on globalization than the rest of the US top thirty, and the non-US top ten a little more than the US top ten. But despite such a variation, the basic picture that emerges is fairly consistent: leading business schools around the world publicly emphasize globalization and, as enabling levers, student diversity and international partnerships.

What top business schools do

Having characterized what top business schools say about globalization on their websites, now let us consider what such schools actually seem to be doing. Data from the *Financial Times* list of the top 100 MBA programs and AACSB surveys do in fact indicate significant activity around diversity and partnerships – the latter focused predominantly on student exchange programs. Looking across regions, top European schools average higher scores along both dimensions than their US counterparts, and within regions, measures of diversity seem to increase systematically with status. But the scope expansions implied by increased student diversity and mobility do not seem to have been matched by efforts to globalize course development and research. We shall consider international/global diversity, partnerships, course development and research in turn.

Diversity

The two types of national diversity highlighted by the websites analyzed in the previous section, related to students and faculty, are an obvious place to start in assessing what top schools are actually doing about globalization. The websites of all but one of the schools on the *BusinessWeek* top forty list provide information on the percentage of international (nonnational) students enrolled in each one's MBA program. That percentage averages 31 percent for twenty-nine US schools (and ranges from 10 percent to 43 percent), is a little higher for the three Canadian schools in the sample, but significantly higher for the seven European business schools, all of which report 75 percent+ international enrollment.

It is worth adding that the US–European differential does not simply reflect the fact that the USA is one country whereas the EU, roughly its equal in total economic mass (but with nearly two-thirds more population), is fragmented into twenty-seven countries. Consider, for example, my home institution, IESE in Spain, with 80 percent nonnationals among its MBA students. While some 21 percent of IESE students come from other West European countries and another 5 percent by East European ones, non-European sources account for 54 percent of the students – a percentage significantly higher than the international student enrollments encountered among any of the US top thirty.

Within the US subgroup, a simple linear regression confirms a statistically significant (at the 1 percent level) link between status and student diversity across the US schools, with a one-point decrease in numerical rank (that is, improvement by one place in the rankings) being associated with close to a 0.5 percent increase in international students' share of the total.

The *Financial Times'* list of top 100 MBA programs provides a basis for extending this analysis to cover a somewhat larger set of (still-top) schools and broaden it to encompass faculty as well as student diversity. Once again, US and European business schools dominate the list, so those will be the two focal geographies in the analysis reported here. Figure 4 contains some simple descriptive statistics summarizing the two diversity measures disaggregated by geography and ranked within the geography. Examining

Figure 4: Diversity versus rankings

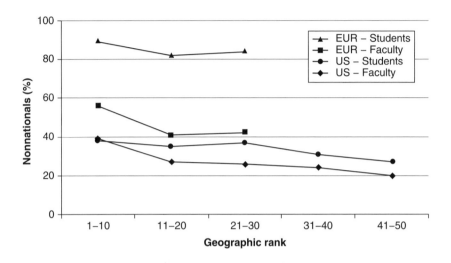

Source: Data from *Financial Times* Survey of Top 100 MBA programs.

Figure 4 suggests that the top European schools exhibit somewhat greater faculty diversity as well as significantly greater student diversity than their US counterparts, as well as that both types of diversity are associated positively with status (that is, negatively with numerical rank).

Visual examination can be supplemented with formal estimates. Table 4 presents the results of simple linear regressions of both measures of diversity on ranks within the two focal geographies, the USA and Europe. All four slope estimates have the expected negative sign: diversity of both types is positively correlated with status in both geographies. But the relationship with student diversity in particular is, for both subsamples, weak in terms of both the sizes of estimated coefficients and their statistical significance. Instead, perhaps the most obvious pattern is the curvilinearity apparent from Figure 4: the top ten schools in both geographies exhibit greater student diversity than schools eleven to thirty; in contrast, schools eleven to twenty are much like schools twenty-one to thirty (another indication of the distinctiveness of the very top schools).

Similar curvilinearity also seems to apply to faculty diversity. Despite that, the linear regression shown in Table 4 indicates a stronger link for faculty diversity

Table 4: International diversity versus rankings

DEPENDENT VARIABLE	USA (n = 55)			EUROPE (n = 31)		
	Intercept ("Rank Zero")	Slope (Rank–Sensitivity)	Adjusted R^2	Intercept ("Rank Zero")	Slope (Rank–Sensitivity)	Adjusted R^2
Student Diversity	39.9	−0.23[a]	13	88.9	−0.24	< 0
Faculty Diversity	37.9	−0.42[a]	36	60.0	−0.87[b]	13

Note: a = significant at the 1% level; b = significant at the 5% level.

Source: based on *The Financial Times* Survey of Top MBA programs.

with status, in terms of both size of estimated coefficients and explanatory power, than for student diversity, in both the USA and Europe. Yet, according to the data presented earlier in the chapter, the US top ten, in particular, seem to deemphasize faculty diversity on their websites – even though the data presented in Figure 4 (based on the *Financial Times'* somewhat different ranking scheme) suggest that that is the one subgroup of schools for which average faculty diversity exceeds average student diversity. The imbalance may simply be indicative of the type of diversity deemed by the top US schools to afford them more leverage, but there are other possibilities too that might usefully be examined.

Various AACSB surveys extend the coverage to a larger, broader group of schools – still relatively highly-ranked but not selected on that dimension – and provide a temporal perspective. From the most recent survey, international students accounted, on average, for 16 percent of the total MBA enrollments with AACSB's US respondents, and for 27 percent of its European respondents. Note that the drop-off in student diversity from the top schools discussed above is relatively moderate in the USA but very large in Europe. And going back through past surveys, average student diversity has been stagnant for at least three years in Europe and at least eight in the USA.

Partnerships

Partnerships were the other globalization lever highlighted by the websites analyzed earlier in this chapter: thirty-six out of the top forty schools mention being involved in them. Their near ubiquity suggests that it would be useful to supplement a binary indicator of involvement/noninvolvement in partnering with a partnership count/intensity data. Unfortunately, none of the standard ranking schemes provides such data. Instead, I shall rely on the results from a still unpublished AACSB "collaborations" survey carried out in 2008–9 to which I was kindly given access, as well as an earlier "alliances" survey from 2004 that was undertaken jointly by the AACSB, the European Foundation for Management Development (EFMD) and the Canadian Federation of Business School Deans (CFBSD).

A total of 244 schools responded to the 2008–9 survey regarding whether the school had existing collaborations (243 respondents) and desired to create new collaborations (237 respondents). Of these respondents, 201 schools reported that they had existing collaborations, and 200 supplied additional information about them. Some 69 percent of the 244 respondents are based in the USA, 13 percent in Europe, 8 percent in Asia and 7 percent in other Anglo offshoots – Canada, Australia and New Zealand – and the rest in Latin America.

Eighty-three percent of the respondents to the survey report being involved in some interorganizational partnership, and 94 percent express interest in entering into additional partnerships in the future. Disaggregating by geography, of the US schools responding to each question, 76 percent report current involvement in partnerships and 94 percent express interest in entering new partnerships. The corresponding averages for European schools are 100 percent and 90 percent, and those for all non-US schools 99 percent and 93 percent, respectively.

The rest of this analysis focuses on the subset of the 200 schools supplying additional information about existing partnerships. For such schools, the mean number of partnerships reported is 15.6, the median 4.5 and the mode 1. The histogram in Figure 5 supplies more information on the distribution of partnerships across schools.

Disaggregating on a geographical basis reveals a number of important differences across the two main geographies – the USA and Europe:

- Even if conditional on engaging in partnerships, which they are less apt to do, US schools engage in them less intensely than schools in the rest of the world, and particularly those in Europe. The median number of collaborations is 4 for US schools versus 18 in Europe, and the means are 9 and 44, respectively (of the six schools reporting more than 100 partnerships, five are European).

Figure 5: Distribution of existing partnerships across schools

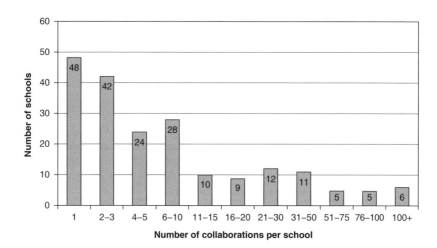

Source: Data from AACSB (2008–9) "Collaborations" survey.

- Disaggregating on a geographical basis reveals a number of important differences across regions: geographically, 54 percent of European schools' partners are in the same region, versus 24 percent for Asian schools. US schools are the most likely to engage in intra-national partnerships (13 percent), followed by schools from two other geographically large countries: China (9 percent) and Canada (7 percent).

- The USA–Europe difference, in particular, does not just reflect differences in the focus on or attributes of those two home regions. Thus, compared to European schools, US schools are less likely to have partnerships in a third region.

Reaggregating geographically to simplify disaggregation along other dimensions, student exchanges (79 percent) are the most commonly reported partnership type, followed by faculty exchanges (21 percent), joint programs (9 percent) and joint research (6 percent). Partnerships involving master's programs (35 percent of the total) are somewhat more popular than programs at the undergraduate/first degree level (31 percent); the difference in partnership-intensity between these two program levels is actually much greater than that, since undergraduate enrollments tend to be several times larger than enrollments in master's programs. And since 71 percent of all existing partnerships began in the year 2000 or later, much of the activity in this regard has been relatively recent.

In summary, the conclusions can be compared with the ones presented in the earlier subsection concerning diversity. The similarity is that partnership incidence and intensity are, despite some regional variation – the USA again lags behind Europe – being already significant-to-high, at least somewhat in line with the emphasis attached to partnerships on top schools' websites. The difference is that engagement in international partnerships is ubiquitous, whereas the very top schools do tend to do better than the other top schools at student diversity. This is probably related to underlying reputational assets, since there are only a limited number of global brands in the business school business.[2]

Curricular content

The previous two subsections indicated substantial activity at top business schools around international diversity and partnerships, in line with the emphasis on these levers for globalization on top schools' websites. But what about some of the activities that the websites do not emphasize as much but that would seem to be just as essential for success? Content-related activities, most obviously curriculum development but also the research required to develop the underlying knowledge about globalization and its business implications, are obvious candidates, and will be taken up, respectively, in this subsection and the next.

On curricula, it is useful to begin by citing some overall evidence.[3] A recent analysis by Professors Srikant Datar and David Garvin of the core MBA curricula at ten top business schools concluded that, while the coursework content converged significantly in most functional areas, virtually no convergence existed in terms of how to handle globalization-related issues. While one could, in principle, celebrate this in the name of diversity, that was *not* the reaction of the deans and recruiters who gathered at a March 2008 colloquium on "The Future of the MBA" at the Harvard Business School, at which the findings from the Datar–Garvin analysis were discussed. Given the participants' general sense that business schools had not grasped globalization, the divergence in curricula is probably better interpreted as evidence of overall disarray.

Figure 6: First-year MBA program of a top US business school

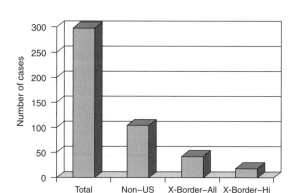

For somewhat finer-grained evidence, consider one of these top schools in more detail. This particular school actually emphasizes the internationalization of its curriculum on its website by claiming that about one-third of the cases developed each year by its faculty are international in scope. To analyze these claims, I relied on the work of a research assistant who had graduated from that school in 2006 and who had maintained a contemporaneous log of all the cases he had studied in his first year (2004–5) in that school's MBA program. The results of his reconstruction of the international/global content of all the cases in the core first-year curriculum apart from the country/macroeconomic cases from the international economy course appear in Figure 6.

To explain, about 35 percent of the cases did indeed have significant content related to activities outside the United States, as the school proudly pointed out. But if we exclude cases without cross-border content (in other words, domestic cases set in countries outside the United States), the percentage falls to 15 percent. Even more subjectively, cross-border issues seem to be highly important in only 6 percent of the cases.

Of course, this procedure does exclude cases on comparative management that might be deemed to have meaningful content relevant to globalization/internationalization. However, many of the single-country "international" cases in this school's records were in fact context-free in the sense that it did not really matter whether a particular business situation was set in, say, Georgia, the former Soviet Union, or Georgia, the former Confederacy. And in any case, a recent recalculation at the same business school that attempts to fix this omission concludes, I am told, that only about 10 percent of the cases in the first year of the MBA program have significant globalization-related content.

One can gain additional perspective by looking at globalization-related content in a particular area across a broad range of schools as well as by looking, as in Figure 6, across a broad range of areas at a particular school. I conducted another study in this vein in 2007, with Jordan Siegel. We compiled a list of faculty members who taught core strategy courses, with a focus on business schools ranked in either *BusinessWeek*'s 2006 Top 30 guide or the *Financial Times*' 2006 Top 50. We sought core strategy MBA syllabuses from fifty-six schools from this list, omitting Harvard Business School, to which both of us were affiliated at the time. We also contacted twenty-one schools that did not make the above lists but that were still well-recognized, to make a total of seventy-seven total contacts. This yielded fifty-eight core strategy MBA syllabuses from fifty-one business schools for 2007.[4] Of these, forty-three syllabi were from thirty-eight schools ranked in the *BusinessWeek* or *Financial Times* lists and seventeen came from outside the USA. A total of nine of the seventeen came from Europe.

Based on our analysis, 33 percent of the courses in this sample do not have a single case set outside the USA. For the average course, the non-US percentage comes to only 34 percent. The most common non-US settings are Europe or Israel, accounting for 21 percent of the cases. About 7 percent are set in Asia or Australia, but very few cases are found for Latin America or Africa. Even in the relatively globalized European subsample, the two regions of North America and Europe/Israel together comprise 85 percent of case settings.[5] Few courses seem to teach global strategy concepts or tools, and when they do, they tend to focus on market entry issues.[6] Discussions of global strategy issues such as locational advantages, scope decisions, adaptation and arbitrage appear to be very rare, as does the specification of any particular world-structural/historical view of globalization. And a sample of fifty global strategy electives generated at the same time offers similarly miscellaneous coverage – and averages only fourteen sessions.

Research

Business school research, like course content, remains largely unglobalized. Perhaps the best indication is provided by surveys of the articles published in the top twenty academic management journals, a focus that concentrates the analysis on research that has high impact, or at least high visibility. About 6.2 percent of articles published in the top twenty management journals between 2002 and 2006 appear to have specifically cross-border content, up very marginally from 5.5 percent over the period between 1996 and 2000.[7] The *Journal of International Business Studies* (*JIBS*) accounts for more than 40 percent of the articles with cross-border content in both periods; excluding it pushes the percentage of articles with cross-border content in the remaining nineteen journals below 4 percent.

The top twenty academic management journals studied by these researchers consist, in addition to *JIBS*, of journals with either a general management orientation or a focus on strategy, organizational behavior or human resources. The top research in other functional areas seems to have even less of a cross-border component. One simple indication is provided by my analysis of the percentage of articles with titles containing the words "international", "multinational", or "global" in top academic journals focused on marketing, finance, accounting and operations over the period between 1950 and 2006.[8] The results of the analysis are summarized by decade in Figure 7.[9] The patterns are obviously

Figure 7: Cross-border content* of leading functional journals

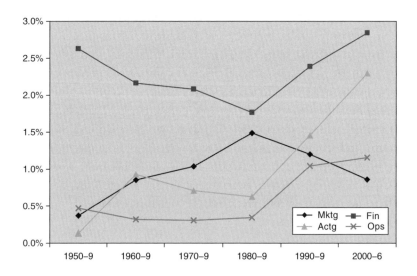

Note: *Percentage of articles by function including "multinational" or "global" or "international" in title.

mixed: accounting, in particular, has greatly expanded its international horizons, but marketing has actually regressed since the 1980s. Also note that, despite such variation, the percentage of articles with cross-border content in each of these four functional areas appears to be smaller than the corresponding percentage for the top twenty academic management journals.

Finally, one might look at the links between research on international business and the various underlying disciplines – economics, sociology and so on. Here too, low rather than high impact is indicated for international research: there is more than a tenfold asymmetry in reciprocal citation patterns between articles published in the *Journal of International Business Studies* and those published in the leading disciplinary journals, for example.[10]

Low status may provide part of the explanation for the limited attention to internationalizing research, but there are other reasons, including:

- *Lack of data.* The last major effort to compile cross-border data of the sort that would facilitate large-sample analysis of hypotheses was Raymond Vernon's Multinational Enterprise Project at Harvard Business School, which concluded in 1986.

- *Data incommensurability.* Even where some cross-border data does exist, we encounter especially serious incommensurability/quality problems, since most data are still collected at the national level.

- *Multifunctional/disciplinary problems.* Many globalization-related topics do not fit well with the increasingly functional or disciplinary orientation of business school research.

- *Physics envy.* Business school research increasingly shows a preference for documenting patterns that apply across time and space.

- *US-dominated editorial control of the top journals.* Home bias is well-known in business, and may exert its effects in this arena as well.

I have elaborated elsewhere on these problems and possible (if partial) remedies.[11] The point to be made here is that change is likely to come slowly.

Assessment: a curricular globalization gap

This section will focus, in the first instance, on establishing that the pattern of globalization efforts observed at the top schools and summarized in the previous section indicates a significant gap in the globalization of curricula.

It will then consider the curricular gap at lower-ranked schools, with a particular focus on the large numbers of schools and by the large number of expected new schools, and the social gap inherent in the fact that the business school community tends to be significantly more pro-global than people at in general. All of these attempts to broaden the analysis reinforce the importance of curricular gaps: the development and deployment of better globalization-related content would have a large social multiplier as well as yielding private benefits.

The gap at top schools

There is obviously a large gap between international diversity and partnership-incidence measures in the 30–80 percent range for the top schools, and international course development and research efforts that appear to account for 10 percent or less of the respective totals.[12] But how this gap is interpreted depends on whether diversity and partnerships are substitutes for or complements to content development activities.

To gain a better idea of the nature of this key relationship, reconsider, first, what top business schools typically are trying to achieve with their emphasis on student diversity and partnerships. The emphasis on student diversity is intended to give students personal exposure to and experience of peers from different countries. And the emphasis on partnerships – not just the dominant collaboration type, student exchanges, but also the second and third most common types, namely faculty exchanges and joint programs – is meant to provide personal exposure to and experience of different locations (as well as different sets of peers). In other words, the effects of both diversity and mobility through partnerships are, to a large extent, intended to be experiential. How one thinks of their relationship to content development activities depends, then, on how one thinks of the link between experiential and academic knowledge.

Augier and March provide, I think, the right perspective on this issue while acknowledging that agreement on it is far from complete:

> Experiential knowledge and academic knowledge are in many ways better seen as intertwined than as in opposition. Experience is interpreted within frames of reference that reflect academic sensibilities, and the research on which academic knowledge is based is deeply affected by the observations and understandings of experience.[13]

To make a case for this kind of complementarity in the context of globalization, imagine what would happen if schools pulled only the experiential levers. Let us start with diversity. Attempts to build and maintain a student body comprising many nationalities often simply assume that this will lead to greater mutual understanding or other positive outcomes. Yet, as research on business organizations shows, that is not necessarily true. Consider Williams and O'Reilly's (1998, p. 120) summary of forty years' research on this topic:

> Consistent with social categorization and similarity/attraction theories, the preponderance of empirical evidence suggests that diversity is most likely to impede group functioning. Unless steps are taken to actively counteract these effects, the evidence suggests that, by itself, diversity is more likely to have negative than positive effects on group performance.

How much attention do business schools and their faculty actually pay to managing diversity to exploit its potential while minimizing its pitfalls – as opposed to merely achieving diversity? This is a particularly interesting question to ask about what happens inside the classroom, because most common mechanisms – diverse study groups, extracurricular niches and community support structures – mainly operate outside it. We know that increasing student diversity – whether on a permanent basis or through shorter-run exchange programs – complicates what goes on in business school classrooms by, among other things, requiring more attention to be paid to varying national expectations about "student empowerment".[14] It would seem that outcomes could be improved by the inclusion and discussion of some content on these and other international differences, as argued on broader grounds in later sections of this chapter.

Similar points apply to mobility through partnerships or other means. The importance of first-hand experience of different locations is sometimes described in terms of the indispensability of "soaking and poking". But most immersion programs I have looked at do not offer much of a framework, if any at all, for thinking about the different locations being visited. Nor do they seem to have assimilated modern approaches to building cultural and emotional intelligence, which stress the limits of simply learning about the different characteristics of different countries/cultures (see, for example, Earley and Mosakowski, 2004). Given this state of affairs, business schools' activities in terms of moving people around would seem to place them within a specialized segment of the travel and hospitality sector as much as in the educational sector. If this seems far-fetched, consider that one ranked business school actually partners with a leading resort to offer a program in which participants from different countries play golf with one another to hone global leadership skills.

Overall, then, it seems that top business schools' globalization efforts focus very heavily on diversifying the national origins of their students and on international partnerships – with European schools well ahead of US-based ones. But schools have not done nearly as much to globalize themselves along the critical content-related dimensions of course development and research. This globalization gap is a problem because diversity and mobility initiatives, far from substituting experience for globalization-related content, seem to increase the need for such content by expanding the scope of business schools' activities across borders.

Corroboration that there is a problem at the top schools, and that curriculum is a key constraint, is provided by the conclusions from several groups of experts:

- Of 150 deans and directors of business schools assembled by the EFMD in 2007, 5 percent thought that the schools were delivering on their globalization promises.

- At a colloquium I organized at IESE in 2007, the participants – mainly deans and other faculty members (of top schools) – ranked "utilizing courses and methods to successfully deliver key material on international business/management" in last position among thirteen globalization-related dimensions of school performance.[15]

- At the Harvard Business School colloquium on "The Future of the MBA", in March 2008, both the idiosyncrasy of top schools' globalization-related efforts and general dissatisfaction with the outcomes were given particular emphasis.

- In a more recent survey of leading academic thinkers (discussed in more detail in the next section), only 4 percent thought that the attention business schools pay to globalizing their educational programs should remain the same; while the others agreed that it should increase or increase significantly.

A globalization gap is a more plausible diagnosis in the presence of such general angst about top schools' globalization-related efforts than in its absence.

The gap at other schools
Lower-ranked schools generally place less emphasis on globalization – a pattern that was already evident in the first two sections of this chapter, with

their examination of the variation within the top-ranked schools. But for lower-ranked schools, the curriculum is even more critical to the achievement of such globalization-related objectives that they do set for themselves: most of the experiential levers relied on by top schools are not ones that lower-ranked schools can pull, and global research seems a less promising basis for them to compete against top schools than (even) research in general. Similar arguments about the criticality of curricula apply to the very large (and growing) number of business schools in emerging markets. Let us consider both sets of arguments in a little more detail.

We shall begin by reconsidering the globalization levers that have been discussed so far – at the greater level of disaggregation identified by Datar *et al.* (2010) and summarized in Table 5. The curricular initiatives in the table (items 1 and 2) are the obvious points of focus for lower-ranked schools: diversity and mobility (items 3 through 6) are likely to be restricted relative to the top schools, and setting up multiple campuses or global research centers (items 7 and 8) is going to be out of the question.

The varying extents to which different schools can progress down the list of initiatives in Table 5 suggests a tiered approach to thinking about the universe of business schools that is summarized in Table 6. Given the roughness of the attempt, only ranges are provided for the number of schools in the top two tiers. Tier I schools – schools that can afford to make substantial cross-border investments to pursue their globalization-related objectives – and Tier II schools – schools that can hope to derive financial gains directly from their cross-border activities – account for only 10 percent of the total

Table 5: Initiatives to globalize MBA programs

1. Increasing the global content of functional courses.
2. Creating integrative global management courses.
3. Increasing the percentage of international students and faculty at the school.
4. Developing international exchange programs.
5. Organizing immersions and treks that take students abroad for several weeks or months.
6. Assigning global field studies and projects.
7. Offering students the opportunity to take courses on multiple campuses located on different continents.
8. Establishing global research centers.

Source: Based on Srikant M. Datar, David A. Garvin and Patrick Cullen, *Rethinking the MBA: Business Education at a Crossroads*, Harvard Business School Press, 2010.

Table 6: Three tiers of business schools

Tier (# Schools)	Scope	Resources	Globalization objectives	Globalization initiatives
Tier I (10–100)	Global	High	Professional obligation + Direct financial gains + Status/altruism/ transformation	Curriculum + Diversity/ mobility + Investment in knowledge creation and dissemination
Tier II (100–1,000)	Multidomestic/ regional	Limited	Professional obligation + Direct financial gains	Curriculum + Some diversity/mobility
Tier III (10,000+)	National/local	Negligible	Professional obligation	Curriculum

number of business schools if one uses the higher end of the ranges, and only 1 percent if one uses the lower ends. Either way, to focus on Tier I and Tier II schools in discussing business schools' globalization requirements is to miss out not just the bottom of the pyramid but also its middle. And for the Tier III schools – the bottom 90–99 percent – curriculum stands out as the lever for pursuing their globalization-related objectives. Curriculum is, in fact, the greatest common factor: the only constant in terms of broad class of initiatives if not specific contents cross Tiers I, II and III.

It is worth adding that the problem of developing globalization-related curricular content for Tier III schools that cannot dazzle students with diversity, mobility and knowledge development is more than just a problem for the Tier III schools. Given what the social mission of business schools is, or should be – to improve the practice of management throughout the world through education – there is a clear case for top schools to spend some time thinking not just about how they are going to confront globalization-related curricular challenges but also what kind of content would best to help the overwhelming majority of institutions in their sector to cope.

The points made here are particularly worth reemphasizing with regard to business schools (and education) in emerging countries, which already represent 64 percent of today's universe of business schools, and which will account for all the growth in formal management education over the next several decades. Some of this reflects pressures on demographics in developed markets. In the USA, growth in total enrollments has decelerated; in addition, apart from the top twenty schools, there has been a hollowing out, with a big shift to part-time programs. In Europe, MBA programs are less well-established and, partly as a result, two-year courses are experiencing significant pressure from shorter or more specialized programs. Even worse, the number of 20–29-year-old Europeans – the key demographic from the perspective of MBA programs – is projected to drop by 25 percent by 2025.[16]

But much more of the shift reflects explosive growth in emerging markets rather than shrinkage in developed ones. China and India, for example, now possess something like 3,000 institutions that award business degree programs at the undergraduate level or above – roughly the same number as the USA and the European Union combined. Even more remarkably, less than 10 percent of these degree programs are estimated to have been in existence back in 1990. Since then, both China and India have raised the number of such institutions per million inhabitants from about 0.1 to 1.

To think of what will happen to these markets in the future, look at Figure 8, which relates business school "density" – the number of schools per million inhabitants in a country – to its per capita income. The countries included

Figure 8. Business school "density": the ten most populous countries

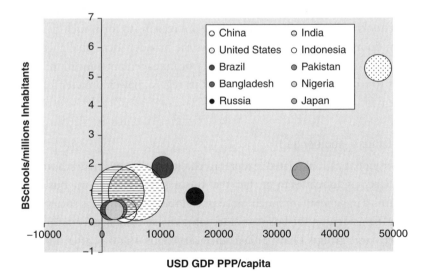

Source: Based on data from AACSB and the World Bank.

in the figure are the ten most populous in the world, and the areas of the circles are proportionate to their populations. Eight are emerging markets – though if the European Union is counted as one entity, that number would fall to seven. Since densities in developed economies range as high as 5+ in the United States (Japan is an outlier among developed countries at only 1.75), and since China is predicted by sources such as Goldman Sachs as coming close to achieving present-day US levels of per capita income in the next few decades, and India to make substantial progress as well, Figure 8 implies a possible doubling or tripling of volume of activity in what are already large emerging markets.[17]

This explosion of quantity will ideally be accompanied by investments in deepening quality, which is an issue for many nascent schools. And all this will have to be accomplished without too many experienced faculty members, who are subject to particularly long development lags and therefore tend to be quite scarce in such markets. Meeting the globalization-related component of this challenge – which surfaces in all subject areas – is likely to hinge on curricular development for most of these schools to an even greater extent than for schools in developed markets.

Given that this represents, once again, one of the biggest challenges in the globalization of management education, it probably is not something that the top schools internationally should simply observe from the sidelines. Note, however, that the usual "marriage games" involving tying in with the best local schools may not suffice. While there are reasons to form such ties, they will not do much by themselves to address the broader social challenge of ensuring an adequate quantity and quality of management education. For top schools to truly play a leadership role in this regard, newer, broader forms of involvement are required.

The business–society gap

Another globalization-related leadership challenge that business schools need to face up to relates to the fact that business schools and the business community in general are much more pro-globalization than is society at large. Consider, on the business side, some casual evidence from three relatively large groups I have polled since early 2009 – that is, after the current economic crisis had attracted people's attention:

- 400 business school deans during a plenary presentation at the AACSB Deans' Conference (San Francisco, February 2009).

- 600 (mainly) strategic management academics during the opening keynote address at the Strategic Management Society Annual Meeting (Washington, DC, October 2009).

- 1,200 business leaders during the opening keynote address at the Young Presidents' Organization/World Presidents' Organization Global Leadership Summit (Barcelona, February 2010).

Asked whether the effects of globalization had been basically good, bad or mixed, less than 1 percent of each of the three groups, by my count, characterized globalization as basically bad or mixed. Business undergraduate and graduate students tend to feel a bit less gung-ho about globalization than do business school deans, but they remain significantly more so than the general population (overwhelming majorities of students eventually believe that globalization is basically good).[18]

On the one hand, this degree of agreement around a nontrivial proposition is unusual in the social world and so should be celebrated. But on the other, business school deans and faculty members need to ask themselves whether they are equipping their students adequately to preserve the power of their convictions – let alone proselytize for further opening up – in a world that is generally much more hostile to globalization, particularly in developed economies. Thus, even before the global financial crisis became apparent, a plurality of US college graduates surveyed tended to agree that globalization had basically been bad for the United States – a big swing away from globalization in just one decade (see Figure 9). The general population tends to be significantly more skeptical about globalization – and markets. And such skepticism has clearly swelled in the two years since the survey: economic downturns and high unemployment can be counted on to fan the flames of protectionism.

By implication, the business–society gap with regard to how globalization is understood has widened significantly in recent years. Yet perhaps because there is such broad agreement at business schools that globalization has basically been good, their students are taught very little about this gap and how to deal with it. Avoiding spending time in the curriculum on anti-globalization ideas that most business school professors are convinced are nonsense frees up time for other, more "constructive" pursuits, but it does leave business school graduates ill-equipped for the real-world interactions they are likely to have. So this is also a globalization-related curricular gap, albeit one of a more

Figure 9: Educated opinions? Percentage of agreement among US college graduates

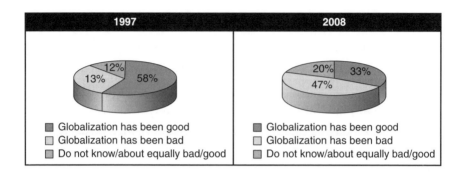

Source: Based on data from *The Wall Street Journal*/NBC Survey 2008.

specific kind than the sort discussed above. And it does reinforce the broader sense of a globalization gap that business curricula need to bridge.

What should be done to globalize curricular content?

We could, in the fashion just illustrated, try to identify other globalization-related curricular gaps. But it seems preferable to be more systematic – and less subjective. The trouble is that another systematic look at what top schools are currently doing in this regard seems unlikely to provide clear guidance, given the diversity of the curricular responses to the globalization challenge that were remarked by Datar *et al.* (2010) –though there may be one recent (mini)trend that is an exception to that rule, which I shall discuss below.

Given the limitations of these other alternatives, this section focuses on leading academic thinkers' recommendations as to what globalization-related content schools *should* put into their MBA programs. These recommendations were elicited through a survey I recently conducted in conjunction with Dean Bernard Yeung of the National University of Singapore Business School, and with the support of AACSB International, particularly Juliane Iannarelli, its Director of Global Research. Our first step was to settle on a categorization of business fields – listed in Table 7 – that would serve as the basis for identifying survey participants as well as analyzing survey responses.

Table 7: Leading thinkers surveyed by field

Field	Number of invitees	Number of respondents
Accounting	20	5
Economics	16	2
Finance	34	7
Information Systems	14	4
Management	28	8
Management – Human Resources	16	3
Management – Organizational Behavior	32	11
Management – Strategy	70	28
Marketing	36	14
Operations	12	2
Total	**278**	**84**

We then sought to identify individuals who might be considered leading thinkers in their respective fields. Lacking an established method for doing so, we employed a variety of ad hoc procedures including a review of faculty biographies for evidence of an extensive publication record in a particular field, active engagement in disciplinary associations (especially leadership positions), and receipt of awards offered by disciplinary associations. We also scanned historical records on disciplinary association websites for past award winners and past leadership work (board and committee). Finally, we considered editors, consulting editors and editorial review board members of the *Journal of International Business Studies* (*JIBS*) with a strong record in one of the specific fields identified.

While this focus on *JIBS* did skew the sample toward academics personally involved in international business, such individuals seemed less numerous, in both the sampled set and the set of respondents, than those not particularly involved in such work. Table 7 characterizes the sampled set and the set of respondents by field. Note that Strategy, Marketing and Organizational Behavior each yielded respectable numbers of respondents, more or less.

Also remember, though, that the intent was not to drill down to the level of individual fields but, ideally, to devise generalizations that would cut across fields – which suggests that the totals in the table may be more relevant than the numbers for individual fields.

Geographically, the coverage was, as in most such efforts, skewed towards the USA, though we obtained significant representation from Europe and, to a lesser extent, Asia/Oceania. US representation accounted for about 60 percent of the total – or what one would encounter among general members of the Academy of Management – and probably pales in comparison with USA-based academics' dominance of areas of leading thinking, particularly editorial control of the major journals. In any case, sample selection was driven by the desire to produce a distinguished roster rather than to meet preset geographic quotas.

While the survey was focused mainly on compiling suggestions about the content of the "global core", it also sought to elicit thoughts about the amount of attention business schools ought to pay to globalizing their educational programs, the obstacles they face in doing so, and other complementary mechanisms. The responses to these ancillary questions are worth summarizing before concentrating for the rest of this section on their suggestions about content:

- Only 4 percent of the respondents thought the attention that business schools pay to globalizing their educational programs should stay the same; the others agreed it should increase or increase significantly.

- "Lack of a clear globalization strategy" and "Insufficient faculty resources" were rated in all three major regions as being among the top three substantial/significant obstacles (out of a list of eight) to business schools' efforts to globalize business education. "Insufficient funding" was next on the list, and 41 percent of respondents also cited inadequate pedagogical materials as a substantial/significant obstacle.

- The survey also reveals a perception that schools rely excessively on certain activities at the expense of others. Of thirteen mechanisms for reinforcing "global" concepts and perspectives within business education, respondents cited national diversity of the student body, joint ventures with foreign institutions, treks, and student exchanges (in decreasing order) most frequently as being overemphasized, and named cross-border collaborative projects most frequently as underemphasized. European respondents seemed particularly jaded in relation to student diversity, but excited about cross-border collaborative projects.

Turning to content, we asked questions such as: "What international elements of [function] do you believe are important for functional/general managers with expertise in the international dimension of business to master? (The expectation is that graduates' knowledge in the areas you identify should exceed simple awareness and be sufficient to support application of the concepts in a global context.)" We initially collected open-ended responses to these questions by primary field of expertise of the respondents (for example, accounting, finance and so on). Most participants identified multiple topics in their responses to each question; we separated these, so that in the data's next version each topic would appear as a unique response (that is, there was a one-to-many relationship between the participant and the topics deemed relevant for each question.)

After lists of topics had been compiled for each field, one of us (Iannarelli) grouped together those with similar themes without the other two "pre-structuring" the results. Iannarelli based the grouping decisions on the utilization of similar terms and on her own knowledge of the identified topics. Grouping enabled us to identify subjects that survey respondents had expressed more frequently in each functional area. It also set up a second research stage in which we tried to determine if common themes were reported across the various disciplines.

We quickly determined that many of the responses referred to various dimensions and effects of cross-country differences, and that these dimensions and effects featured distinctively in the international context. Six areas of environmental/contextual differences appeared to emerge naturally from the data, relating to many of the individual topics that were cited: *cultural, legal/ regulatory, political, economic, financial, and "other" differences*. We created a matrix that arrayed these six categories of cross-country environmental differences against the ten fields discussed above. For each field or row, topics corresponding to each environmental category or column (if any) were inserted into the relevant matrix, letting us identify managerial implications of a country context's broad aspects (for example, its political environment) across the various fields. Of course, presentation in terms of differences does run the risk of underemphasizing the extent to which the respondents had

firms' *responses* to such differences in mind as well as the differences themselves. The original results from this process are reproduced in Appendix A on
pages 213–15.

What leapt out from the matrix was the breadth and depth of the feeling
that an understanding of cultural, legal/regulatory, political, economic and
other differences across their countries and their implications should be a key
component – probably the central one – of what we teach our MBA students
about globalization.

This focus on differences may seem odd, given the common conception of
globalization as a leveling force that increases similarities but has both
empirical and conceptual underpinnings.[19] Empirically, there is a tendency –
even among people with significant international experience – to overestimate
similarities and underestimate differences. This induces some predictable
biases that must be recognized to enable them to be countered – on the basis
of a concentrated effort, since it is not usually sufficient merely to point out
that other countries are different. An overarching emphasis on the differences
themselves is what is helpful in this regard – but both differences and similarities
are important, of course.

Even more compelling in some respects is the conceptual point that fundamental differences across countries are essential for global thinking to have
content qualitatively different from single-country thinking: otherwise, the
world could simply be thought of as one giant country. And it is worth adding
that, to focus on differences is not purely negative: cross-country differences
can be powerful sources of value creation rather than merely constraints to be
adapted to or overcome.

Design challenges and a response

Moving to close the curricular globalization gap requires not just a sense
of what globalization-related content to include – discussed, at a high level,
in the two previous sections – but also *how* to include it. Most attempts
to do so have employed one of two approaches: *insertion* of a stand-alone
global course (for example, a general/survey course, a specialized functional
course, or an internationally-oriented non-business course such as world
politics or comparative economic systems); or *infusion* of global content
into functional courses or other existing business courses to the point of
pervasiveness.

Ray Vernon (1994), the prime mover behind a very early and influential experiment at the Harvard Business School, summarized the lessons from attempting, at different times, both insertion and infusion:

> When the School decided in the early 1960s to adopt a formal structure based on functional areas, international business was designated one such area. I could teach what I liked; but at the same time I could exert little or no influence over the content of other courses at the School ... When in the late 1960s, the Dean of the Business School proposed to me the abolition of the international business area, it seemed to me a reasonable and logical step. Thenceforth, according to the proposed plan, the various functional areas would internationalize their respective curricula. And to ensure that the shift occurred, the handful of faculty members associated with the international business area would be distributed strategically among the various functional areas. With hindsight, it seems evident to me that the shift came too early.

Since then, a number of other top schools have also figured out this point for themselves. Thus, in 1999, Stanford decided to insert a required course on global management in the first year of its MBA program, to follow on from a strategy course. Over the next few years, issues with overlapping content and student acceptance led to the decision to infuse the content of the global management course into the strategy course, which was lengthened as a result. But problems staffing this new format led to it being scaled back and much of the international content being eliminated. Several years later, in 2006, Stanford attempted another insertion: a course on the global context of management was introduced at the very beginning of the first year of the MBA curriculum. This course has been restructured significantly since it was first introduced, and has also come to focus on the differences across countries.

The broader point from these examples is that insertion is a recipe for isolation and infusion potentially for invisibility. Given those problems, what is to be done? I find myself attracted to a third model, *interlock*, in which a globalization module provides a cross-functional platform for talking about an important phenomenon that the functional courses then build on to at least some degree (see Figure 10). Note that insertion and infusion can be seen as degenerate versions of interlock: insertion involves zero degree of interlock between the course or module on globalization and the functional courses, and infusion can be thought of as involving such a high degree of

Figure 10: Models of curricular globalization

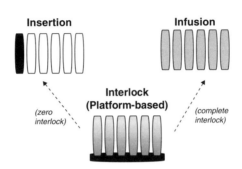

interlock that there is no room left for a distinct focus on globalization as such: it is supposedly everywhere in the curriculum. Given the problems with the two endpoints of this continuum that were highlighted by Vernon, it seems reasonable to look for an interior solution.

Specifically, I envision this interlock model as having two components: the first component (*zero interlock*) *insertion* of a platform (*complete interlock*) relatively early into the core of an MBA program that is focused on covering the differences between countries flagged by the columns in Appendix A so that it can serve as a feeder for globalization in other core courses in addition to providing visibility and focus for globalization-related issues;[20] the second component involves *infusion* in the form of the requirement that follow-on functional courses have a 10–20 percent cross-border component focused on covering at least some of the topics listed in the relevant row of Appendix A – and monitoring to prevent this infusion from becoming invisible over time. This approach accepts that schools and curricula are generally partitioned by function, rather than also requiring them to completely transform themselves, and connects directly to the functions – or other existing structures.

I developed the first component of this model, a platform course called the Globalization of Business Enterprise (GLOBE), during 2009 and piloted it as a required course in the second term of the first-year of the MBA program at IESE Business School, in Winter 2010. The GLOBE platform was designed as a 12-session course. It is split into three modules that are intended to acquaint students with basic facts about globalization, expose them to a broad view of the differences between countries that underlie limited levels of cross-border integration, and get them to begin to think about the broader implications of such differences for public and business policy – and for their own personal development. We shall consider the modules in a little more detail below:

I. *Introduction: semiglobalization* The first, short module of GLOBE looks at levels of and changes in the cross-border integration of markets and of firms, as well as the widespread tendency to overestimate actual levels of cross-border integration of markets. It also provides an opportunity to discuss how recognition that the world is semiglobalized – that levels of market integration fall far from the extremes of complete isolation and complete integration – helps businesses to avoid some basic biases in operating across borders.

II. *The differences between countries* The second and longest module in GLOBE focuses, as recommended by the survey of leading thinkers, on the differences between countries that underlie limited levels of cross-border integration. The discussion is organized in terms of the CAGE distance framework – "CAGE" is an acronym for Cultural, Administrative (institutional and political), Geographic and Economic distances among countries – which seems to be used for country analysis at the majority of the top business schools I have surveyed.[21] More important than these four precise categories or the myriad subcategories presented is the idea of looking broadly at cross-country differences in ways that go beyond the handful of economic (and sometimes, geographic) variables that customarily receive attention. Bilateral (country-pair) attributes are to be examined, not just the unilateral ones that are the focus of most country analysis, because bilateral attributes are necessary to capture ideas such as "France is closer to Spain than is Japan". And finally, the CAGE framework derives much of its power from being customized to the particular industry being studied.

III. *Leading in a semiglobalized world* This short module considers some of the broader implications of a semiglobalized perspective for governments, businesses and individuals. The focus on public policy permits a discussion of some the gains from additional opening up – and how they are being affected by the global economic downturn. The focus on business policy shifts the focus from the social context to the organizational context, and permits a review of some of the barriers to globalization *within* companies that they need to tackle. And the focus on the individual level enables discussion of additional opening up at the level of one's own mindset and behavior.

See Table 8 for a session-by-session outline of GLOBE. A complete overview of the course is available at www.ghemawat.org.

To add some characterization of course flow and pedagogy to that discussion of content, the three modules of GLOBE move from the macro to the managerial, and in terms of the emphasis in the discussions, from data to analysis to judgment. The individual sessions offer a mix of case discussions, presentations by instructors, and other pedagogical elements (for example, in-class polling and role-plays). The design exploits at least minimally the national diversity of the typical MBA student body at leading global business schools and taps into advances in information technology. As already noted, it also appears to afford some external modularity, as in some degree of connectivity to most of the ways in which the rest of the relevant curriculum might be organized, not just functionally. In addition, the internal partitioning eases adjustment of the basic design to, for example, significant time constraints: to offer a shorter version of GLOBE, one could choose to focus only on the second module, or it and one other, while perhaps assigning one short reading per omitted module. Additional flexibility stems from the possibility of shortening the second module: while it is central, it does have six sessions earmarked for it in the outline in Table 8. When teaching a four-session prototype of GLOBE at IESE in spring 2009, I obviously had to compress the treatment of cross-country differences. Note that modularity, partitioning and flexibility are some of the other important design principles in dealing with differences, alongside platforms.

One could easily expand the GLOBE platform course and, more broadly, the focus on globalization, in a variety of ways. I will simply cite half-a-dozen:

- Elaborating on what is, even at 12 sessions, a very, very compressed treatment

- Including a project component

- Incorporating debates, panels, town halls et cetera

Table 8: GLOBE outline

Module	Session
I Introduction: Semiglobalization	1. **Globalization of markets**. Levels of and changes in cross-border integration of markets. Noneconomic integration. Overestimation bias.
	2. **Globalization of firms**. Cross-border connections by firms. Causes and consequences of overestimation bias.
	3. **Grolsch: growing globally**. Key questions in globalizing: why, what, where, when, how, who…? The importance of evaluating globalization moves. Industry and competitive analysis in a semiglobalized context.
II Cross-country differences: the CAGE distance framework	4. **International interactions, differences and the CAGE framework**. The law of gravity and extensions. The CAGE distance framework: cultural, administrative, geographic and economic differences. Typical coefficients in gravity models of trade and other cross-border interactions.
	5. **Star TV**. Cultural differences between countries and their business implications. The myth of cultural convergence. Overlay of administrative/institutional and economic differences.
	6. **Administrative differences**. International variation in ownership, external finance and labor rights. Underlying determinants. Varieties of capitalism literature and their implications for business functions.
	7. **Geographic differences**. Typical geographic differences and trends, including regionalization. Impact on trade and other kinds of interactions. The myth of the death of distance. Recent supply chain reconfigurations.
	8. **The Indian IT services industry**. Globalization in the service sector. Labor cost differences. Arbitrage strategies and their sustainability.
	9. **Economic differences**. Focus on offshoring, employment and income levels. The implications of the European context. Other dimensions of economic differences.
III. Leading in a semi-globalized world	10. **ADDING value by opening up**. ADDING economic value through merchandise trade; through trade in tasks and capital, labor and knowledge flows. Noneconomic gains from openness. Resisting and reversing protectionism.
	11. **Globalizing Kraft** (role play). The organizational context of globalization. The impact of industry contingency and company heritage. Mechanisms for achieving more effective intracompany integration.
	12. **Globalization: a personal agenda**. Internal as well as external. Globalization. A self-diagnostic. Course summary with a focus on GLOBE's links to other required courses.

- Building in time to take an explicitly (international) regional perspective (more important, for instance, in the EU than in the USA)[22]

- Discussing the diversity and mobility (and more experiential) components of a school's globalization initiative and offerings

- Drilling deeper into one or more individual functions for greater concreteness as well as functional foreshadowing, and so on

In practice, though, trying to include everything one desires will likely prove more of a challenge than filling up the number of sessions available for such a globalization module. Instead of focusing on expanding the scope of GLOBE, I plan to concentrate in the near-to-medium term on moving farther in implementing the second component of the interlock design: ensuring that globalization-related content is infused into functional courses as well. Some limited coordination with the functional courses *was* achieved in the pilot offering of GLOBE in winter 2010: the results of a cultural intelligence questionnaire administered earlier by colleagues in organizational behavior were reused, and GLOBE was explicitly leveraged to add more of an international perspective to the required strategy course. But that teaching experience and follow-up with students did suggest that achieving the interlock with the functional courses is the single most important determinant of the long-term success or failure of an initiative that aims, ultimately, to broaden and deepen the discussion of globalization-related issues throughout the curriculum. That is, of course, a tentative conclusion: having gotten through just the first phase of what might be seen as a multi-year action research program, it is clear that much learning remains to be done.

Conclusions

Very briefly, this essay suggested that to think of more globalized content as just another mechanism for globalizing business schools would be a serious mistake: such content is a strategic factor because it is the critical constraint on business schools' ability to address the gap that has developed between the globalization of their reach and the globalization of their offerings. A survey of academic thought leaders suggested that content aimed at bridging this globalization gap should focus on cross-country differences and their business implications. The essay concluded with a specific proposal for a globalization course with such a focus that is designed to be inserted into the core MBA curriculum and to serve as a platform for globalization-related discussions that continue in follow-on functional courses.

Acknowledgments

I am grateful to Dean Jordi Canals and the IESE Business School for providing multiple forms of support for the development of the ideas expressed in this essay, to AACSB International and its Globalization of Management Education taskforce chaired by Dean Robert Bruner for stimulating discussions as well as help in assembling and interpreting some of the data that I rely on, and to Dean Bernard Yeung of the National University of Singapore Business School for his collaboration on the survey of academic thought leaders reported on herein as well as for many helpful discussions on this broad topic. I have also benefited from comments on earlier drafts by Thomas Hout, Gerald McDermott, Riel Miller, Carlos Sanchez-Runde, Jordan Siegel and seminar audiences at Darden, INSEAD and Wharton. Steven Altman provided research assistance and Seth Schulman editorial assistance. However, the views expressed in this article are purely personal and should not be assumed to coincide with the perspectives of any of the individuals or institutions listed above.

NOTES

1 Despite the focus here on a 12-session module, it is compressible – of particular interest in shorter-format executive programs.

2 Of course, there is probably related heterogeneity in the partnership data, since one expects partnership formation to share some aspects of a (polygamous) marriage game, with top-ranked schools more likely to form ties with each other.

3 Additional evidence and discussion of this point is provided in Ghemawat (2008a).

4 Some business schools had more than one approach to teaching core strategy, and hence the unit of analysis is the course and not the school.

5 It is interesting to contrast this focus with projections that these two regions will account for one-quarter to one-third of total global economic growth through 2030.

6 In our preliminary analysis of the European subsample, we found that 45 percent of the cases were set in Europe or Israel, 39 percent in the United States, and 2 percent in Asia and Australia, with 6 percent focused on multi-location global firms.

7 This despite the inclusion of the *Journal of International Business Studies* in the top twenty in both periods. See Pisani (2009) and Werner (2002).

8 The following journals are included by function, based on suggestions from colleagues at IESE Business School:

- Marketing: *Journal of Marketing* (1950–2006), *Journal of Marketing Research* (1964–2006), *Marketing Science* (1982–2006), *Journal of Consumer Behavior* (2001–6).

- Finance: *Journal of Finance* (1950–2006), *Review of Financial Studies* (1988–2006), *Journal of Financial Economics* (1974–2006), *Journal of Financial and Quantitative Analysis* (1966–2006), *Journal of Empirical Finance* (1993–2006).

- Accounting: *Accounting Review* (1950–2006), *Journal of Accounting Research* (1963–2006), *Accounting Organizations and Society* (1976–2006), *Journal of Accounting and Economics* (1979–2006), *Review of Accounting Studies* (1996–2006).

- Operations: *Management Science* (1954–2006), *Operations Research* (1952–2006), *Journal of Operations Management* (1980–2006), *Production and Operations Management* (2002–6).

9 Data for the early years included in this analysis are based on very small sample sizes (small number of total articles) and the conclusions concerning them are correspondingly less reliable.

10 Henisz (2007).

11 Ghemawat (2008b).

12 The cross-border components of content development activities are also smaller than cross-border flows such as trade or even FDI in relation to GDP – without even making any adjustments for the greater-than-average importance of cross-border activities for most large firms or the greater (and distinctive) complexities entailed by them versus purely domestic activities.

13 Augier and March (2007).

14 Kragh and Bislev (2008).

15 It tied in this regard with "utilizing innovations from executive education for MBA courses" and "finding an institutional solution to chair, develop and fund their international efforts".

16 "The Global Management Education Landscape: Shaping the Future of Business Schools". Report of the Global Foundation for Management Education, 2007, p. 13.

17 It would be preferable to conduct the analysis in terms of student enrollments rather than number of business schools, but systematic cross-country data on the former are unavailable.

18 This statement is based not just on my surveys of my graduate students at Harvard Business School and IESE Business School but also on others' surveys of their students: for example, Peng and Shin (2008).

19 For further discussion of these points, see Ghemawat (2007).

20 While interlock could, in principle, be achieved at the end through a capstone course rather than towards the beginning, my experience – admittedly, back in the 1990s – of running the integrative exercise that was then the capstone to the first year of the MBA program at HBS suggests that the really powerful role for that slot, given the predominantly functional organization of most MBA programs, is one of cross-functional rather than cross-border integration.

21 See Ghemawat (2001) and ch. 3 in Ghemawat (2007). The wide diffusion and integrated logic of this framework are the reasons for preferring it to the six categories of differences that emerged from the survey of leading thinkers.

22 A more expansive adaptation event might aim to tailor multiple sessions to a particular national or regional context – often a good idea. Thus, in teaching this material in Spain, I use Spain as an anchor for some of the specific discussions, particularly those involving CAGE differences.

REFERENCES

AACSB (Association to Advance Collegiate Schools of Business) Available at: http://www.aacsb.edu/dataandresearch/.

Augier, M. and March, J. G. .2007. "The Pursuit of Relevance in Management Education". *California Management Review* 49(3): 129–46.

BusinessWeek MBA Ranking. Available at: http://www.businessweek.com/business-schools/.

Datar, S., Garvin, D.A. and Cullen, P. 2010. *Rethinking the MBA: Business Education at a Crossroads*. Boston, MA: Harvard Business School Press.

Earley, P. C. and Mosakowski, E. 2004. "Cultural Intelligence". *Harvard Business Review*, October: 139–46.

Financial Times MBA Ranking, http://rankings.ft.com/businessschoolrankings/global-mba-rankings.

Ghemawat, P. 2001. "Distance Still Matters: The Hard Reality of Global Expansion". *Harvard Business Review*, September: 137–47.

Ghemawat, P. 2007. *Redefining Global Strategy: Crossing Borders in a World Where Differences Still Matter*. Boston, MA: Harvard Business School Press.

Ghemawat, P. 2008a. "The Globalization of Business Education: Through the Lens of Semiglobalization". *Journal of Management Development* 27(4):391–414.

Ghemawat, P. 2008b. "Reconceptualizing International Strategy and Organization". *Strategic Organization* 2:195–206.

Global Foundation for Management Education. 2007. "Global Management Education Landscape: Shaping the Future of Business Schools"Tampa, FL.

Henisz, W. J. (2007). "Research Programs in International Business". *Progress in International Business Research* 1(1):15–25.

Kragh, S.U. and Bislev, S. 2008. "Business School Teaching and Democratic Culture: An International and Comparative Analysis". *Research in Comparative International Education* 3(2): 211–21.

Peng, M. W. and Shin, H.-D. 2008. "How Do Future Business Leaders View Globalization?". Published online in Wiley InterScience (www.interscience.wiley. com), DOI: 10.1002/tie.20192.

Pisani, N. 2009. "International Management Research: Investigating Its Recent Diffusion in Top Management Journals". *Journal of Management* 35(2):199–218.

Vernon, R. 1994. "Contributing to an International Business Curriculum". *Journal of International Business Studies* 25(2): 215–28.

Werner, S. 2002. "Recent Developments in International Management Research: A Review of 20 Top Management Journals". *Journal of Management* 28(3):277–305.

Williams, K. Y. and O'Reilly, C. A. 1998. Demography and Diversity in Organizations: A Review of 40 Years of Research. *Research in Organizational Behavior* 20: 77–140.

Appendix A

Table A.1: Relevance of country-specific environmental conditions to understanding/applying various business disciplines in a global context

	Cultural Environment	Legal/Regulatory Environment	Political Environment	Economic Environment	Financial Environment	Other Environment
Accounting		• National tax systems			• Financial reporting standards & expectations; • Approaches to evaluating financial performance; • Currency valuation.	
Economics	• Cultural and ideological conditions	• Impact of laws and policies on trade • Strategies by firms to 'get around trade hindrances'	• Effects on trade, business systems	• Economic conditions • Trade regimes		
Finance		• National tax systems (influence on subsidiary capital structure, dividend policies)	• Political risk management (as related to international investments)		• Financial markets; • Currency valuation; • Interest rates; • Foreign exchange risk.	
Information systems	• Influence on management of information resources	• Influence on management of information resources • Influence on availability of suppliers • Regulations on open-source systems	• Influence on management of information resources	• Influence on management of information resources		• Electronic markets.

(continued)

216

	Cultural Environment	Legal/Regulatory Environment	Political Environment	Economic Environment	Financial Environment	Other Environment
Management	▪ Influence on management strategy ▪ Influence on human resources ▪ Gender division of labor	▪ Governance of business activity	▪ Political system	▪ Economic conditions	▪ Foreign exchange rates.	▪ Impact of national business structure/systems on MNC strategy.

Management – HR	▪ Influence on:
	  – Work values;
	  – Motivation;
	▪ Performance management;
	▪ Compensation;
	▪ Perceptions of equity;
	▪ Succession planning;
	▪ Management development
		▪ Employment regulations:
		  – Who can be employed and how;
		  – Motivation;
		  – Performance management;
		  – Compensation;
		▪ Existence of labor management policies, unions.
				▪ Impact of economic development level on degree to which foreign HRM practices are welcome, appropriate or understood.		

Management – OB	▪ Influence on:
	  – interactions (communication, negotiation);
	  – values, assumptions, perceptions;
	  – leadership styles;
	▪ existence and acceptance of corruption					

Management – Strategy	• Implications for human behavior; management, HR; strategy and competitive advantage	• Implications for managing human capital	• Implications for human behavior; • Government–business relationships	• Business/economic context (planned versus free market; socialist versus capitalist) • Implications for human behavior • Implications for strategy and competitive advantage.	• Currency valuation.	• Role of government (including business ownership, relationships to business); • Structure of business environment, including public markets; • Role of location-specific resources; • Implications for strategy and competitive advantage.
Marketing	• Impact on: • Customer demand, preference, and behavior (including B2B and B2C); • Marketing strategy; • Reporting norms (metric variance across countries on international surveys)	• Impact on customer demand and preference • Reporting norms (e.g. on surveys, data collection) • Impact on export marketing, grey/parallel marketing	• Impact on marketing function	• Impact on: • Marketing management decisions; • Execution of marketing strategy; • Customer demand and preference		• Technological environment (effect on customer demand & preference).
Operations	• Impact on HR management					

Leadership Development in Business Schools: An Agenda for Change*

JEFFREY PFEFFER, Professor, Graduate School of Business, Stanford University

B usiness schools see themselves as being in the business of producing leaders for both public and private sector organizations. For example, Harvard Business School's mission, frequently articulated by the former dean, Kim Clark, is to educate leaders who make a difference in the world. Clark would begin presentations to the school's visiting committee with examples of people who had graduated from HBS and held major leadership positions in organizations of all types and sizes. Many, perhaps most, other business schools have similar aspirations and take pride in their graduates who have gone on to hold significant leadership positions. This focus on educating leaders pervades not just business schools but is part of the mission of US colleges and universities more generally. Some observers have noted that educating leaders who could guide a new nation was one of the founding tenets of America's first institutions of higher education (Gomez, 2007).

"Leadership" is also a topic that many companies take seriously. Numerous organizations have, at least prior to the economic turmoil of 2008, expanded their leadership development activities under various rubrics. Such efforts have sometimes taken the form of appointing Chief Talent Officers to focus on the attraction, retention and development of key performers. Such roles have been particularly prominent in professional services firms such as Morgan Stanley and Deloitte (see, for example, Benko and Weisberg, 2007). In other cases, leadership development efforts have entailed building internal corporate universities, sometimes modeled on General Electric's center in Crotonville, NY. For example, in 2008 Apple hired former Yale School of Management dean Joel Podolny to head a new internal corporate university, possibly signaling an increased commitment to training and leadership development. In some companies, leadership development has encompassed diversity initiatives designed to ensure that leadership opportunities reach different demographic groups that have traditionally not been represented in senior management ranks. Organizations have become partners with external providers of leadership education and development, including business schools, for internal custom programs, and have sent executives to external, open enrollment programs.

Developing leaders has at least three components. There is a knowledge component – effective business or nonprofit leaders should have the technical skills required to help them and their colleagues make better decisions, organize their enterprises more effectively, and be able to think in a scientific, critical way about strategy and business models. There is also a dimension of leadership development that entails helping people not only to "think" smart but also to "act" smart. This involves being able to turn technical knowledge into action – to be able to surmount the knowing–doing gap (Pfeffer and Sutton, 1999) and actually behave in ways consistent with the theories and information that leaders possess. And third, given the importance of values to both organizational effectiveness (see, for example, Collins and Porras, 1994) and societal well-being, leadership development entails inculcating values and standards for conduct that are socially beneficial and able to engage the workforce.

The growing emphasis on leadership development and its importance to business success has prompted a few external assessments of companies on their ability to build leadership pipelines. In 2001, Hewitt, the large human resources outsourcing and consulting firm, began a periodic survey designed to "identify those factors that allow … successful organizations to consistently produce great leaders", and in the process producing a list of the "Top Companies for Leaders" (Hewitt, 2008) that has appeared in *Fortune* magazine. Hewitt's survey data showed, not surprisingly, that companies that were more effective in their leadership development efforts were able to fill more positions through internal promotion. These companies did better in developing leaders because they devoted more resources as well as more senior executive time and attention to leadership issues.

Hewitt, and for that matter, business schools, emphasize what companies or schools might *do* to develop leadership talent. But it is also possible that what looks like good leadership development is the result of a more effective sorting and selection process, in that companies that are more effective at leadership development simply have more opportunities, because of how they

are structured, to give more people general management responsibilities earlier in their careers and then select those who are most capable at performing
those jobs. In other words, being better at leadership development may be a
result of running a better, larger, more robust tournament to find people who
are already great leaders and promoting them to more responsible roles rather
than doing anything to change the skills of people in the system. Similarly,
high prestige business schools may be effective in their leadership development more because of their selection and sorting activities than because of
their education and development abilities.

But whether leadership development is a matter of selection or of the actual
development of leadership skills, there is little doubt that leadership education
and development has become a big business and an important focus of attention for both business schools and companies. Companies have recognized
that going outside to fill leadership positions is both riskier and more costly.
Business schools, sensing an opportunity to raise money and build their
brands, have opened centers for leadership development and research, and
raised and filled endowed chairs in leadership.

After briefly reviewing a few facts about the growth of leadership education
and development, I argue that notwithstanding all this attention and activity,
the data suggest that leadership development at business schools is not all that
it could or should be. Of course, any assessment of performance at the task
of leadership development must begin with the criteria to be used.[1] There is a
paucity of data that speak directly to the three dimensions of leadership development previously mentioned. Attempts to assess whether students who attend
business schools acquire substantive, technical skills by means, for example, of
implementing some form of certification testing as is required for becoming a
certified public accountant or practicing law, have met with fierce resistance.
Consequently, the idea that people who attend business school classes actually
acquire and, more importantly, retain specific knowledge is essentially based
on faith rather than data. This faith exists even though there is evidence suggesting that graduation rates are high and getting ejected from leading business
schools is a rare event (see, for example, Armstrong, 1995) and even though
authors who have written about their own business school experience (such as
Robinson, 1994) self-report that they did not understand much of the material.

There are also few, if any, direct assessments as to whether, having acquired
some technical knowledge, business school students have acquired enough
of the skill to implement that knowledge as part of their education. As

Armstrong (1995) has noted, assessment centers and similar methodologies could measure the ability to turn learning into practice in realistic situations. But while assessment center methodologies are sometimes used inside companies, they are virtually absent in business schools. There is a perception that, when confronted with real business situations, few business leaders (with or without MBAs) display much analytical skill. Randy Komisar, a business author, high-technology entrepreneur, and partner at the important venture capital firm of Kleiner, Perkins, has observed that relatively few executives, even those with MBAs, are able to think analytically and critically about business strategy and business models. Instead, many people respond to challenges by relying on benchmarking and seeking to emulate apparently successful models. Finally, with respect to education in values and ethical behavior, as discussed below, data from the Aspen Institute suggest that business education is inculcating values while students are in school, but quite possibly the wrong ones.

The evidence on the effects of business education on leadership development tends to be indirect. At a minimum, leadership development should be judged successful if people who have gone through the educational experience do better at attaining higher-level positions than those who have not. After all, leadership development is about developing *leaders,* so presumably a relevant criterion is the level of leadership people achieve. Beyond mere career attainment, leadership development might also be evaluated by its development of the values and character, possibly exhibited through behaviors associated with being an effective leader and demonstrating good values. And though it would be useful to have assessments of these leadership competencies and whether they are enhanced by particular leadership development experiences, certainly one intended outcome of effective leadership development is better-organizational performance.

By these criteria, the evidence suggests that business schools have not been particularly successful in their leadership development role. Note that this overall assessment does *not* mean that no school, or no specific program in some individual school, has achieved positive results. Nor does this statement imply that there are not specific leadership development efforts that are successful. Clearly, there are some specific executive education interventions, for example, that have achieved good results (see, for example, Tushman *et al.,* 2007). The issue is whether, overall, business schools, with their intention of developing leaders, have been successful in that effort, and if not, what stands in their way. While the data at present are limited and imperfect, the existing evidence does not show strong evidence of success.

I conclude the chapter by noting some sources of the problem of leadership development in business schools – what gets in the way of the schools fulfilling their mission. This discussion leads logically to what the schools, if they are serious about leadership development, need to change.

The leadership "business"

Leadership training and development is a large and expanding business. There are estimates that some US$45 billion is spent annually by companies on leadership development, an amount that has grown more than 400 percent over the past twenty years (Gomez, 2007). Surveys show that about 60 percent of all companies offer leadership development training and even more organizations have such activities in the planning stages (Gomez, 2007). In their executive education activities, business schools run both custom and open-enrollment programs designed to help companies with their leadership development activities. A nonprofit organization originally started by the Smith-Richardson Foundation, The Center for Creative Leadership, today runs programs all over the world designed to foster individual and group leadership capability as well as doing research on leadership.

Business schools, responding to the demands of the recruiting marketplace and alumni, as well as to the implications of their mission to develop effective business leaders, have launched a number of significant efforts focused on educating leaders. Many of these activities are more experiential and skills-focused than the rest of the curriculum. For example, the University of Chicago, responding to early MBA program rankings that viewed the school as too technical and oriented only to economics and finance, instituted a LEAD program required of all entering students. The program includes a required 360 degree assessment, a three-week orientation which incorporates an outward-bound type of experience, quarter-long leadership labs and experiential learning, and a one-quarter course used to train the second-year students who facilitate these activities for first-years. Stanford, beginning around 2005 under the impetus of significant funding from a number of alumni, launched a Center for Leadership Development and Research. This entity also runs leadership labs and a set of class-wide experiences, including a business simulation judged by alumni and faculty. Harvard Business School requires all entering students to take part in a three-week "foundations" program that provides basic skills for working in teams and lays down appropriate classroom norms of conduct. Harvard also runs a business simulation as part of its leadership development activities. Michigan has a week-long session before regular classes begin for all entering students, something that has become increasingly common in many schools. Michigan also has self- and peer assessments, a required project emphasizing the importance of corporate global citizenship, and seminars on executive skills.

Such efforts are widespread. It is difficult now to find any major, or for that matter, minor, business school that does not have some sort of leadership development experience as part of its first-year curriculum. Schools have added outward-bound types of activities, assessments, coaching (including coaching from more advanced students), and group activities. Business school leaders feel pressure that comes from shared expectations concerning the role of business schools as well as from what other schools are doing that virtually guarantee every business school is, or at least says it is, in the leadership development business. Because of the interest from both alumni and companies in leadership, it is relatively easy to raise money for leadership activities, positions and centers.

At the same time, many of these leadership development initiatives are tied weakly to the rest of the curriculum or, for that matter, the tenure-line faculty. Leadership programs are frequently organized and staffed by non-tenure line people hired specifically to fill that role. Leadership development activities are often offered at times different from regular classes – for example, during a pre-enrollment period or on days and times such as weekends or evenings, when regular classes do not meet. As such, leadership development often seems not quite central or core for many of the business schools' other activities. There is a sense that leadership development is important to external constituencies but is not quite as high status as other research and teaching efforts, at least in some schools. This somewhat marginal position of leadership development makes it less likely that it will be effective, and that is certainly what the available data appear to show.

Are business schools doing a good job of developing leaders?

At the outset it is important to note the paucity of evaluation of leadership development efforts, either in business schools or in companies. Without evaluation, it is difficult to know what is working and what is not, so that appropriate changes in the allocation of effort and resources can be made. This absence of evaluation exists even though assessments have become an important and expected component of elementary and secondary education, with both schools and teachers evaluated on their ability to improve students' performance, while controlling statistically for student characteristics such as parental income and socioeconomic status that might affect their mastery of the material.

As an example of the absence of evaluation of leadership development, a report by Audit Scotland noted that good leadership was essential in Scotland's public sector, and that more than £5 million was spent each year on identifying and training leaders. However, the report noted that 75 percent of the public agencies were unable to say what impact their spending had had on performance; 60 percent had no process for directing their spending; and some 20 percent could not even estimate accurately the amount they spent on leadership development (Audit Scotland, 2005) let alone the effects of such expenditures. This state of affairs of little or no evaluation and good intentions substituting for systematic planning is not at all unusual. Therefore, the evidence on the important question of the effects of business schools on the education and development of leaders is not yet as extensive as one might like. But what evidence there is paints a reasonably consistent picture.

If business education matters for leadership development, people in leadership roles who have such an education should do better in those roles than those that do not have comparable training. One recent study of the effects of CEO education (a measure of the CEOs' human capital) on firm performance examined the financial performance over a period of several years of almost 500 CEOs. The authors claimed this was the first study to examine the effect of educational credentials on senior executive results. The findings concerning the effects of a business education are decidedly mixed. On the one hand, the data show that, by the early 2000s, about one-third of all CEOs held MBA degrees. This empirical finding is consistent with the institutionalization of the MBA credential as a factor in selecting senior level executives, with many senior leadership roles now being filled by people with MBAs. On the other hand, the study found no effect of having an MBA, controlling for other factors, on CEO compensation. And as for organizational performance, the research found that "there is no evidence that firms run by CEOs from higher prestige graduate business … schools perform any better than firms led by CEOs with educations from less prestigious … schools" and that "firms managed by CEOs with MBA or law degrees perform no better than firms with CEOs without graduate degrees" (Gottesman and Morey, 2006, p. 12).

In fact, there was some evidence in the study that firms led by CEOs who had neither MBA nor law degrees had a slightly better risk-adjusted market performance.

Another possible way of assessing the effects of business education on leadership development would be to see whether possessing the MBA helps people to access senior leadership positions, under the assumption that companies' selection processes would recognize superior performance and ability. The existing, albeit sparse, data on the effects of MBA education on career progression – as contrasted with the possible effect of an MBA degree on starting salaries – tends to show little or no effect of attaining an MBA degree on salary or position attainment, controlling for other individual factors (Pfeffer, 1977; Dreher et al., 1985). The absence of an effect for the MBA holds even in investment banking and consulting, where training in finance and analytical thinking might be expected to be an advantage (see, for example, Lieber, 1999; Leonhardt, 2000; and see Pfeffer and Fong, 2002, for a review), and for industries that are historically large employers of students from leading business schools. Furthermore, studies finding small to null effects of MBA grades on performance (for example, Weinstein and Srinivasan, 1974; Pfeffer, 1977; Dreher et al., 1985) are consistent with the idea that the MBA degree, particularly from an elite school, is a good sorting and selection device, which is why there are observed effects of having an MBA on starting salaries. But what students learn, as measured at least by their grades in classes, and the extent to which such learning actually leads to better real corporate decision-making is more problematic.

Data have also been collected on the educational backgrounds of high-technology executives which permit some initial understanding of the relationship between business education and entrepreneurship. A study of more than 650 CEOs and heads of product development in more than 500 engineering and technology companies established between 1995 and 2005 found that the largest group held terminal degrees in science or technology-related fields, and about one-third had degrees in business, finance and accounting (Wadhwa et al., 2008). The study also found that tech company founders with MBA degrees tended to establish companies more quickly – earlier in their careers – compared to the others. The study did not, however, ask whether the companies founded (or led) by MBAs were more successful, using various criteria, than those led or founded by people with technical degrees.

More proximate data on the effects of business education on values and behavior do exist, though again more research and data would be helpful. Perhaps the most disturbing data on the effects of MBA education on leader development come from the Aspen Institute's periodic surveys of MBA students' values and attitudes, and how these change during their time at business school. The initial study (Aspen Institute, 2001) found that during the two years on full-time MBA programs, students came to place a higher priority on shareholder value and a lesser emphasis on customers, employees and product quality. This finding is not that surprising, given the prominence of shareholder return as *the* measure of a company, and by extension, leader performance in business school curricula and by the business press. The Aspen Institute's most recent study reported that business school students' confidence in their preparation to manage values conflicts at work fell throughout their time in the program, as did the proportion of people agreeing that they had opportunities to practice ethical/responsible decision-making as part of their MBA (Aspen Institute, 2008). The recent survey also showed that the importance students placed on "having a positive impact on society" decreased the longer respondents were in the MBA program, a result that was observed particularly for male students.

In addition to the Aspen Institute studies demonstrating the change in values during business education, several studies on cheating in school – a manifestation of moral malfeasance that must certainly be inimical to good leadership and character development – consistently revealed that both under-graduate and graduate business school students cheat more than students in other majors (see, for example, McCabe and Trevino, 1995; McCabe, 2001; McCabe *et al.*, 2006). These data do not permit us to distinguish between self-selection and "learning" or socialization effects that are produced by the business school experience, but it cannot be a good thing for business leadership that business students cheat more than others (see also Brown and Choong, 2003). One plausible explanation for these results is that the emphasis in business education on "ends" rather than means, and the instrumental, careerist orientation of some business students who are more interested in getting a job rather than being driven by intellectual curiosity or a desire to learn leads individuals not to worry about what they are learning or their conduct, but just to focus on obtaining the credential, getting a job, and getting out.

While some people might be surprised by the evidence, or lack of it, for positive effects of business schools on leadership development, the very dynamics of the current business education marketplace virtually guarantee these observed outcomes. Understanding these dynamics and what might be done to change them is therefore important.

Causes of the problem – and what needs to change

Making changes that would make business schools more effective in their mission of leadership development requires an understanding of what gets in their way or diverts them from this task, and then working to change those things. The list of potential problems is long, but here I focus on three of what I believe to be the most important: (i) the fact that business schools are measured and evaluated using criteria that are at best unrelated to leadership development and at worst are antithetical to that goal;(ii) because of competitive dynamics and the ranking game, business schools have tended to market themselves and create identities that would be unlikely to attract the right people for the right reasons; and (iii) the evaluation of faculty is, for the most part, either orthogonal to or inconsistent with producing an emphasis on leadership development.

Measurements and rankings

Khurana (2007) argued that business schools were originally founded to educate a professional class of managers and have subsequently retreated from that task, leaving the professionalization of the management project largely uncompleted. Others, such as Howell (1984), have argued that business schools have always been vocational or trade schools with a limited, careerist orientation and few professional aspirations or accomplishments. But regardless of what business schools may have set out to do, there is little doubt that under various institutional pressures – including pressures in some instances from their universities to become not only self-sustaining but also cash cows – business schools today face an identity crisis as to how much they want to emphasize the "business" and how much attention they pay to the "school" part of their name. Or, as Dipak Jain, the dean of the Kellogg School at Northwestern University, put it so nicely during one conversation, business schools and their students struggle with the tension between "earning" and "learning".

In this navigation of their social and institutional environment, most business schools are quite concerned about their position in the various rankings or league tables published by ever more newspapers and magazines. Such concern on the part of business schools leaders is quite rational. Fee *et al.* (2005) found that the turnover of deans increased following a drop in a school's *BusinessWeek* ranking, and following deterioration in the student placement score as assessed by *US News and World Report*. Recruiters, potential applicants and alumni all pay attention to where schools rank and to changes in these ranks, and are quick to voice concerns should there be any negative publicity involving school rankings. There is therefore little debate that such rankings are important and have influenced business school curricula (Morgeson and Nahrgang, 2008). Indeed, many writers have expressed the view that there is too much attention paid to the rankings (see, for example, Gioia and Corley, 2002; DeAngelo *et al.*, 2005). Unfortunately, there is also evidence that the rankings, as measures of school quality, are not necessarily very good. Dichev (1999), for example, found that there was little correlation between changes in the *BusinessWeek* and *US News* rankings, and that business school rankings had a tendency to revert to what they had been earlier. Morgeson and Nahrgang (2008) also observed that school rankings were highly stable over time and that some of the best predictors of school rankings were stable characteristics of institutions that were difficult, if not impossible, to change.

One of the oldest findings in organization studies is that measurements affect behavior – that what gets measured gets done, and this effect holds in settings ranging from medical practice (McGlynn, 2004) to education (Wilson *et al.*, 2006). What the various rankings measure primarily are indicators of job market success and "customer" (student) satisfaction, along, in some cases, with indicators of school selectivity. Morgeson and Nahrgang (2008) found that recent business school rankings were driven largely by student perceptions of placement results. Such measures focus both students' and business schools' attention on outcomes emphasizing brand-building and job-finding, and ignore learning and character development. They are therefore, at best orthogonal to the mission of leadership development.

So, for example, the *Wall Street Journal's* ranking of executive MBA programs assesses the increase in salary on completion compared to the cost of the program in an effort to measure return on investment. *BusinessWeek* bases its rankings on the survey responses of students and recruiters, with a small weighting given to faculty research output. The *Financial Times* includes both recent salary level and the growth in salary in the three years following earning the MBA degree, among other factors, and *Forbes* also assesses the additional salary earned over five years after the MBA compared to the cost of tuition. *US News* incorporates starting salary as a significant component of its rankings (DeAngelo *et al.*, 2005).

Maximizing income or increases in income favor some industries and jobs over others. In the recent past, consulting and various financial services firms, ranging from investment banks to private equity to hedge funds, have paid the highest salaries. Consulting and financial service jobs invariably offer more money than line management positions, or government or social sector jobs. There is at present little evidence on the question of whether the rankings, with their emphasis on salary, affect students' career preferences or what business school placement offices do to encourage higher-pay job placement. But there is also little doubt that large economic offers to people who may have both overhanging graduate school and college debts will affect job choice to at least some degree. So, career dynamics and the concern with placing students in high-paying positions work against job placements that are likely to provide as many opportunities for the development of leadership skills.

Furthermore, the rankings do not follow students over their whole career to see to what extent they achieve leadership positions and how well they perform in those positions. Nor do the various league tables measure values, leadership skills or ethical behavior, including cheating. Assessing these other, possibly better measures of leadership development requires more time and resources than the publications – which are, after all, mainly interested in selling copies and advertisements – want or need to expend. Indeed, the overemphasis on starting salary and salary increases after graduation as the primary criteria by which business schools are evaluated has prompted the Aspen Institute, among other organizations, to try to create alternative measures that could assess other dimensions of the effects of business education and its social impact. But the business publication rankings dominate the media as well as the attention of deans and the schools' various constituencies. Unless and until such rankings concern themselves with schools' performance in developing leaders rather than job candidates, it will be difficult for leadership development to gain much additional traction.

Some observers have noted correctly that nothing can be done about the rankings, and that only a few, very high-status schools can afford to opt out of the process. While it is certainly true that various media have free rein to do and to measure what they want, it is important to recognize the extent to which the business schools have, collectively, made the problem worse. If, instead of endlessly complaining that the various publications use the wrong measures often inaccurately or incompletely assessed, the schools – through one of their associations such as the Graduate Management Admissions

Council or the AACSB – promulgated their own, more desirable and more accurate assessments, there would at least be a competitive alternative to the various rankings published by the newspapers and magazines that currently control the rankings game. The point is that, in the absence of better, more accurate information, any information is going to receive attention. If business schools are serious about their mission of leadership development, they should measure this activity and their effectiveness, and make such assessments public.

Self-created business school identities

If the media rankings were not bad enough, business schools themselves are complicit in creating an emphasis on immediate job market outcomes as a measure of their success, and promulgating a focus on short-term financial benefits for their students. Many schools market themselves in ways that almost certainly mitigate against attracting the right people for the right reasons. These marketing messages, found in advertisements in magazines and newspapers, in brochures and literature, and on websites, are important. The content of such messages help to establish a brand identity and, more important, help to set client or, in this case, student and others' expectations for the product or service being offered.

For the most part, business schools present themselves as placement agencies that help their students find better jobs and meet more people – network – more efficiently. So, for example, in an advertisement in the *Wall Street Journal*, the Columbia–Berkeley Executive MBA Program promotes itself as networking squared:

> Your formula for success. Combine the best of two top MBA programs in a 19-month format. Connect with world-class faculty and a worldwide network earning the same degree as our full-time programs. Attend classes every three weeks on two exciting campuses. Double your network and advance your career.

Rice University's business school in Houston, Texas has, as the first statement on its online home page, "The Rice MBA gets you where you want to go, faster." Such ads and messages are typical, not just from these particular schools or in specific publications.

Pfeffer and Fong (2004) noted that this emphasis on finding a job was not an inevitable result of graduates needing to find work, and that other professional schools such as law and medicine created very different sorts of identities in their efforts to attract students to enroll for reasons other than increasing one's pay. It is almost certainly the case that if business schools are serious about leadership development as part of their mission, they will have more success in such efforts if they brand themselves and present their offerings to the world in ways consistent with such an objective. As an example, the home page of Northwestern University's Kellogg School of Management states, "Developing global leaders who make contributions of lasting significance for the world."

Until the branding and identity creation activities of business schools are congruent with a leadership development focus, it is unlikely that leadership development will be much more than window dressing. And schools that advertise themselves as great places to make contacts and get a better job are unlikely to attract students with a professional or substantive interest in learning compared to a careerist orientation toward finding the best-paying job.

Research and faculty evaluation

Faculty members do, or might do, the teaching and research that form the foundation for leadership development. It is generally recognized that successful implementation of any strategy requires a set of human resource policies that attract, retain and motivate people to execute the strategy successfully. This would be the case for leadership development as it would for any other organizational effort.

But here too the evidence suggests that most business schools have policies and practices in place that are unlikely to generate the activities required to make leadership development a reality. In the first place, schools have largely outsourced the faculty evaluation process. Faculty teaching is assessed by the students taught. Though this might seem sensible at first glance, the existing evidence shows little to no correlation between student ratings of faculty members and what the students actually learn (see, for example, Attiyeh and Lumsden, 1972). It is far from clear that students would necessarily value highly the sorts of experiences, and particularly the direct feedback, necessary for leadership development. MBA students are often admitted on the basis of a track record of outstanding individual success. Confronted by a large group of equally talented peers, students sometimes feel insecure and competitive, and can be more interested in enhancing their feelings of self-worth than in learning what they need to do better to be effective leaders. It is also not evident that at the time a course is taken and evaluated, students are completely capable of assessing the course's value for their subsequent activities, or even how much they learned and whether or not they will retain and use that learning in the future.

In addition to teaching, faculty careers depend on the professors' ability to publish high quality scholarly research. Because research performance is assessed via the ability to publish in prestigious, refereed journals, it is the journals more than the schools themselves that decide what will happen with faculty careers. This may seem like a good idea until one considers the evidence that indicates the peer review process used by virtually all journals is basically unreliable, in the measurement sense of providing consistent, replicable evaluations of work (see, for example, Ceci and Peters, 1982; Miller, 2006), and that journal prestige is only loosely correlated with the impact of articles published in those journals (Starbuck, 2005). Evaluations by external faculty are also part of the research assessment process, though such evaluations are inherently subjective and, as a consequence, undoubtedly affected by things such as likeability of the individual being judged as well as by the halo effect of the status of where the person works. Moreover, with the increasingly common hiring of people from the social sciences into business schools, and with the implicit "contract" that such individuals will be evaluated using the standards and criteria of their discipline, business schools have further outsourced the performance evaluation process to somewhat related but none the less distinct academic fields.

In the faculty performance assessment process, any effects of either teaching or research on leadership development are assessed only implicitly, if at all. Teaching is assessed mainly through student evaluations and, to a lesser degree, by peer evaluations of the courses' rigor and design. Except in some leadership development workshops, there is little or no measurement of whether students' leadership qualities change as a consequence of their specific educational experiences. And while some schools require an assessment of research impact as measured by citation counts, not all schools do so, and in any event, the assessment of the faculty member's impact on the leadership development literature is not necessarily part of the assessment of scholarly impact. It seems fair to assert that measuring students' leadership development through classes or the research contribution to leadership development knowledge is largely a voluntary and accidental part of the faculty performance evaluation process. The contrast of this situation in business schools with companies, most of which assess people directly on their contributions to the achievement of the company's mission and the execution of its business strategy, is notable.

It would, of course, be possible to change the performance evaluation process to link it more directly to the ostensible leadership development mission of business schools. Faculty research could be assessed more generally for its impact on management, and more specifically for its effects on leadership development (Pfeffer, 2007), and so could faculty teaching and course material development. It goes without saying that such information could be part of, but not determinative of, faculty evaluations for promotion and tenure. But without such information being available, leadership development is very much in the background of the faculty evaluation process and rational faculty will not pay it much heed unless there is some intrinsic interest in doing so.

Conclusion

Some people will undoubtedly ask how I can indict business schools for their failure at leadership development given the tremendous expansion of such efforts in the recent past. The answer is simple. While there are many experiential activities, leadership labs, self-assessments and group project work taking place in business schools, there is little peer-reviewed research evaluating such efforts, and the available, albeit limited, evidence is almost completely inconsistent with the idea that business schools are having positive effects on the development of student values and attitudes, or on graduates' ability to attain higher-level positions or their organizations' performance once in such positions.

If business schools are serious about their mission of leadership development, then the implications for action seem clear. The schools need to practice what they teach. Because measurement matters, schools need to measure not just the starting salaries of their graduates but also outcomes that are proximately related to their stated mission of leadership development. Based on the results of such measurements, schools need to learn what seems to working well and what is working less well, and adjust their activities accordingly. Schools should emphasize leadership development in their marketing to prospective students and in how they brand themselves. Organizational identities matter, and if leadership development is a critical part of the mission of business schools, it needs to be a more central part of the schools' identity.

It cannot be the case that leadership development remains disconnected from the core processes of faculty evaluation and development. While not all faculty and all courses need to be held accountable for accomplishing the schools' stated mission of leadership development, at least some of the evaluation of research and teaching ought to incorporate this objective.

Otherwise, business schools will be like many other organizations with mission statements that are designed largely for social legitimation and marketing but that have little relevance for the organization of day-to-day life.

The frequently-articulated mission of business schools to develop leaders for organizations in all sectors and in many countries is a good one. It is a mission that is clearly able to attract both financial support and behavioral engagement from alumni and organizations. It is a mission that is consistent with the role of higher education in society. It is a mission that has a precedent in the history of business schools, with their efforts to promote management as a profession, and with the historical role of colleges and universities. It is a mission that ought to be taken a lot more seriously, not just in organizational rhetoric but also in organizational action. As a number of observers of business education such as Rakesh Khurana have noted, a continuing failure on the part of business schools to advance management as a profession – complete with a sense of mission and values, and a commitment to learning and instilling values of service in their students – puts the continued success and possibly even the legitimacy and existence of business schools at risk.

NOTES

*My thanks to Charles A. O'Reilly, III, Rakesh Khurana and Jordi Canals for their very helpful and perceptive comments on an earlier draft of this chapter, and to Beth Benjamin for some unpublished research she so generously provided.

1 Some argue that leadership development can and must be assessed solely by whether or not the experience – for example, of attending an MBA program – makes a given individual more effective; for example, more capable of making better decisions and more effective in enlisting the support of others to implement those decisions. But individual increases in effectiveness as a result of some "treatment" must manifest themselves as differences in the mean levels of skill and performance between those who have experienced the "leadership development" and those who have not. Unless one assumes that people attending MBA programs or other leadership development experiences begin at a lower level of competence and skill than those who do not go through such programs – and in fact the reverse assumption is probably more sensible – then people who attend leadership development experiences should, in the aggregate, perform better, be more effective, and reach higher levels than those who do not.

REFERENCES

Armstrong, J. S. 1995. "The Devil's Advocate Responds to an MBA Student's Claim That Research Harms Learning." *Journal of Marketing 59*:101–6.

Aspen Institute for Social Innovation Through Business 2001. *Where Will They Lead? MBA Student Attitudes About Business and Society.* New York: Aspen Institute.

Aspen Institute 2008. *Where Will They Lead? 2008 MBA Student Attitudes About Business and Society.* New York: Aspen Institute, Center for Business Education.

Attiyeh, R. and Lumsden, K. G. 1972. "Some Modern Myths in Teaching Economics: The UK Experience". *American Economic Review* 62:429–33.

Audit Scotland 2005. "Scotland's Public Sector Spend More Than £5 million a Year Developing Its Leaders of the Future, 17 November 2005. Available at: www.audit-scotland.gov.uk .

Benko, C. and Weisberg, A. 2007. *Mass Career Customization: Aligning the Workplace With Today's Nontraditional Workforce.* Boston, MA: Harvard Business School Press.

Brown, B. S. and Choong, P. 2003. "A Comparison of Academic Dishonesty Among Business Students in a Public and Private Catholic University". *Journal of Research on Christian Education* 12:27–48.

Ceci, S. J. and Peters, D. 1982. "Peer Review: A Study of Reliability". *Change: The Magazine of Higher Learning* 14(6):44–8.

Collins, J. C., and Porras, J. I. 1994. *Built to Last: Successful Habits of Visionary Companies.* New York: HarperBusiness.

DeAngelo, H., DeAngelo, L. and Zimmerman, J. L. 2005. "What's Really Wrong With U.S. Business Schools?" Unpublished manuscript. Marshall School of Business, University of Southern California.

Dichev, I. D. 1999. "How Good Are Business School Rankings?" *Journal of Business* 72:201–13.

Dreher, G. F., Dougherty, T. W. and Whitely, B. 1985."Generalizability of MBA Degree and Socioeconomic Effects on Business School Graduates' Salaries". *Journal of Applied Psychology* 70:769–73.

Fee, C. E., Hadlock, C. J. and Pierce, J. R. 2005. "Business School Rankings and Business School Deans: A Study of Nonprofit Governance". *Financial Management* 34:143–66.

Gioia, D. A. and Corley, K. G. 2002. "Being Good Versus Looking Good: Business Schools Rankings and the Circean Transformation from Substance to Image". *Academy of Management Learning and Education* 1:107–20.

Gomez, D. 2007. "Practitioner's Corner: The Leader as Learner". *International Journal of Leadership Studies* 2(3). Available at: http://www.regent.edu/acad/global/publications/ijls/new/vol2iss3/prac.

Gottesman, A. A. and Morey, M. R. 2006. "Does a Better Education Make for Better Managers? An Empirical Examination of CEO Educational Quality and Firm Performance". Unpublished working paper. New York: Pace University.

Hewitt Associates 2008. *Top Companies for Leaders 2007*. New York: Hewitt Associates.

Howell, J. 1984. "An Interview with Professor James E. Howell". *Selections*: 9–13.

Khurana, R. 2007. *From Higher Aims to Hired Hands: The Social Transformation of American Business Schools and the Unfulfilled Promise of Management as a Profession*. Princeton, NJ: Princeton University Press.

Leonhardt, D. 2000. "A Matter of Degree? Not for Consultants". *New York Times*, 1 October 2000, Section 31, 1 ff.

Lieber, R. 1999. "Learning and Change: Roger Martin". *Fast Company* 30:262.

McCabe, D. L. 2001. "Academic Integrity: A Research Update". Paper presented at the Center for Academic Integrity, College Station, Texas, October.

McCabe, D. L., Butterfield, K. D. and Trevino, L. K. 2006. "Academic Dishonesty in Graduate Business Programs: Prevalence, Causes, and Proposed Action". *Academy of Management Learning and Education* 5:294–305.

McCabe, D. L. and Trevino, L. K. 1995. "Cheating Among Business Students: A Challenge for Business Leaders and Educators". *Journal of Management Education* 19:205–18.

McGlynn, E. A. 2004. "There Is No Perfect Health System". *Health Affairs* 23: 100–2.

Miller, C. C. 2006. "Peer Review in the Organizational and Management Sciences: Prevalence and Effects of Reviewer Hostility, Bias, and Dissensus". *Academy of Management Journal* 49: 425–31.

Morgeson, F. and Nahrgang, J. 2008. "Same As It Ever Was: Recognizing Stability in the *BusinessWeek* Rankings". *Academy of Management Learning and Education* 7, 26-41.

Pfeffer, J. 1977. "Effects of an MBA and Socioeconomic Origins on Business School Graduates' Salaries". *Journal of Applied Psychology, 62,*

Pfeffer, J. 2007. "A Modest Proposal: How We Might Change the Process and Product of Managerial Research". *Academy of Management Journal* 50, 1334–5.

Pfeffer, J. and Fong, C. T. 2002. "The End of Business Schools? Less Success Than Meets the Eye". *Academy of Management Learning and Education* 1:78–95.

Pfeffer, J., and Fong, C. T. 2004. "The Business School Business: Some Lessons from US Experience". *Journal of Management Studies,*1501–20.

Pfeffer, J. and Sutton, R. I. 1999. *The Knowing–Doing Gap*. Boston, MA: Harvard Business School Press.

Robinson, P. 1994. *Snapshots from Hell*. New York: Warner.

Starbuck, W. H. 2005. "How Much Better Are the Most Prestigious Journals? The Statistics of Academic Publication". *Organization Science* 16: 180–200.

Tushman, M. L., O'Reilly, C. A., Fenollosa, A., Kleinbaum, A. M. and McGrath, D. 2007. "Relevance *and* Rigor: Executive Education as a Lever in Shaping Practice and Research". *Academy of Management Learning and Education* 6:345–62.

Wadhwa, V., Freeman, R. and Rissing, B. 2008. *Education and Tech Entrepreneurship*. Kansas City: The Kauffman Foundation, May.

Weinstein, A. G. and Srinivasan, V. 1974. "Predicting Managerial Success of Master of Business Administration (MBA) Graduates". *Journal of Applied Psychology* 59:207–12.

Wilson, D., Croxson, B. and Atkinson, A. 2006. "What Gets Measured Gets Done". *Policy Studies* 27:153–71.

PART 3

The CEOs' Perspective: What Companies Expect from Leadership Development

How to Develop and Promote Leadership from the Top*

MIREIA LAS HERAS, Assistant Professor, and **NURIA CHINCHILLA**, Professor, IESE Business School, University of Navarra

Since the 1980s, leadership and career development, as well as the organization of work, have changed significantly. More than ever before, career development has become defined more by personal choices through which individuals create their own career paths. Job relationships have changed dramatically from a relational to a transactional contract (Hall, 2002, p.13). This shift towards a transactional relationship reflects the desire of firms to cut fixed costs and become more flexible. Previously, organizations used to decide the possible and optimal pathways for the individual. The individual is now a pilgrim who needs to decide not only about his or her own future but also about the different ways to get there. Thus, each person is forced to make decisions repeatedly (Hall and Mirvis, 1996, p.15), and can no longer rely on the organization to make them for him or her.

It is not, however, only personal career development that has changed noticeably over the past few decades. Leadership and the necessary competencies to develop it have also changed. Managers in organizations constantly face numerous strategic and practical challenges. These change the organization of work repeatedly by downsizing, restructuring, diversifying, globalizing, flattening organizational hierarchies, and/or outsourcing functions (Cappelli, 1999, p. 146). In this context, in which leaders operate and work and where non-work roles frequently overlap, continuous learning and adaptability have become the key to successful leadership. Moreover, change is the hallmark of the times, rather than the exception to the norm. Our age reflects a period of transformation (Drucker, 1992, p. 95).

This chapter first presents some notions about leadership and distinguishing between three types of leadership style: transactional, transformational and transcendental. This first section presents the assumptions under which each type of leadership is based and the main characteristics of those styles of leadership. Then the chapter moves on to present five central points of how CEOs can develop leadership in their organizations.

What styles of leadership are we talking about?

Leadership is a relationship of influence, in which all parties involved play an important role; it is the art of mobilizing others to attain shared aspirations (Kouzes and Posner, 1987). Thus, in complex and competitive markets, leadership is crucial for business sustainability. Leadership abilities should be fostered, not only for top executives and managers but also among employees across all levels in the organization. The goal is to have leaders who help to develop other leaders.

Most theories distinguish between two main types of leadership: transactional and transformational (Weber, 1947; Burns and Stalker, 1961, Bass, 1985). However, there is also a third level of leadership: transcendental leadership (Chinchilla and Pérez-López, 1990). Recognizing the distinctive traits of each style of leadership is crucial in understanding how to develop leaders that are comprehensive, effective and sustainable. Through identifying the characteristics of each style, we can understand the consequences of promoting one style of leadership over another.

Transactional leaders are those who apply the "physical Newtonian rules" of action–reaction to human interaction. These leaders base their behavior on strict rules of rewards, incentives and promotions. Through these approaches, they encourage people to act in a certain way, and if they do not, they are punished accordingly. This is a leadership style based on the tacit assumption that human beings are reactive and passive. And that they lack the capacity to decide whether to respond when facing a problem or when they are under stress.

Transactional leadership is based on a give-and-take relationship with specific extrinsic incentives and rewards, such as financial income, promotion and recognition. These rewards are given to employees in exchange for their contributions. Leaders tend to act toward increasing their extrinsic rewards, and thus these leaders surround themselves with people whose priority is to be rewarded by others in exchange for doing their job.

The principles behind transactional leadership drove the movement toward scientific management, which had a profound impact on how companies were managed at the beginning of the twentieth century following the Industrial Revolution. Scientific management was influential because it sought to create efficiency, and the basic principles seemed generally to work and apply to companies using industrial automation. In *Principles of Scientific Management* (Taylor, 1911) the author argues that, left to their own devices, workers will do as little as possible and engage in "soldiering" – working more slowly together in order to keep management ignorant of their potential. Similarly, if left to plan their own work, workers' output is further lowered. They will do things in the customary manner rather than the most efficient way. The solution is for management to "relieve" workers of the necessity of planning their own tasks, particularly those with a mental component. Workers will learn from management how best to increase their output for the benefit of both. The best inducement, Taylor believed, is money or economic reward. According to his principles, people are primarily interested in achieving a level of pay commensurate with the effort they have expended, and expect a fair day's pay for a fair day's work; thus piecework ensures that individual effort is rewarded. As Taylor notes in his book from 1911:

> So universal is soldiering for this purpose that hardly a competent work-man can be found in a large establishment, whether he works by the day or on piecework, contract work, or under any of the ordinary systems, who does not devote a considerable part of his time to studying just how slow he can work and still convince his employer that he is going at a good pace …
>
> When accurate records are kept of the amount of work done by each man and of his efficiency, and when each man's wages are raised as he improves, and those who fail to rise to a certain standard are discharged and a fresh supply of carefully selected men are given work in their places, both the natural loafing and systematic soldiering can be largely broken up.

Under this paradigm, the problem of leadership development is exclusively a problem of incentives: leaders need to learn how to pay a fair amount of money for a fair day of work (Taylor, 1916, p. 66). CEOs who seek to develop employees under this paradigm of leadership should develop their negotiating skills, in order to obtain the maximum benefit from the economic influence that it creates.

Transformational leadership is a relationship of professional influence. Transformational leaders understand that people are not only interested in extrinsic rewards, but also in many aspects of their jobs, such as learning and developing skills. Transformational leaders surround themselves with people who are largely intrinsically motivated. They like to feel rewarded by the job itself, either by the tasks that allow them to develop their creativity and acquire skills, or by the feeling of being intellectually stimulated (Betz *et al.*, 1989, p. 26). Whereas extrinsically motivated people perform their jobs with the hope of receiving rewards and benefits, people with intrinsic motives perform the activity even "in the absence of operationally separable consequences" (Aldrich and Pfeffer, 1976, p. 12). Thus transformational leadership is not opposed to transactional leadership, but it is more comprehensive and deemed to be more effective.

According to Chinchilla and Pérez-López (1990), a transformational leader is able to:

> discover the talents and skills of the people he manages. He discerns a potential in people that they themselves may not be aware of, then organizes and distributes tasks in such a way as to make the saleable product also producible. Transformational ability presupposes outstanding skill in communicating difficult objectives to a large number of individuals and requires an in-depth understanding of the weaknesses and positive traits of each individual.

Transformational leadership is based on the assumption that people are inclined toward growth, and thus they seek the means that foster such development. Transformational leaders are very effective in engaging people in change processes. They communicate the benefits that change will bring for those involved in the change process in terms of learning, enjoying and creating career opportunities. However, transformational leaders can also engage people in actions that might not be noble, such as environmentally or socially damaging actions. Unfortunately, some directors might be poor examples of this kind of leadership. Finally, transformational leaders will exhaust their power when the projects are monotonous and require contributions from employees that are not regarded as being personally stimulating: employees will not be willing to "go the extra mile" if they do not foresee a plausible extrinsic or intrinsic reward.

Organizations are essentially cooperative systems that need to integrate the contributions of individual participants (Barnard, 1996[1938], p. 181). Implicit in this formulation are the ideas that: (i) participants must be induced to contribute; and (ii) efforts must be directed toward a common purpose. One of the functions of the executive is to inculcate the belief in the existence of a common purpose. The first advocate of this type of leadership was Chester Barnard, who argued that the most critical factor in creating a successful organization is forming a collective purpose that becomes morally binding to the participants. Thus, the distinguishing mark of the leader is that he or she is required not only to conform to a complex code of morals, but also to create moral codes for others. This leads to the discussion of transcendental leadership.

Transcendental leadership is based on a relationship of personal influence, in which the aim is to achieve a shared mission. This kind of leadership seeks to engage employees who commit themselves to pursue a mission that appears worthy for both the company and for the person who pursues it (Pérez-López, 1996). Leaders not only influence others with rewards and penalties, but they also offer attractive assignments during which employees can personally learn and develop their interests and competencies, as well as to see that their work has a positive effect on others. This type of leader may also simplify work arrangements, and create a culture that facilitates employees' abilities to take care of their families and other personal commitments outside their job. Leaders working under this paradigm facilitate employees to understand the positive consequences of their job on other people and on society at large. By establishing these leadership aspects, leaders engage employees on projects as they increase their job mastery; thus those employees remain employable, while also sharing in the mission of the company.

As Chinchilla and Pérez-López (1990) wrote, referring to such leaders:

> They are not only concerned that things are done in a way that makes the organization efficient; nor is it enough for these leaders that tasks are more or less appealing to those who have to do them. Above all, they want people to develop their full potential and to internalize the organization's mission. They are, therefore, concerned with problems such as developing a sense of responsibility among their subordinates, so that they are capable of acting out of a sense of duty, and so on.

The value created by transcendental leaders depends on the value of the mission within which their actions are based (Cardona and Rey, 2006). A mission that goes beyond shareholder value to include all stakeholders' interests, such as the interests of the employees and their families, the clients and society at large, is deemed to be much more engaging than one that is restricted solely to maximizing profits.

Transcendental leaders seek to foster prosocial motives in those who work with and for them. People who have those kinds of motives – prosocial or transcendental – have the impetus to commit to their jobs and to perceive that such work makes a difference in someone's life (Grant, 2007). People with transcendental motives may perform activities even in the absence of positive consequences for themselves; provided that those activities have a positive impact on others, and that the action satisfies the needs of another person or group of people.

In contrast with the first two styles of leadership, transcendental leadership is based on the assumption that define the human person more completely and clearly. This assumption is that people are active rather than passive; thus, they are influenced but not determined by their environment. And they are naturally inclined toward growth and development. This assumption means that people are not programmed by the social environment, because each person has a unique and inalienable free will and subjectivity (Deci and Ryan, 2000; Coughlin, 2003, p. 227). Human beings have a desire to engage in relationships, and they depend on other people and on their surroundings. Therefore, people cannot achieve their maximum potential on their own, but rather they need to be in relationships with other humans, and need, in turn, to be able to influence them (Ferreiro and Alcázar, 2002). Finally, people have a set of basic innate psychological needs for autonomy, competence and relatedness (Amit and Zott, 2000; Deci and Ryan, 2000).

The objective of leadership development for transcendental leaders is to promote prosocial (Grant, 2007) or transcendental (Pérez-López, 1996) motives, so that those leaders act in a way that has a positive effect on others' lives and outcomes. To foster such motives is a two-step process. First, employees need to understand what the objective of the executive is, in order to be motivated to produce such an outcome (Pérez-López, 1985). That objective includes not only the product or service, but also the mission to which that service is targeted and what kind of needs the service will meet. Second, once employees understand the objective of the outcome, they need to understand the value of the outcome in order to be attracted to the assignment. Thus, to develop transcendental leaders, CEOs do not only need to teach the existence of transcendental outcomes but also to facilitate situations in which employees can experience their value.

A CEO may communicate the existence of transcendental outcomes to the company's executives in various ways. For example, top executives may try to include employees in specific corporate information, such as explaining to employees why certain decisions have been made or in which direction the company is headed. And, most important, top executives can facilitate others to value those outcomes by putting them in touch with those who receive the services or products generated in the company.

Compartamos Banco, the biggest microfinance bank in Latin America, sends its executives for a one-week visit every year to the bank's clients. The executives learn how their decisions have affected not only their clients, who are mainly very poor families in rural areas, but also the employees of the bank, also living in poor rural areas, who serve the bank's clients. By doing so, the bank's executives are likely to value the positive effects of their decisions on the clients and the employees much more than if they had not met them at all. Some biotech companies invite those who have been cured by the drugs that their company has developed to meet their researchers. There is also a university that put their fundraisers in contact with the beneficiaries of the respective scholarships. Afterwards, those fundraisers were substantially more effective in meeting their targets than those who were not in contact with the beneficiaries (Grant *et al.*, 2006, p. 53).

The next section moves on to present five central points that CEOs and senior executives need to take into account in order to develop transcendental leadership in organizations in today's business context. CEOs need to realize that they play crucial roles in fostering a culture of development that helps to develop the right capabilities and a strong leadership pipeline.

How do CEOs think about leadership development?

Leadership development is the CEO's responsibility

The availability of talented managers is one of the top challenges that CEOs face. However, it is well known that the match between an executive and a job is often unsatisfactory. This regularly results in placements that are unsuccessful either because managers fail to deliver results or because they are unhappy in the job and decide to leave. By and large, executives make poor promotion and staffing decisions. One-third of such decisions turn out to be correct; one-third of the managers are minimally effective; and the rest are outright failures. In no other area of management would we put up with such a miserable performance (Drucker, 2004, p. 58). Yet failure in hiring effective executives is expensive in terms of management time and as well as a loss of specific human capital. It can have a serious effect on the financial well-being of a company, resulting in the loss of money, reputation and competitive advantage, among other things. As Rafael del Pino, chairman of Grupo Ferrovial, S.A., a leading Spanish infrastructure and construction company, states:

> You have to keep in mind while you manage a large organization or a smaller one the balance of the skills that you have within the group of people you are leading. There is no one perfect at every task, so try to balance out what the skills of the different team members are, and also what their long-term potential is. Try to get people better than you, working for you, and that's something I look for with people we have within our workforce. Team building is the capacity to attract and develop management talent within their smaller groups. People who are not able to do that, I think, have a limited career in any organization.

CEOs need to realize that leadership development is one of their main responsibilities. This means that talent detection and talent management tools can be delegated to others in the organization, but it is the CEO and his/her team who are ultimately responsible for leadership development. CEOs have to lead the development of strategic competences among their collaborators (such as entrepreneurship), interpersonal competencies (such as empathy), and intrapersonal competencies (such as self-leadership, proactivity and integrity) (Cardona and Chinchilla, 1999, p. 10). They hand over leadership development tools and rely on HR information and support: but, ultimately, CEOs are responsible for developing strong pipelines of leaders who will be able to confront future challenges and market needs. It is the CEO who knows what capabilities will be necessary to implement the strategy sustainably and address future challenges. Thus, it is him or her who should foster those competencies and decision-making criteria among people in the organization.

Alfredo Sáenz, CEO of Grupo Santander, explains this process:

> We have set up a high potential development committee, which I chair, that reviews the top 300 people at Santander. This committee meets once a month for a full day. The committee's members are the bank's executive committee members and other senior executives. We discuss each day

around twenty people: we make an assessment of their capabilities and skills, their performance and their career paths. It is a very time-consuming process, but necessary, and is giving us terrific value to better develop our people.

In this context, Rolf Breuer, former Chairman and CEO of Deustche Bank, says:

> I highly appreciate the work of HR. I love HR, I need HR, and I couldn't have done without HR's work. But leadership development is the responsibility of the CEO. Don't try to delegate it. You can rely on HR to provide tools for leadership development, such as performance management, talent management, and training and coaching programs.

When Rolf Breuer was serving as the CEO of Deutsche Bank, he made leadership development his personal responsibility. For example, he used a tool that he named "The CEO's Challenge". This allowed him to choose twenty highly potential employees each year from all areas within Deutsche Bank. Those twenty people worked in groups of five, and the groups were asked to undertake a task: to answer four crucial and relevant strategic questions for which Breuer himself had no answers. Breuer would ask these four groups of potential senior executives to work on these questions for a year. This work was added to these employees' usual responsibilities, since they remained in their existing jobs. These groups had to communicate with each other by email, and met face to face with a coach a few times throughout the year. Breuer corresponded with them after three, six and nine months, to learn about the progress of their work. At the end of the one-year term, they presented their recommendations and findings at the annual senior management conference. In 2008, three of the people who had participated in "The CEO's Challenge" program were members of the executive committee of Deutsche Bank.

Board members have a responsibility to coach, guide and develop the CEO and the first executive of the company (Canals, 2004). Such guidance should not interfere with the course of action of the company or the operational decisions he or she needs to make in his or her day-to-day work. Canals clearly explains that the members of the board should develop leadership skills while at the same time offering support to the CEO and the executives of the firm. In fact, what the CEO should do with high-potential leaders is just a reflection of what the board members should do for him.

This development process has to take place during the day-to-day work. Carlos Costa, Managing Partner of The Boston Consulting Group, argues that:

> there is so much emphasis on distinguishing between strategy design and implementation. Implementation actually starts at the very conception of the design, and senior managers have to help high potentials think about how they develop the capabilities necessary to do a great job at integrating strategy design and implementation. They need to provide clear references on how to do it.

Thus, as we have just argued, leadership development in the company is the CEO's and senior executives' task; as much as the CEO's supervision, support, and development should be the board members'. Such a task requires that their behaviors provide a model for what is expected from others in the company, what the firm stands for, and how the mission and values are put into practice.

Developing leadership by example

In a world overloaded by information and where change is continuous, examples teach better than words. To build on leadership skills, CEOs need to set an example for others to follow. The CEO and the executives' behaviors should be aligned with the principles that, explicitly or not, they consider to be important for the organization. Developing leadership by example means that executives communicate better through what they do, rather than through what they say. CEOs also need to develop shared values among their future top leaders. Values have two components, which require: (i) guidance to learn the formal content of these values and what they entail; and (ii) learning how to put these values into action and the consequences of doing so.

Leading by example is basic to transmitting values to the future leaders of the organization and to the company as a whole. An organization must have a set of values that are deeply rooted and shared by the people in the organization. Values are normative and help in setting priorities when an individual makes a decision. They have a direct effect over the long-term success of the company as well as over their strategies, since they guide people's decisions

(Argandoña, 2002). Values are learned mainly by acting, perceiving the consequences of one's actions, and reflecting on those consequences. Such reflection should also include a consideration of alternative courses of action that could have been taken. This learning process is enriched by putting the decision-maker in touch with the people who experience the consequences of one's decisions. And values have a transcendental impact on others, such as meeting the needs of a third party, or creating a problem for someone (Pérez-López, 1996).

Leading by example is necessary because, for good or ill, the CEO and the executives are perceived as ideals. As Rolf Breuer puts it, "The CEO as a leader is regarded as some sort of role model, rightly or wrongly, but it is a fact." It is really passed on to others when people witness how the leader works in his or her day-to-day tasks, how others are treated by the leader, and if the CEO is consistent in what he or she says and does. As Gildo Zegna, Ermenegildo Zegna's CEO, explains:

> I think that my responsibility is to try to coordinate the team. I think another important trait that I try to transfer is the attitude in leading the team ... Leadership at Zegna is appreciation and care for each other. Discipline and excellent execution, and unless there is discipline, there is no excellent execution.

CEOs should strive to be coherent, sincere and forthright. For example, it is not a rare situation that a CEO remarks that team work is essential to generate value in the company, and yet he or she repeatedly acknowledges and rewards individual contributors. Or that the CEO repeatedly spreads the word around that people are the company's best asset; yet goes on to lay off employees without much consideration simply to cut costs. On the other hand, whenever a CEO or executive flies economy class instead of chartering a plane, particularly during times of financial trouble, his or her actions speak louder than words.

In family businesses, leading by example is of the utmost importance because the family members of different generations have shared values and want to prevail even when businesses and markets evolve. As Gildo Zegna described it, "I do believe that the first criterion is to lead by example in regards to other family members, and to try to emulate what other generations before yours have done." For Zegna, preserving the values in the company is key because, as he says, "You share the same values as other family members, the brand becomes stronger, and its value increases."

CEOs also need to set an example in their attitude toward work and relationships. In these times of complex decisions and rapid change, leaders' character attributes are even more important than their educational background, practical skills, specialized knowledge or work experience. Jim Collins says that it is not specific knowledge or skills that are important; rather it is those attributes such as character, work ethic, common sense and values that can ultimately decide whether a person is able to lead, decide under pressure, be a team player and handle complex situations effectively (Collins, 2001). And character attributes and personal attitudes cannot be imposed or rewarded, but shown and fostered.

The ability to develop relationships is also important. Alfredo Sáenz says: "We need people capable of creating and sustaining relationships. This means healthy people who are committed to having a positive influence on their colleagues and employees, who do not destroy others to achieve results, who are psychologically stable and who can develop their people and teams".

When CEOs and executives lead by example, it helps others in the company to understand the mission and values the company stands for, minimizes ambiguities, and sets a standard for others' behavior. In this context, as Andrea Christenson, CEO of Käthe Kruse, describes: "Authenticity, as well as trust, is an indispensable quality for leaders and professionals, and the source of your identification and loyalty to any professional project, and trust as well." All these benefits bring us to the next point: leading by example creates a climate of trust, in which people know what is expected from them, and feel valued and secure. It is in that climate of trust that leadership competencies develop and mature.

CEOs develop leadership by creating trust

The dynamics of a knowledge-based economy impose one clear imperative: every organization has to build the management of change into its very structure (Drucker, 1992, p. 95). And change implies that leaders need to make decisions in the face of uncertainty, lack of information, contradictory cues and uncertain outcomes. In a panorama of clarity and complete information, leaders would not be necessary: a sophisticated algorithm would be sufficient. But leadership is not about set rules or clear-cut steps: it is about ambiguity and risk. As Nicholas Schreiber, former CEO of Tetra Pak explained, "One of the most important and pervasive traits of good leaders is to deal with ambiguity and be able to tackle conflicting goals. Good leaders have to pursue goals that seem to contradict one another."

Trust has the following characteristics: it is a dynamic phenomenon (Pérez-López, 1996; Flores and Solomon, 1998, p. 205; Vaux Halliday, 2003, p. 405); it is rational and manifests itself in conditions of uncertainty and risk (Mayer et al., 1995, p. 709; Wicks et al., 1999, p. 99); it lowers the perceived cost of the transaction; it involves emotions (Drolet and Morris, 2000, p. 26); and it has a clear moral element (Becker, 1998).

Trust fosters employees' willingness to contribute and fuels their desire to make decisions that aim to maximize productivity and efficiency for the company. This is because they believe that the mission is worthy, and that their actions will also benefit themselves. Employees who have the desire to contribute will go beyond the task requirements and job descriptions when it is necessary for the well-being of the organization. Willingness to contribute is reflected in individual behaviors, such as: working on tasks that are out of the scope of his or her own domain or responsibility; acting on changes proposed by others; and even accepting changes that in the short run may be negative to him or her. The moral element of trust implies that both the employee and the leader will seek the long-term survival of the company, and that the leader will consider seriously the impact of his or her decisions on the well-being of others.

Leaders frequently have to make decisions in the face of incomplete data and uncertain outcomes for their companies, as well as for the short- and the long-run. CEOs, however, need to set a stage in which all leaders in the company make decisions with the goal of maximizing the company's long-term sustainability, rather than minimizing personal risks. This will sometimes result in what some authors refer to as intelligent failures (Sitkin, 1992, p. 231), which are a byproduct of the risks inherent in addressing challenging problems.

Intelligent failures result from thoughtfully planned actions that have uncertain outcomes, which are designed to test ideas, products and strategies. Uncertainty denotes unpredictability, which by the nature of unpredictability, may lead to possible losses, negative consequences and failures. When leaders need to make decisions in the face of uncertainty, they must be confident that possible, moderated and unavoidable failures will not be held against them. This requires trust between the CEO, management and employees. As Ermenegildo Zegna describes it, "Leadership is to accept mistakes. I think that I am the first one making mistakes, hopefully not too many, but I think in particular with a new team, you have to sometimes accept failures. Leadership is about accountability and taking responsibility."

To develop leadership competencies in others, CEOs should create environments in which people can trust each other and the organization as a whole. CEOs can provide a good example by valuing competence and passion above success, as Carlos Costa, managing partner of The Boston Consulting Group, likes to highlight, "We have to treat our people, our clients and our projects with passion. Our people have to be passionate about what they do. It shows commitment, and commitment helps develop trust." With a common understanding of trust, all counterparts will cooperate in a way that results in a joint gain. A leader who never fails is a leader who never plays hard. Or one who hides their mistakes. Or one who minimizes his or her own personal risks even if that is not the best option for the company. As Zegna says:

> I remember when 9/11 happened. I was in the United States. I tried to use my deepest values and instincts to respond to a terrible event that actually stopped our business. So I took a plane with my team, and in two weeks we visited every [one] of our fifty clients in the States, and we said, "Listen, we are in the same boat, we are in trouble. It's going to be a rough six months, but what can we do together? Let's share the risk and try to make a comeback together."

Failure, however, can always be regarded as a personal threat or as an opportunity to enhance knowledge. In the absence of trust, failure is perceived as a threat, and activates defense mechanisms that lead to blaming others, hiding mistakes or withdrawing from the process. In the absence of trust, failure will lead to distorted learning processes by making external attributions and locating the cause of failure in some external force (Lant and Milliken, 1992, p. 585). External blame for failure fosters persistence in the wrong actions and prevents managers from learning about the negative impact of their behavior on organizational outcomes. Positive illusions also lead people to perceive that the "external forces" that have led to failure are changing in favorable ways, and so individuals tend to search for information that confirms their belief that these external causes of their troubles are temporary.

CEOs, therefore, need to breed trust in order to develop real transcendental leaders within the organization who act to achieve both extrinsic and intrinsic outcomes, but most importantly, transcendental effects. Only in the presence of trust, can intelligent failures associated with the risks inherent in addressing challenging problems be used to enhance knowledge and gain experience.

Failure, in the presence of trust, draws attention to potential problems because it challenges the status quo and stimulates a search for possible solutions. Thus, trust allows people to learn from failure. This is very important for transcendental leadership, which is concerned with creating good outcomes for others. To learn and increase their leadership competencies, leaders need to know whether they have achieved the goal of creating good outcomes for others, and if not, they need to learn how to do so in the future. During this process leaders make companies more sustainable, since people witness the leaders' desire to have a positive impact on others. Trust facilitates motivation to adapt and to consider different alternatives. Trust, then, is necessary to create a culture of diversity, in which different voices, opinions, backgrounds and alternatives are considered, welcomed and valued. This leads us to the next point, which considers the necessity of fostering diversity as a way of developing leadership and effectiveness.

CEOs should promote diversity

Leaders must understand the company's peculiarities and strengths to be able to calibrate future challenges and competition, and to be devoted to its long-term welfare. This requires talented people. Talented people are men and women of different cultures, ethnicity and socio-economic backgrounds, who can bring diverse knowledge, perspectives and experience to the company. In most developed countries at the start of the twenty-first century, women make up more than 50 percent of college graduates. And as most countries have high immigration rates, minorities have a growing representation in the labor market and graduate schools. Under these conditions, for companies to attract and retain the best talent, they need to set up policies, leadership styles and cultures that welcome these constituencies (Chinchilla *et al.*, 2010).

In recent years, the distribution of purchasing power has also changed. Women and minorities now have a growing share in the purchasing decision processes. Having leaders that resemble and understand the diverse employees' needs, interests and priorities will allow companies to serve clients effectively.

Leadership teams that do not mirror the market they serve are disadvantaged when attempting to serve a diverse customer base adequately. Additionally, leaders should be considered from a generational perspective. As Ermenegildo Zegna illustrates, he seeks to attract diverse young talent: "We work with business schools; we work with head hunters, like any other company does, to attract talents. I do believe that without young talent, not just talent, but young talent, there is no future."

Effective leadership teams need to have the most capable people and to represent the target audience composition, Most important, diverse groups are better equipped to take creative approaches to problem-solving, contributing with varied expertise perspectives and personal life priorities. Because of their varied experiences and backgrounds, diverse groups can manage decisions better than those in cohesive groups. In his initial address, Rafael del Pino stressed the fact that no one is perfect at every task that is required in a company, or even in a team. Thus, to complement each other and create positive synergies, CEOs need to ensure that people in the leadership pipeline and in current leadership teams balance out and enrich each other. Again, leadership pipelines that lack the variety of perspectives that diversity brings would be at a disadvantage. Gildo Zegna explains how he attempts to ensure diversity of strategies and ideas: "What I try to teach is to be inclusive. I try to invite people, consult people, and listen to people and that's very important in an organization. A CEO should be curious and open. I think that this is especially important in emerging markets."

Diversity in strategy and perspectives is necessary now more than ever before. We are living in times of globalization, rapid changes in technology, crises, and increasingly competitive environments that place growing demands on managers and leaders. As leadership roles become increasingly complex, effective job performance requires managers to develop a comprehensive understanding of the business environment by seeking out and learning from many diverse experiences (Weick, 1979).

As Rafael del Pino mentioned, this need for complex understanding is especially important as people develop their careers. In the first steps of those careers, people are valued for their technical skills, whether in finance, accounting or operations. However, as del Pino pointed out, "As they move up in the organization, they will be mostly judged by their people skills. The question is how do you survive the first step without killing the second?" One key mechanism for developing the needed complex understanding and people skills is through a variety of job assignments and career roles (Karaevli and Hall, 2004, p. 62). Therefore, to develop effective leaders, CEOs need to facilitate and ensure that people have diverse and enriching experiences. Rolf Breuer says that, "Diversity means not only having people from all sorts of ethnic and geographical backgrounds, but even more, to have them with a lot of different experiences that can contribute to the success of the position they hold."

Diversity is also necessary to avoid group biases. Group biases are a result of the environmental characteristics of the group, which causes the group members to process information irrationally. Those biases range from false consensus to "groupthink" to group polarization (Jones and Roelofsma, 2000, p. 1129). For example, Rakesh Khurana (Khurana, 2001, p. 91) recommends that special teams, such as those who are involved in a CEO search, consist of diverse people, not only in terms of age and functional background, but also concerning knowledge of the company and its culture in order to increase the chances of effective placement decisions. To avoid such biases, Rafael del Pino suggests that CEOs should, "try to balance out what the skills of the different team members are, and also what is their long-term potential".

Surrounding oneself with those who are too similar (Cross and Brodt, 2001, p. 86) causes false consensus. The false consensus bias refers to a form of social projection: individuals overestimate the degree to which others share their opinions, ideas and beliefs (Bauman and Geher, 2002, p. 293). False consensus distorts decision-making processes because the leader undervalues objective assessments and ideas of those with opposing views, and turns away constructive feedback.

Diversity means aiming at more capable people. Anna Ruewell (British Petroleum) points out that:

diversity is not only about background, gender, career or nationality. It involves different ways of thinking, seeing problems and challenges, and observing the world. When I go to LBS or IESE to recruit MBA students, I do not only look for people from certain countries. I go to the world's top business school to find the world' s top people, and this includes a diversity of perspectives, experiences and capabilities.

The crucial contributions that spring from a strong international background are also emphasized by Franklin Johnson (chairman, Asset Management):

When dealing and trying to promote entrepreneurship, diversity is essential. Starting a new business in Silicon Valley is not the same as doing it in China or Eastern Europe. Entrepreneurs and business leaders need to understand those differences and learn on the ground and from other leaders with that specific expertise. In this way, they can improve their own understanding of policies and execution in different geographical contexts.

Diversity in executive teams is also more liable to avoid groupthink bias. This is the process by which people in a cohesive in-group strive for unanimity. Such a desire overrides their motivation to appraise alternative courses of action realistically (Whyte, 1989, p. 40). In unified teams, the desire to maintain cohesiveness potentially leads to a decline in mental efficacy and realistic decision-making. The ultimate effect is that the number of options considered in decision-making is lowered systematically, which possibly leads to poorer decisions.

Finally, diversity in executive teams and in general, in any decision-making team, also helps to avoid group polarization. Group polarization is the tendency of individuals in a group setting to engage in making more extreme decisions than their own private, individual decisions would be (Myers and Lamm, 1976, p. 602). Group polarization leads to decisions that are more daring than the average risk that any one of the group members would rationally tolerate individually. The implication of the phenomenon of group polarization is that group dynamics have the potential to change the group's final decision without necessarily changing any of the underlying facts that led to that decision (El-Shinnawy and Vinze, 1998, p. 165).

A. M. Konrad and V. W. Kramer illustrate the beneficial effects of gender diversity in both executive teams and boardrooms (Konrad and Kramer, 2006, p. 22). Their research shows that gender diversity might ameliorate those potential biases. When women are present on boards, three things happen: first, they broaden the board's discussions to better represent the concerns of a wider set of stakeholders; second, they tend to be more persistent in pursuing answers to difficult questions; and third, they tend to bring a more collaborative approach to leadership.

Diversity facilitates attracting, retaining and promoting the best talent in the job market. It also serves the customer base in a more direct and effective way by making more valuable decisions. Such diversity is not only composed of people of different cultural backgrounds and nationalities, but also of people with diverse priorities and life circumstances. This is of utmost importance, since a growing segment of talented people are seeking to enjoy a fulfilling family life while also developing their professional careers. People are searching increasingly for flexibility and a better work–life balance, so companies need to offer more individualized career opportunities in order to foster their commitment to the company. This leads to the next point, in which we consider how and why CEOs and executives should facilitate work and family integration for the people in the company as a leadership development tool.

CEOs should facilitate work and family integration as a way to develop leadership

The family is the natural space in which the person, and thus the leader, can recharge energies, develop competencies and gain support. The aim of forming a family is to personally nurture one another and grow together, to protect, educate and love any children in the family and to care for the elderly, if necessary (Vidal Gil, 2007; Guitián, 2009). Within the family, the person develops his or her capacity to think and reflect, to be surprised, and to admire. He or she also develops the capacity to be resilient and bounce back after setbacks. The family is the natural space in which the person learns to be open to others, to be just, compassionate and empathic. Thus, leaders require family life to reenergize, feel supported and gain confidence. As Professor Robert Kegan has stated, only when challenge is coupled with support are people able to mature and grow in a complex understanding of reality.

As Rafael del Pino suggested, great leaders need their spouses' guidance to keep a balance in their lives. The spouse is a person who can give feedback, fulfill the need for affective support, and teach the individual to be a good follower:

> If you do not have a balanced personal life, it is very difficult for you to perform correctly in your work. You see that when you have people going through tough personal periods in their life, because they have lost something they love, or because they are divorced, or are in a divorce process. You can see that at work. They perform poorly when they go through personal stress periods. So keeping the balance is essential.

Leaders should strive to be whole individuals. And to develop holistically, a person needs to grow in mastery, connection and autonomy (Deci and

Ryan, 2000, p. 227). It is only then that the person achieves psychological growth, integrity and well-being; and thus is more likely to be a good leader. When a person feels supported he or she can provide support to others, and when a person has the proper space to grow he or she can create space for others to do the same. It is within the context of a family that people are loved and respected regardless of their productivity or capacity. And it is within families that people tend to develop their abilities to build lasting and healthy ties, to learn to trust and to cooperate, and to grow in self-awareness as well as in the acknowledgement and recognition of others (Roback Morse, 2001). Work and family are two important areas in which personal and professional development take place. Family life enables people to become better leaders, and more aware of the needs, priorities and motivations of others. Leaders who have discovered their own professional purpose and family mission can be more effective in engaging their employees in the firm's mission.

Leaders not only learn among and develop their own family lives, they also need to acknowledge that other people also desire and need a family life. Transcendental leaders must acknowledge fully that people today pursue different goals in their careers, so they need to hire, manage and reward those people differently, according to their diverse contributions to firms. Only people who are moved by the three different types of motive – intrinsic, extrinsic and transcendental – are able to understand fully people with varied needs and preferences (Chinchilla and Moragas, 2008). Therefore, only those sort of people are likely to be effective leaders in contemporary organizations.

Finally, CEOs should facilitate work and family integration, since participation in other life spheres fosters transcendental leadership development. Family life makes leaders more aware of others' needs and of the repercussions of his or her actions on others. Work and life do not have to be in conflict but can be enriching (Stanko, 2008); leadership at all levels is about being real, being authentic and being whole (Friedman, 2008). A person who is able to develop his or her interests in different life spheres is better off as a leader and better equipped to understand and manage others. Work and life integration is not a matter of tradeoffs but of mutual enrichment and harmony.

Conclusion

In this chapter, what we have highlighted illustrates that one of the main tasks of the CEO is to develop transcendental leaders. Transcendental leadership is much richer than transactional or transformational leadership paradigms. The transactional leader is concerned exclusively with the results of the working relationship. He or she focuses on negotiating extrinsic exchanges and on controlling the actions of his or her collaborators as well as ensuring that they follow his or her will. Transactional leaders can only influence their collaborators on the basis of extrinsic rewards and punishments.

Transformational leaders go one step further in their understanding of leadership and seek to be charismatic in such a way that they push their collaborators to go beyond what is formally demanded of them, and motivate them to achieve intrinsic goals and increase the attractiveness of the organization. However, only transcendental leaders manage others by a contribution-based exchange relationship. In this relationship, the leader promotes unity by providing fair extrinsic rewards, appealing to the intrinsic motivation of the collaborators, and developing their desire to act for transcendental motives – that is, effects that the action has on other people (Pérez-López, 1985). Those are the real leaders that aim for efficiency, attractiveness and unity in organizations.

As this chapter has shown, to develop transcendental leadership is the responsibility of the CEO. It is important for the long-term sustainability of the company, having an impact on daily decisions as well as on long-term strategic actions. The CEO can delegate tasks and tools for talent development and attraction, but leadership development is his or her own responsibility. A CEO develops transcendental leadership via his or her own experience, decisions and discourse. The example and discourse of the CEO can teach people to value transcendental motives, but it is the actions of the CEO in particular that teach what he or she values, and why, and whether he or she uses power in a proper way.

It is undeniable that leadership poses a great many challenges to those developing such roles. Contemporary leaders need to be well-rounded, strong and flexible, technologically capable and, most importantly, good at human relationships. Transcendental leaders need to be willing to put themselves out for the good of their people. They need to value the positive effects of their actions on others, knowing that in the long term it will pay off for the company as a whole, and for themselves. To acquire the strengths that transcendental leaders need, business schools can help by developing curricula that prepare new generations to face these challenges. However, it is mainly the task of CEOs and business leaders to develop the skills of younger people. They will do so through challenging assignments and developmental opportunities, helping them reflect on their responsibility toward the company, the clients and all the stakeholders, and fostering in them the pride of having a positive impact on all those constituencies. CEOs that live up to this challenge will reap the benefits for their both companies and themselves.

NOTE

* Senior executives quoted in this chapter were speakers in the IESE Conference on "The Future of Leadership Development and the Role of Business Schools", which took place on 17 and 18 April 2008. We were very privileged to count as keynote speakers Rolf Breuer (former Chairman of Deutsche Bank), Andrea Christenson (Käthe Kruse, CEO), Carlos Costa (The Boston Consulting Group, Managing Partner), Rafael del Pino (Grupo Ferrovial, Chairman), Franklin Johnson (Asset Management, Chairman), Anna Ruewell (British Petroleum, Talent Development Manager), Alfredo Sáenz, (Banco Santander, CEO), Nicholas Schreiber (former CEO of Tetra Pak), and Gildo Zegna (Ermenegildo Zegna, CEO).

REFERENCES

Aldrich, H. and Pfeffer, J. 1976. "Environments of Organizations", *Annual Review of Sociology* 2:79–105.

Amit, R. and Zott, C. 2000. *Value Drivers of E-Commerce Business* Models. Research paper, University of Pennsylvania and INSEAD.

Argandoña, A. 2000. *Fostering Values in Organizations*, IESE Research paper, Barcelona.

Barnard, C. I. 1996 [1938]. "The Executive Functions". In J. S. Ott, ed. *Classic Readings in Organizational* Behavior. Belmont, CA: Wadsworth: 181–8.

Bass, B. M. 1985. Leadership: Good, Better, Best. *Organizational* Dynamics 13(3): 26–40.

Bauman, K. P. and Geher, G. 2002. "We Think You Agree: The Detrimental Impact of the False Consensus Effect on Behavior", *P*sychology 21: 293–318.

Becker, H. S. 1998. *Tricks of the Trade: How to Think about Your Research While You're* Doing It. Chicago, IL: University of Chicago, Press.

Betz, N. E., Fitzgerald, L. F. and Hill, R. E. 1989. "Trait Factor Theories: Traditional Cornerstone of Career Theory". In M. B. Arthur, D. Hall and B. S. Lawrence, eds. *Handbook of Career Theory.* New York: Cambridge University Press: 26–41.

Burns, T. and Stalker, G. M. 1961. The Management of Innovation: Mechanistic and Organic Systems. In J. M. Shafritz, and J. S. Ott, eds. *Classics of Organization Theory*, 4th edn. Belmont, CA: Wadsworth.

Canals, J. 2004. "Tasks and Responsibilities of CEOs", Technical Note, DGN 645.IESE Publishing.

Cappelli, P. 1999. "Career Jobs Are Dead", *California Management* Review 42: 146–68.

Cardona, P. and Chinchilla, N. 1999. "Evaluación y Desarrollo de las Competencias Directivas", *Harvard Deusto Business* Review 89:10–27.

Cardona, P. and Rey, C. 2006. "Management by Missions: How to Make the Mission a Part of Management", *Problems and Perspectives in M*anagement 1:164–74.

Chinchilla, N. and Pérez-López, J. A. 1990. "Business or Enterprise? Different Approaches to the Management of People in Organizations". Technical note, FHN-216-E. IESE Publishing.

Chinchilla, N. and Moragas, M. 2008. *Masters of Our* Destiny. Pamplona: EUNSA.

Chinchilla, N. Las Heras, M. and Masuda, A.D. 2010. *Balancing Work and Family. A Practical Guide to Help Organizations Meet the Global Workforce* Challenge. Amherst, MA: HRD Press.

Collins, J. 2001. *Good to Great: Why Some Companies Make the Leap... And Othe*rs *Don't.* New York: HarperCollins.

Coughlin, J. J. 2003. "Pope John Paul II and the Dignity of the Human Being". *Harvard Journal of Law & Public* Policy 27:65–80.

Cross, R. L. and Brodt, S. E. 2001. "How Assumptions of Consensus Undermine Decision Making". *MIT Sloan Managem*ent Review 42:86–94.

Deci, E. L. and Ryan, R. M. 2000. "The 'What' and 'Why' of Goal Pursuits: Human Needs and the Self-Determination of Behavior". *Psychologica*l Inquiry 11:227–68.

Drolet, A. L. and Morris, M.W. 2000. "Rapport in Conflict Resolution: Accounting for How Face-to-Face Contact Fosters Mutual Cooperation in Mixed-Motive Conflicts" *Journal of Experimental Social P*sychology 36:26–50.

Drucker, P. F. 1992. "The New Society of Organizations". *Harvard Busine*ss Review 70:95–105.

Drucker, P. F. 2004. "What Makes an Effective Executive". *Harvard Busine*ss Review 82:58–63.

El-Shinnawy, M. and Vinze, A. S. 1998. "Polarization and Persuasive Argumentation: A Study of Decision Making in Group Settings". *MIS Quarterly/The Society for Information M*anagement 22:165–98.

Ferreiro, P. and Alcázar, M. 2002. *Gobierno de Personas en l*a Empresa. Barcelona: Ariel.

Flores, F. and Solomon, R. C. 1998. "Creating Trust". *Business Ethics* Quarterly 8: 205–32.

Friedman, S. 2008. *Total Leadership: Be a Better Leader, Have a Ri*cher Life. Boston, MA: Harvard Business Press.

Grant, A. 2007. "Relational Job Design and the Motivation to Make a Prosocial Difference". *Academy of Managem*ent Review 32:393–417.

Grant, A., Campbell, E., Chen, G., Cottone, K., Lapedis, D. and Lee, K. 2006. "Impact and the Art of Motivation Maintenance: The Effects of Contact with Beneficiaries on Persistence Behavior". *Organizational Behavior and Human Decision* Processes 103:53–67.

Guitián, G. 2009. "Conciliating Work and Family: A Catholic Social Teaching Perspective". *Journal of Busine*ss Ethics 88;513–24.

Hall, T. 2002. *Careers In and Out of Orga*nizations. London: Sage.

Hall, T. and Mirvis, P. 1996. "The New Protean Career: Psychological Success and the Path With a Heart" In *The Career Is Dead: Long Life To The* Career. San Francisco, CA: Jossey-Bass:15–46.

Jones, P.E. and Roelofsma, P. H. M. P. 2000. "The Potential for Social Contextual and Group Biases in Team Decision-Making: Biases, Conditions and Psychological Mechanisms". *E*rgonomics 43:1129–52.

Karaevli, A. and Hall, D. T. 2004. "Growing Leaders for Turbulent Times: Is Succession Planning Up to the Challenge?". *Organizational* Dynamics 32:62.

Khurana, R. 2001. "Finding the Right CEO: Why Boards Often Make Poor Choices". *MIT Sloan Managem*ent Review 43:91–5.

Konrad, A. M. and Kramer, V. W. 2006. "How Many Women Do Boards Need?". *Harvard Busine*ss Review 84:22.

Kouzes, J. M. and Posner, B. Z. 1987. *The Leadership Challenge: How to Get Extraordinary Things Done in Orga*nizations. San Francisco, CA: Jossey-Bass.

Lant, T. K. and Milliken, F.J. 1992. "The Role of Managerial Learning and Interpretation in Strategic Persistence and Reorientation: An Empirical Exploration", *Strategic Managem*ent Journal 13:585–608.

Mayer, R. C., Davis, J. H. and Shoorman, D. F. 1995. "An Integrative Model of Organizational Trust". *Academy of Managem*ent Review 20:709–34.

Myers, D. G. and Lamm, H. 1976. "The Group Polarization Phenomenon". *Psychological* Bulletin 83:602–27.

Pérez-López, J. A. 1985. "Human Motivation". Technical note, FHN-161-E. IESE Publishing.

Pérez-López, J. A. 1996. *Fundamentos de la Dirección de* Empresas, 3rd edn. Madrid: Ediciones Rialp.

Roback Morse, J. 2001. *Love and Economics: Why the Laissez-Faire Family Doesn't Work*. Dallas, Tx: Spence.

Sitkin, S. B. 1992. "Learning Through Failure: The Strategy of Small Losses". *Research in Organizational* Behavior 14:231–266.

Stanko, T. 2008. *From Scout Leader to Business Leader: How Participation in Multiple Roles Shapes Behavio*r at Work. Dissertation research. University of California: Irvine.

Taylor, F. W. 1911. "The Principles of Scientific Management". In *The Principles of Scientific M*anagement. New York: Cosimo: 4–5.

Taylor, F. W. 1916. "The Principles of Scientific Management". In J. M. Shafritz and J. S. Ott, eds. *Classics of Organizati*on Theory, 4th edn. Vol. 6. Belmont, CA: Wadsworth: 66.

Vaux Halliday, S. 2003. "Which Trust and When? Conceptualizing Trust in Business Relationships Based on Context and Contingency". *The International Review of Retail, Distribution and Consumer* Research 13:405–21.

Vidal Gil, E. 2007. *La Visión De La Fa*milia Hoy. Barcelona: Pasder BCN.

Weber, M. 1947. *The Theory of Social and Economic Organization.* Trans. A. M. Henderson and T. Parsons. New York: Free Press.

Weick, K. 1979. *The Social Psychology of Organizing,* 2nd edn. Reading, MA: Addison-Wesley.

Whyte, G.1989. "Groupthink Reconsidered". *Academy of Managem*ent Review 14: 40–56.

Wicks, A. C., Berman, S. L. and Jones, T. M. 1999. "The Structure of Optimal Trust: Moral and Strategic Implications". *Academy of Managem*ent Review 24: 99–116.

Managing Managers as Professionals: Leadership Development and Talent Transfer in a Global World

M. JULIA PRATS, Assistant Professor, and **REMEI AGULLES**, Research Assistant, IESE Business School, University of Navarra

Introduction

Today's business landscape calls for better managers. However, several trends complicate the nurturing of management professionals for firms that must identify, develop, retain and transfer them.

This chapter discusses some current paradoxes and challenges that firms face in incorporating, training and transferring a new generation of leaders. Our main proposition is that considering managers as professionals broadens the perspective on their contribution to business and society at large, and calls for the development of a more comprehensive set of competences. This suggests opportunities for further collaboration between firms and business schools. It is from this standpoint that leaders should be developed to meet successfully the complex demands of today's world.

Managing the complexities of current business requires both the sharp diagnostic of a well-trained specialist and the implementation skills of an expert craftsman. Modern management has become one of the most powerful contemporary institutions. As Khurana has pointed out, "Neither owner nor worker, this new economic actor, the manager, performed work that ... was ... critical to the development of the large-scale business enterprise" (2007, pp. 1–2). But, as Khurana noted, the rise of this new job was controversial: "it was not obvious who they were, what they did, or why they should be entrusted with the task of running corporations" (2007, p. 3). Management had to struggle to gain legitimacy, and in this battle, business schools – with their goal of professionalization – had an important place.

Business schools and management have shaped each other as institutions, which is why they are discussed hand-in-hand in this chapter. Academic research has improved our understanding of management; at the same time, academic programs in management have contributed greatly to framing the new corporate leader. Major firms have also been influential, thanks to their demands regarding the design of business school programs.

In this chapter, we discuss salient challenges that today's firms face and propose a broader viewpoint for management development. The next section considers the manager as a professional. Immediate consequences for managers are the need to master a body of knowledge, the commitment to contribute to the managerial community and society at large, and the pledge to follow ethical standards. The following section reviews aspects of our business landscape, including business context and new generations of managers, to point out the potential mismatches – first, between an increasingly disjointed context and the need for integral training; and second, between a firm's needs and a new generation of managers' expectations. The third section makes clear how organizations are coping with that landscape. In the final section, we conclude that managers who want to live up to the standards of a good professional must incorporate to their development career a carefully designed plan to foster all the competences, with special attention to personal competences – the foundation of all the others. We approach leadership development as a task that firms and business schools must undertake side by side, to make sure that both pay attention to all spheres of a manager's development, putting stronger emphasis on the intrinsic commitment to the public good.

Managers as professionals

Discussions concerning the similarities and differences among managers, professionals and leaders have been at the forefront of academic research and in the business media. In addition to the mainstream view that considers managers as leaders, we argue that considering management as a profession and, hence, managers as professionals, provides an interesting avenue for exploring how to develop, train and transfer managers.

Business schools appeared as a response to economic and social changes at the end of the nineteenth century and the beginning of the twentieth. They sought to create a new profession – management – and based their model on that of law or medicine (Khurana *et al.*, 2002; Khurana, 2007). Since then, the literature on management as a profession has grown. A closer look at the subject first requires a characterization of what is a profession.

A profession may be defined as a certain kind of occupation or employment and, at the same time, a body of persons engaged in this occupation.[1] More specifically, Khurana et al. (2005, p. 45) say:

Our criteria for calling an occupation a bona fide profession are as follows:

- a common body of knowledge resting on a well-developed, widely accepted theoretical base;

- a system for certifying that individuals possess such knowledge before being licensed or otherwise allowed to practice;

- a commitment to use specialized knowledge for the public good, and renunciation of the goal of profit-maximization, in return for professional autonomy and monopoly power;

- a code of ethics, with provisions for monitoring individual compliance with the code and a system of sanctions for enforcing it.

In summary, a profession is articulated around three concepts: *knowledge* (both theoretical and practical); *association* (it is more or less organized as a community of practitioners with a recognized identity and a group spirit that entails personal contribution and mutual support); and *ethics* (service: commitment to public good and renunciation of profit-maximization). Consequently, professionals engaged in a profession commit to mastering the specific knowledge, contribute to the community and follow ethical standards.

A few professions lack some of the traits listed above. For example, consulting and investment banking do not have established barriers to entry or a reputation for ethical aims; however, these professionals possess a considerable level of expertise (knowledge) for which they are well paid. On the other hand, nurses in general do not hold the high social status and level of remuneration of other professions, but they have the other characteristics (Empson, 2007). Since the profession of management also lacks some of the basic traits, its identification as a profession, and its members as professionals, is still controversial. However, there is no doubt that many changes in the business world are leading to more professional-like forms of management.

Historically, the knowledge required for the managerial practice had been mainly of the implicit and practical type. However, the increasing complexity of both the practice and the environment necessitated the creation of explicit theoretical, abstract knowledge that could be learned only in an academic setting (Nanda, 2004). The increasing demand for MBAs and other degrees is proof that the consideration of management has evolved: there are still no rigid barriers to entry for the managerial practice, but, increasingly, university management studies are a requirement for holding certain positions.

Managers are also far from constituting a body of practitioners. However, trends in organizational structure and job configuration signal a more precise delineation of a manager's identity. One of the most outstanding transformations is the gradual generalization of flatter organizations, which has transferred to managers some of the salient characteristics of professional work. For example, there is less reliance on power derived from hierarchical position and more reliance on authority given by colleagues. This shift challenges, from very early in the managerial career, his or her basic leadership competences. Also, jobs are more project-based. Consider, for example, the so-called "portfolio careers", where a manager is called in to take a new venture to the next level; or trends such as "interim management", where a manager is hired to perform a specific task. Finally, strategy becomes much more "emergent". Though firms may have a well-designed "intended" strategy, complexity and continuous change in the environment push managers at all levels to adapt quickly without waiting for strategic reviews. Managers' knowledge, skills and values will ultimately shape the firm's strategy. As in a professional services firm, managers' behavior becomes the strategy itself.

In summary, manager's job content increasingly resembles the one of an expert able to act upon its knowledge, experience and discernment. The development of this professional, which entails expertise that goes beyond explicit knowledge, requires the cooperation of other professionals that confront and resolve similar problems. Indeed, managers find support and make invaluable contributions in getting involved in diverse development forums either inside the firm or in the broader managerial community.

Perhaps the most salient objection to considering management as a profession is the one raised by those who believe that business and professions are in complete opposition to each other. The former would be devoted to profit, while the latter to public good (Marshall, 1939; Parsons, 1939; Meadows, 1946; Khurana et al., 2002). In response to this view, some scholars have pointed out that what underlies the conception of business as mere money-making is the introduction of neoclassical economic theory, according to which every human action is performed out of self-interest (Maister, 1997; Khurana *et al.*, 2002; Nanda, 2002a; Khurana *et al.*, 2005; Khurana and Snook, 2006; Gintis and Khurana, 2008). Gintis and Khurana (2008, p. 300) have explained:

> Neoclassical economic theory thus fosters a corporate culture that ignores the personal rewards and social responsibilities associated with managing a modern enterprise, and encourages an ethic of greedy materialism in which managers are expected to care only about personal financial reward, and in which such human character virtues as honesty and decency are deployed only contingently in the interests of personal material reward.

Later cases of corporate misbehavior show clearly how unsustainable this style of business practice is, and that cooperation and mutual regard could improve both the moral character of business and the profitability of corporate enterprise (Gintis and Khurana, 2008). However, this behavior calls for higher ethical standards, which include, as suggested by Khurana *et al.* (2005) certain margins of gratuity. Indeed, by abjuring professional standards for managers in favor of a culture of generosity, we are advancing not only healthier and more human corporate cultures but also the notion of public good; the idea that those who lead and manage our society's major private institutions might provide, or be responsible for contributing to, a sustainable society. Undeniably, the best business schools are aware of this necessity, and they include leadership development in their curriculum design. However, leadership development models are often somewhat biased toward knowledge or practical skills, almost leaving out the development of stable personal characteristics that in fact inform the rest. If, as previously noted, a manager's job is increasingly similar to the work of a professional, a manager's development model must be focused on developing an individual who is capable of mastering knowledge, contributing to the managerial community and the public good; in summary, behaving in a way that is guided by ethical responsibilities.

As a tool to aim for these high managerial standards, in this chapter we follow Pablo Cardona's model (Cardona and García-Lombardía, 2005; Cardona and Wilkinson, 2009). These authors propose a classification of leadership (that is, managerial) competences into three groups: *business competences, interpersonal competences* and *personal competences*. Though there are many different models of competences, the main advantage of this model is that it includes all spheres of a manager's behavior: the practical expertise and theoretical knowledge specific to the profession; the abilities required to form interpersonal relationships; and, finally, the competences that are indispensable for self-leadership, the base that enables ethical behavior.

Business context, firms and managers: a reality check

Managing a business at the beginning of the twenty-first century is very different from managing one ten or twenty years ago. Not only has the scenario changed by becoming more complex, world-sized and technologically sophisticated, but also the expectations of firms and new generations of managers are different. In this section, we briefly explore these three elements – firms' requirements; managers' characteristics and expectations; and the environment in which they operate – starting with the latter. If we want to develop strong leaders, a realistic view is indispensable.

A difficult landscape and a paradox

Today's business landscape is characterized by higher uncertainty, knowledge complexity, geographical distance and speed. Developing managers as professionals in this environment must take into account the effects of such characteristics. We shall now examine them more closely.

First, a common basis of theoretical knowledge is an essential trait of professions (Meadows, 1946; Mason, 1992; Empson, 2001; Hitt *et al.*, 2001; Løwendahl *et al.*, 2001; Chang and Birkett, 2004; Khurana *et al.*, 2005). But more learning is accompanied by a gradual specialization and fragmentation of knowledge. Narrow knowledge leads to routine and commoditization (Baumard, 2002; Nanda, 2002b; Coff *et al.*, 2006), a search (even unintended) for pre-established, ready-to-use solutions that take the place of developing the thought process required to solve complex problems. However, it is obvious that in uncertain and rapidly-changing environments, traditional solutions are fairly useless for solving new problems.

Indeed, good managers should have a holistic outlook. They are not "technicians" who solve mechanical problems. Rather, their daily task involves people, which demands an integral view developed through in-depth training. According to Marshall, "The professional man is distinguished by the further fact that he does not give only his skill. He gives himself. His whole personality enters into his work" (1939, p. 328).

Moreover, it is important to note that all decision-making processes involve two stages: an information stage, and a judgment/reflection stage. The increase of information via new technologies may improve the quality of the first stage, but, at the second stage, gathering more information does not add more value. Here, everything depends on the professional's own ability to apply his/her expertise to the particular case he/she must solve. Here we see the insufficiency of relying only on standardized solutions or "recipes". Professionals should be able to integrate all the inputs and decide by considering the nuances of each situation. In summary, they must have the know-how to deal with complexity, and this has a direct impact on how managers should be trained.

The second issue we want to highlight is that the current trend of virtual work may improve some processes, but at the same time it isolates individual agents.

On the one hand, information technology accelerates and facilitates work – for example, many tasks can be performed long-distance with respect to clients, team members or other professionals – which is a great advantage in a global era. But on the other hand, the increase of virtual work leads to the greater isolation of the professional, which has many negative effects, including a potential distortion of the communication process (Valley *et al.*, 1998; Valley *et al.*, 2002) as well as the learning process. Furthermore, having faster communication channels does not guarantee the actual quality of the communication itself.

This consequence directly affects an essential aspect of professions: the idea of professions as *communities of practice* (Hitt *et al.*, 2001; Løwendahl *et al.*, 2001; Baumard, 2002; Greenwood *et al.*, 2002; Khurana *et al.*, 2005; Nanda, 2005). A manager never works – or develops as a professional – alone. Today, concepts such as *mentoring, coaching* and *continuous education* are accepted as indispensable parts of the learning process for anyone who wants to become a good professional (Barr *et al.*, 1993). Non-standardized knowledge, the essence of the professional contribution, needs an "unstructured medium" through which to be transmitted and learned. For example, it requires face-to-face interaction because it involves a great deal of non-verbal communication. In this context, greater isolation in the managerial practice poses a challenge to the development of professionals.

Finally, managers must deal with excessive time constraints when fulfilling their tasks. As noted, new technology enables an increase of speed in many managerial activities. This effect, although positive in itself, has also led stakeholders to expect – and demand – managers to respond more quickly to their requirements. This often means more pressure and less time for professional interventions and talent development (Gardner, 2009).

But judgment and reflection require time both to learn and to act on. Too much pressure on managers may force them to make harsh decisions in which simply doing something is more important than doing it well; again, this goes directly against the concept of professionalism. It affects not only the outcome but also the way experience becomes expertise in a professional's development.

In summary, managers confront a great paradox underlying these problems. On the one hand, more complex knowledge and the incorporation of new technologies – with the possibility of crossing borders of space and time to increase speed and effectiveness – are contextual facts that require from the professional manager a new mastery, a stronger set of competences. On the other hand, these demands seem to be obstacles to this progress. If, as we believe, firms require well-rounded professionals – not only "good technicians", and solid leaders – not only followers, then managerial development should be revisited.

What firms are (really) looking for

Firms looking to fill their managerial ranks demand leaders who can deal with this challenging environment – well-rounded professionals who have the capacity to confront and effectively solve difficult and complex situations. However, this new race of in-demand managers has nothing to do with the popular concept of the *star professional*, someone who pursues his or her own brilliant path, sometimes at the expense of many others. Today's landscape requires the attracting and developing of the *solid citizen*: the professional who transcends his/her personal interests in favor of the firm's, searches out the best team and looks for solutions that go beyond personal capabilities – usually because he/she has ambitious goals that require collaboration and buy-in from others.

Solid citizens are not the opposite of high-potential individuals – those who are usually identified as the promise for the future of the firm. Innovative organizations wisely not only insert high-potential individuals at the frontier to lead the necessary change and innovation, but also develop them into these solid citizens, team builders who are able to move the whole organization toward achieving the firm's goals. As stated by Alejandro Beltrán, Partner and Managing Director in the Iberian Office of McKinsey, "These two terms, high-potential and good citizen, are not exclusive. I think that you need to be a good citizen if you want to be a high-potential guy." Ellen Miller, Executive in Residence at LBS, pointed out:

> High-potentials by definition have to be carriers of the culture and also good corporate citizens. Firms should not promote a 'star culture' because managers have to be able to work well within a team; they have to be collaborative … They have to develop a series of corporate competences. If people don't have concrete examples of how they've contributed to corporate citizenship, they won't be promoted or rewarded.

Before we provide an overview of the different competences firms are seeking, it is important to note that business leaders agree that they expect candidates to have a long-term vision of their professional careers. They consider hiring as an investment: "We're looking for someone we could invest in and who we think could accede to a leadership position at some point," said Julie Fuller, Avon, HR Executive Director and former Director of Leadership Development of PepsiCo. Many companies prefer to develop talent in-house rather than to buy it from outside. This strategy has advantages, both from the company culture side and from the economic perspective. But they are not the only reason: "It would be a kind of contradiction if Nestlé says that the most important strength and asset of the company is people, and then what we do is basically buy people from the outside," said Luis Cantarell, Executive VP and board member at Nestlé. Often they headhunt when they are look-ing for radical innovation, or developing new settings. This mindset means that while companies seek a series of competences when incorporating new managers, they also consider that some of the knowledge, attitudes and habits can be cultivated in-house if the managers have the right potential and suitable development plans are established. We shall unfold this idea in the third section of this chapter. First, however, there is another requirement, the competence that is a condition for all the others: *capacity of change*, or, in other words, the *capacity of effective learning*. When firms demand flexibility in order to implement different successive tasks in different positions, they assume that this competence is present – or, at least, that they can develop it. According to Ellen Miller (LBS), "Firms should be hiring not only for what they can do for the firm at the point of the hire, but also for what they could do longer-term, because the successful ones should be able to do four to six jobs over the years, instead of only one."

At the business level, there are several highly valued competences, most of them in the areas of *business vision, knowledge of functional areas*, and *people and resource management*. Primarily, companies look for a good background in terms of knowledge and experience; these are taken for granted if the candidate comes from an MBA program. In some cases (for example, for a finance position), more specific expertise is required. Any leader must have a holistic approach and maintain a broad overview of the firm's challenges and issues. But, at the same time, this focus must be combined with a very analytical business sense that enables problem-solving. Other related skills are the capability of setting an agenda and of allocating resources and functions.

As Hans Ulrich Maerki, former Chairman of IBM Europe, Middle East and Africa, puts it:

> At IBM we have an inclination to develop T-shaped people, not I-shaped people. I-shaped people are very good specialists, but they do not have a good idea of what is going on in the rest of the organization. T-shaped people also have a training and expertise in a discipline, but they have to understand the organization as a whole and what is happening in the world.

The same concern is shared by David Moon, Head of Talent Management at Merck: "We are trying to develop future leaders who have not only the specific knowledge, but also the general management perspective, people who can make priorities about products and markets, and understand the business in a holistic way, what we call 'end-to-end'".

Passion for quality is required, which in some market sectors must match a passion for the specific business. This is particularly valued in consumer services organizations. According to Julie Fuller, "I have actually spoken to people who've said, 'Oh, I don't really care about the industry; I am just looking for a great leadership experience.' Deal breaker! Don't you tell that to someone from a consumer products organization." Luis Cantarell pointed out, "If you work in our pet food business, you need to like pets; if you'd like to work in an infant nutrition business, you have to like babies; if you'd like to work in a culinary business, you need to love cooking … This is about satisfying consumer needs." The latter citation addresses another business competence: *client orientation*. Considering that the end goal of any company is to satisfy clients' expectations, and that the company cannot exist without those clients, the conclusion should be that client orientation must be present or developed in all the employees, but primarily in managers (Cardona and Wilkinson, 2009).

But great business leaders are also in search of interpersonal competences. As Alejandro Beltrán (McKinsey) stated, "After the interview, you ask yourself the question: would I stay twelve hours straight working with the candidate?" The so-called "soft skills" are very important here, especially empathy and tolerance: a manager must be capable of working with people of different nations, education level and cultural background, and also be capable of integrating into the firm's corporate culture. Therefore, *teamwork* is the first interpersonal competence. But these competences go beyond "getting along" with co-workers or the environment. They include the notion of inspiring them, committing them to the collective project and, moreover, developing others.

In a global context, Hans Ulrich Maerki also highlights the importance of helping the company's senior managers to adjust to this new, more integrated world:

> How do we create a global integrated company? How do we help senior managers change their habits? How do we get our people spread in different countries to think about the global challenge that the firm faces? How can they contribute from their own country with solutions for other countries? These are key challenges for leadership development over the next years for companies that want to become global players.

Other interpersonal competences such as *communication* and *conflict management* are also valued in an increasingly complex environment in which distance, both physical and cultural, and the great number of agents are important factors to take into account.

Interestingly enough, most of the competences demanded by great firms do not belong to the business or interpersonal levels but to the personal one.

The first is *intellectual capacity*. This may seem obvious when talking about managerial positions, especially when the candidate comes from an MBA program. As Angel Cano, CEO of BBVA, explained, "We don't expect to receive people who need to demonstrate they are … clever and so on because the volume and the amount of knowledge are well demonstrated." However, intelligence here is a wider concept, related to *emotional balance*, maturity and judgment. The candidate is expected to give a good reason for his/her previous and present choices regarding studies, work, decisions and so on. This requires a great degree of *self-awareness.*

Another set of personal competences is related to *ambition* or determination: future leaders must have drive, aspirations, the will to achieve, a commitment to do something important in the future and the capacity to carry it out. They must have long-term vision combined with a great deal of pragmatism. This competence is closely related to *resilience*, the combination of resistance, persistence and the capacity to recover after a failure. In addition, it is not only a matter of simply meeting certain goals but of doing it the right way. In the current market environment, having managers who consistently show *integrity* and honesty in their behavior is more necessary than ever. Reliability and trustworthiness are at the root of any human organization.

Finally, there is another group of personal competences in the sphere of innovation. Managers are expected to contribute *creative solutions* to the different challenges that appear. Marc Puig, CEO of The Puig Group, points out that "blending creativity and good management is key in any company; in particular, in luxury products. We have to create an organizational context where teams made up of scientists, creative people and business developers can work together and make good long-term decisions for the firm. We need innovation, but one that is sustainable." Requirements for this disposition are flexibility, open-mindedness and curiosity; that is, a constantly renewed appetite for learning. The *learning attitude* is a key to success. According to Angel Cano (BBVA), "Most of the MBAs who have finally failed, in the end it has been because, from the beginning, they were trying to demonstrate how very clever and bright and knowledgeable they were in their area, when in the first six or eight months the point is to understand very well the company you are working for."

In summary, according to Alejandro Beltrán "Everybody knows what we ask for – it's people leadership, thought leadership, client leadership, entrepreneurship and professionalism." Though this concept is rarely openly acknowledged, everything points toward a new class of managers, professionals that master a wider and deeper body of knowledge; help to develop their colleagues, many times leading by example (walk the talk); and have an attitude of service toward all stakeholders. These professionals are characterized by being opportunity-driven, innovative and creative in all circumstances – and they operate with ethical standards. In fact, they are the source of institutional values, which in turn condition the behavior of the organization's members.

What new generations are looking for, and can offer

In addition to these demands, we must take into account the trends among new generations to ascertain whether they meet the demands we have been reviewing – or if there are maladjustments between them.

According to business leaders from top global firms, recent generations have, on average, a shorter-term vision of their careers: "They do think about their career in stages. Even though you tell them that in six years they can become partners, they are pretty much concerned with what they want to do in the next two years," said Alejandro Beltrán. This career should be attractive, nonlinear, preferably international and include learning and development possibilities, which lead to further opportunities. "They may want to be here for two years and then go into the industry or a nonprofit for the third one, and come back to McKinsey a year later," Beltrán explained. This characteristic differs from how firms usually conceive of their managers' development: as we have seen, plans are designed in a way that requires a long-term commitment to help managers to fit the firm's culture and values in a better way. High turnover is a known source of paralysis, as there is no continuity in strategy implementation; it also results in high expenses and wasted resources, since new managers must be trained from scratch.

Business leaders have also detected in young managers a desire for a better lifestyle. For example, they expect to have more time for themselves; flexibility in terms of time, even to take temporary leave; and flexibility in terms of location, expecting the firm to take their preferences into account. Here is another source of potential conflict: while firms are becoming increasingly aware of the importance of a work/life balance, the truth is that conciliation is not easy in global companies, which challenge managers' availability in terms of traveling, different time zones and even differences in work schedules. In addition, new generations expect financial advantages, such as high salaries and investment possibilities, when traditionally these have been rewards for senior managers who have proved their commitment over time.

Their desire for flexibility extends to other areas, such as clients and the structure of the firm: flatter structures and efficient, fluid communication are preferred. The latter is related to the idea of transparency. A higher sensitivity toward environmental issues and social impact has also been detected. According to Luis Cantarell, "It's not like some time ago, when people were more impressed by the company itself and its products; they want to know the people behind it and the way they behave." They prefer individual relationships rather than impersonal interaction between manager and corporation. Overall, they expect the company to meet their expectations by offering individualized solutions.

Complementing these views, various reports featuring Generation Y, also known as the millennials – portray upcoming professionals as having reduced loyalty to and trust in institutions, with little willingness to fit into an established mold that includes traditional mores such as honor, hard work and so on. They report a strong need for recognition for their efforts and have a low tolerance for failure. They prefer "what works for me" over what benefits the company or the group. Members of Generation Y also appear to have a short attention span and little willingness to do repetitive tasks. This may explain their preference for short-term tasks, positions and even employers. On the other hand, they show a strong ability to perform multiple tasks, and a strong willingness to create and implement new initiatives and to craft tailored programs. These dispositions are accompanied by a broad curiosity. This creative side may be a strength when satisfying clients' demands, and in terms of searching for the best solution that fits both the manager and the firm during times of conflict.

There is no doubt that these traits may signify a considerable challenge for firms eager to hire the most suitable managers. These characteristics are contrary to some of the firm's desires, such as good integration with the firm's culture (as opposed to an aversion to "fitting the mold"); the idea of a long-term career in terms of development within the firm (as opposed to a short-term view of a career that is considered a door to further opportunities); the need to get along with many different people (as opposed to a conception of work centered on one's own interests and preferences); among others. On the other hand, these characteristics may make firms aware that candidates' aspirations and what they require for personal fulfillment have changed with respect to previous generations. According to Luis Cantarell, "It is not only important to look at people and society. You need to adapt your own organization to them, making sure that you have the flexibility to address the upcoming issues. You have to ascertain whether the structures and the way you work are adapted to what clients are expecting, because you are here to satisfy them through the quality of your people."

Business schools play a part in this process. They must craft their programs to provide the leaders society needs at any given time. Through their teachings, business schools can bridge the gap between corporations and candidates, helping their students to align their competences with the ones required by firms and society, and building on the ones they already possess.

Developing and transferring talent

Many global corporations are implementing different ways of coping with these new demands. Their survival depends on this ability to adapt. Most of them are tailoring their development programs according to the demands of the juniors, such as by allowing them to take a break from their job for an agreed length of time (McKinsey); by facilitating local mobility – BBVA has a Chief Mobility Officer; or by means of flexibilizing the firm's organization – Nestlé has started a program called "Nestlé on the Move". Some companies cater to those who want a career with a social profile by giving them the opportunity to work on social projects for a time. Companies are like living organisms, constantly changing and adapting to new conditions. But companies do not limit their objectives to survival; they intend to be ahead of the times, so they nourish creativity and innovation. In this section we shall describe some examples of this ongoing work.

Developing talent: how to train the needed professional

A professional is not deemed to be an expert until after he or she has undertaken considerable practice. This is particularly valid in the case of managers. According to Khurana and Nohria, "Many management scholars and practitioners believe that management is as much art or craft as science, better mastered through experience than through formal education ... Some people ... go so far as to argue that experience is the *only* valid teacher" (2008, p. 73). Hence leading firms realize that, while the investment may be temporary for the reasons stated above, it is in the firm's best interests to give professionals the tools to develop their talent.

Developing talent is not a matter of codes or theory, but a practical issue. However, *practical* does not mean *superficial*. At the end of the day, good leaders are capable of aligning individuals' actions with the meaning they are seeking in their organizational experience without forgetting the firm's purpose. Indeed, organizational survival depends on its members' willingness and ability to adjust collaboratively to changes that could endanger that survival. This wish and capability of collaborative response cannot be induced through bureaucratic structures or only by strong economic incentives. On the contrary, it depends on the extent to which individuals in the organization internalize the common goal and are able to perceive the connection between their actions and the ability of the organization to achieve this common purpose. Therefore, firms must have a clear vision that is appealing enough to encourage professionals to strive to identify with it.

In the second section above, we outlined the capabilities firms are looking for in new hires. It goes without saying that, while a given professional may not have all the desired characteristics, firms ask for and work at developing a balanced combination of them. Alejandro Beltrán explained that "You need to be at least distinctive in one dimension, and in the others you need to be above the bar."

Talent development is a must in companies that, like McKinsey, have an up-or-out promotion system. Alejandro Beltrán insisted that up-or-out should be viewed more as a developmental system than an eliminatory one. McKinsey has well-defined stages, quarterly evaluations and a very personalized follow-up that includes coaching from a group leader. Evaluations are intended to identify strengths and weaknesses, with the aim of helping each professional achieve the desired goal.

This behavior is not exclusive to this kind of company. For example, at PepsiCo, all managers go through tailor-made development programs, where 360-degree assessments are broadly used. Managers are also held accountable for their subordinates' development. Acknowledging the nature of the managerial job, the investment in development is distributed as 70 percent on-the-job training, 20 percent training by others (peer coach or mentor), and 10 percent formal training. This distribution aligns with their consideration of on-the-job training as, according to Julie Fuller, "the key component of development … We develop people through experiences". The exposure to "critical" experiences is crucial, but it is always accompanied by support. Special attention is paid to transition periods in the career, as well as to juniors, for whom they have designed the Talent Sustainability Program, which aims to retain talent and is based on the "5 Rs": Right People in the Right Jobs, in the Right Place, at the Right Time, doing the Right Work.

Nestlé sees development programs as tools for the diffusion of the firm's culture. Luis Cantarell explains that, "Companies that have existed for many years and have been successful normally tend to have a strong culture, and in order to develop their culture there are some values that they need to develop and then push in the organization." One distinct element is a strong dedication to face-to-face encounters with managers. Typically, a regional head spends 40 percent of his/her time in these meetings, which are held on a regular basis, at headquarters or during visits to different countries. Cantarell has pointed out, "At the end of the year, I could have seen around three to four thousand people."

Having a corporate training center is quite common in this kind of company. Nestlé's is in Switzerland, and its goal is to train employees in the firm's culture, with 7,000 trainees a year receiving personalized attention, on both a formal and an informal basis. The entire senior management team is involved in the process. McKinsey's University provides year-and-a-half-long programs that combine classes with real client work. BBVA is also starting a corporate university. In addition, they have just set up a new experience called "Learning Expeditions", with pilot projects in two very different geographic areas (Northern Europe and India). The initiative involves putting together, sharing and then diffusing the expertise of the firm's most talented people.

It is obvious that a primary goal is the development of business competences. By leveraging corporate universities and/or partnering with the best business schools in the world, firms make sure that professionals develop a solid understanding of businesses.

In light of the growing diversity of backgrounds and the increasing mobility of positions, it is no wonder that companies also eagerly cultivate leaders' interpersonal skills. Julie Fuller said "There are a lot of changes going on in the world right now: generational changes, multicultural focus and a global workforce." All these characteristics require leaders to be capable of dealing with different kinds of diversity. Teamwork requires and helps to develop a set of interpersonal competences, including *communicating effectively; implication* or *charisma; delegation;* and *respect*. The emphasis on corporate culture, team-building and community contributions should be managed properly: socialization must not hinder innovation (see Nahapiet and Ghoshal, 1998; Adler and Kwon, 2002). According to Luis Cantarell, "some companies' systems try to put you in boxes, and this is always a paradox, a kind of conflict: you are trying to put people in boxes, and then you promote the people who basically go outside the boxes".

Finally, we have the third nuclear level of personal competences. An important one that firms focus on is fostering creativity. Luis Cantarell (Nestlé) has said, "Innovation means accepting change and disruption." And according to Julie Fuller (Avon), "One of the things we can do with people who are already part of the company, a major focus, is ensuring that risk-taking is acceptable, and that failure is acceptable to some extent. So an innovative culture has to allow risks." Here again, the need for the *capacity for change and learning* becomes apparent.

However, it seems that this and the other personal competences required in a leader, such as *determination*, *integrity*, *tenacity*, *emotional balance* and *self-awareness*, are considered to be requirements for hiring, but not as competences that could be developed within the firm. We suggest that more attention should be paid to this issue. It is true that an existing foundation of personal competences is needed (as in the other levels), but one should expect that potential to also be here. And note that the idea of "potential" is ambivalent: it may suggest improving as much as deteriorating. This is why, once a candidate with the right personal qualities – the right character – has been hired, that person cannot rest on his or her laurels.

How can these competences be developed? Like all the other competences, habits of character are learned through practice. We suggest that, just as corporate and individual practices should be carefully designed to foster all the other competences, personal competences should be included in the design. The first step is to analyze whether there are inconsistencies across the three levels. Recent events in the financial and business worlds show the inconsistency that comes from practices aimed at developing people, for example, while the compensation system may reward self-interest.

What has been said up to now is valid both for firms and for business schools. The latter are also charged with developing leaders of character. Adding supplementary ethics subjects to the curriculum is not enough, just as increasing control and monetary rewards is not enough to guarantee committed managers. The following words from Snook and Khurana (2004, p. 227) are enlightening:

There is a hidden curriculum built into the educational process itself. It is conveyed to students in the form of norms, values, and dispositions that are created simply by living in and responding to institutional expectations and the routines of school … Such an acknowledgement requires educators to explicitly consider the ideological and epistemological commitments they are conveying to students by supporting certain models and pedagogical traditions.

The model of competences we have been using here shows the importance of having an integrated view of a manager, in which all three levels are inter-related. Personal competences are not only in need of further attention but also at the core of the process. As mentioned earlier, these are the competences that allow for the development of rounded professionals, competent managers who are capable of acting for the common good.

Transferring talent

Well-rounded professionals carry their expertise with them, applying it to any situation they face wherever they are. This characteristic is vital in professions with high mobility, which is the case with managers. Large firms face the chal-lenge of transferring talent across boundaries. Knowledge is created in differ-ent parts of the firm, and hence managers need to share it across a number of business units and countries, partly because of the especially demanding nature of global leadership. While processes contribute to this aim, it is *people* who have the knowledge that is applied and transferred in the activities devel-oped by the company (Itami and Roehl, 1987). More explicitly, it is in people that we find the tacit knowledge that characterizes the work of a professional, compared to the mere application of explicit knowledge by a technician. Tacit knowledge is deeply rooted in an individual's experience – though we could also refer to collective knowledge when referring to an organization's culture – and is revealed only through its application; it requires the judgment of a professional for its correct application (Nanda, 2004).

Indeed, it is understood that, for example, international assignments have great potential as knowledge-transfer mechanisms (Brewster, 1991; Bartlett and Ghoshal, 2002). In addition to providing an opportunity to derive additional rents from existing knowledge, internationalization offers learning opportunities by exposing the company to new cultures, ideas, experiences and so on, which can be used to create new expertise that complements and leverages current knowledge. This newly developed knowledge will ensure the future of the organization itself.

However, according to a McKinsey study (Guthridge and Komm, 2008), the movement of employees between countries is still surprisingly limited, and many people who are hesitant to relocate fear that doing so will damage their career prospects. In fact, these expatriates – a scarce and very expensive resource – often fail, and many leave their employers even after they have succeeded overseas (Collings *et al.*, 2007; Lazarova and Cerdin, 2007). In addition, according to recent studies by Groysberg *et al.* (2008), managerial capabilities are less portable than is currently assumed. Finding the right fit between context and capabilities is the path to managerial effectiveness, and when transferring professionals – inside the firm, or even more when hiring talent from outside – that alignment may easily disappear.

The previously proposed classification of personal capabilities may help senior managers to think about transferring talent. In general, narrower knowledge, skills and personal assets will be less efficient to transfer to different contexts; they will require a higher level of adaptation. For example, industry-related business competences – technical and regulatory knowledge, and client and supplier relationships that are unique to the industry – may prove not to be useful in an industry that operates under different rules. Similarly, narrow, functional-based competences may limit transferability across the firm. By contrast, general management capabilities constitute the base for firm flexibility and organizational learning in terms of transferring people wherever they are needed in the firm. We should note that it is easier to develop the former than the latter. Moreover, given the trends previously outlined in this chapter, the temptation to train and develop only within a narrow range of knowledge and skills is huge, which reduces transferability and prevents firms from benefiting from cross-firm learning and sustaining competitive advantage.

Similarly, different development levels of interpersonal skills and personal competences affect the transferability of professionals. We claim that the more successfully both sets of competences are developed, the higher the benefits for the individual and the firm from transferring talent. This is because it speaks to the professionals' capability to learn, change and adapt better and faster, which reduces the cost of adaptation and maximizes the benefits of cross-learning.

This brings us to the point that successful talent transfer that advances a firm's competitive advantage also requires personal competences that enable the manager to make the right decisions in matters that are beyond his or her knowledge. As stated earlier, good professionals need more than economic, technical or intellectual resources – though they must have these too, or at least be able to summon them when required. Even the resources inherent in their own temperament are not enough. Above all, they need to cultivate the habits of character that guide action, allow them to go beyond duty, and form the basis of all they do, regardless of changes in the environment or the emergence of unexplored territories.

Implications for leadership development: a joint task

Today's business landscape and society at large call for better managers. At the beginning of this chapter we proposed to consider managers as professionals, as a better paradigm to respond to this challenge. This consideration makes more salient three important aspects that broaden the horizon for hiring, developing, retaining and transferring talented managers: the professional's business knowledge; the responsibility of each manager to contribute to his/her community; and a set of ethical standards, putting stronger emphasis on the intrinsic commitment to the public good.

This richer consideration of what a well-rounded manager is necessitates developing a broader set of competences that encompass the different aspects of a manager's behavior – business knowledge as well as interpersonal and personal competences. Indeed, we have suggested that professionals that must master business knowledge, have the skills and values to contribute to their managerial community, and care about the public good, should incorporate into their development career a carefully designed plan to foster all the competences, with special attention being paid to personal competences – the foundation of all the others. Certainly, without self-leadership it is difficult to live up to the outlined standards of a good professional, something called for by both firms and society in general.

To strengthen the collaboration that business schools and companies must build up in designing their respective development plans, and taking into account the difficult landscape confronting them, we recommend below some actions that will ensure that the three levels of competences are addressed.

First, firms and business schools must think about the knowledge aspect of management development (Hitt *et al.*, 2001; Løwendahl *et al.*, 2001; Baumard, 2002; Nanda, 2004). *Explicit theoretical* knowledge – the "*know-what*" – is learned by managers mainly in the academic field, typically through the MBA or other programs offered by business schools. And there is another kind of explicit knowledge that belongs to the *practical* area – the "*know-how*", which consists of a range of standardized techniques that result from different practitioners' experiences. It is learned in both academia and companies. Finally, there is a great deal of *tacit* knowledge – individual or collective – that can be transmitted or acquired only on the job, through interpersonal relationships and personal decisions. Thus, the development of the required technical competences typical of a manager goes hand-in-hand with the development of interpersonal qualities, not only because interpersonal relations are crucial for the transmission of tacit knowledge, but also, just as important, because a manager must be a leader of others. Another consequence is that firms should collaborate closely with academic institutions in establishing a range of development programs. External views and cross-industry learning are sources of enrichment for the firm. Business schools must ensure that the explicit knowledge they provide – either theoretical or practical – and the implicit values they transmit complement the companies' activities and culture. In-company programs and in-house training are also relevant, given that the company is the natural place in which managerial behavior occurs.

Second, it is important to reflect on the associational aspect of the profession. As noted earlier, a manager's identity is in the making, and there is no professional association for managers as there is for lawyers or medical doctors. But the increasing number of managers who enter the practice by obtaining a university degree in management is a sign that there are some standards that belong to managerial practice as a profession. On the other hand, managers in top companies constitute real communities of practice, through which the culture of the firm is learned, transmitted or even transformed (Løwendahl *et al.*, 2001; Baumard, 2002; Khurana *et al.*, 2005). Once again, business schools and corporations play a significant role in promoting and building commitment inside the firm and across companies, avoiding the inconsistencies that many times come from teaching and implementing practices aimed at developing certain competences, while at the same time having other practices, or elements in the structure, that encourage the opposite behavior.

Finally, professionals are characterized by their pursuit of high ethical standards, mainly understood as contributing to the common good through their practice. It is true that in some professions there are explicit codes of ethics – companies also display them – that professionals are obliged to adhere to, and that even in some cases are reinforced by law. But it is also true that no code of ethics or regulation has any effect if it is purely external (Khurana *et al.*, 2002; Khurana *et al.*, 2005). Every professional – each manager – develops his or her own ethical principles through the different professional and personal choices he/she makes. Business schools and companies are also, to a certain extent, shapers of this aspect of managers' competences, including personal competences, through the curricula and practices they develop respectively (Snook and Khurana, 2004). In short, the training and teaching provided by both academia and corporations must be integral and not limited to technical skills or intellectual content. The model of competences we have proposed acknowledges this integral consideration by linking the knowledge, skills and ethical aspects of professional practice.

Current global social and economic reality poses new challenges to firms. In addition, clients' expectations regarding quality and professional ethics keep raising the bar. Companies coping with complex contexts and more demanding stakeholders are implementing changes in their structure and practices that demand more well-rounded managers. Business schools are adapting to provide the type of leaders both society and companies need. New breeds of managers have their own ideas about finding personal fulfillment through their work. How can it be possible to accommodate all these different – and, as we have seen, sometimes contradictory – trends? Our proposal is that the consideration of managers as professionals, and of companies and business schools as places where professional competences can be developed, may foster a higher quality of business leadership development.

NOTES

* Senior executives quoted in this chapter were speakers at the 2008 IESE Conference on the future of leadership development. We were privileged to count on the experience and ideas of the following speakers: Angel Cano (BBVA, CEO), Luis Cantarell (Nestlé, Executive Vice-President and board member), Julie Fuller (Avon, HR Executive Director, and former PepsiCo Director of Leadership Development), Alejandro Beltrán (McKinsey, Partner and Managing Director of the Iberian office), Hans Ulrich Maerki (ABB, board member, and former Chairman and CEO of IBM Europe, Middle East and Africa), Ellen Miller (London Business School, Executive in Residence, and former Managing Director and Head of Leadership Development of Lehman Brothers, Europe), David Moon (Merck, Executive Director of Leadership Development), and Marc Puig (The Puig Group, CEO).

1 Profession. *Online Etymology Dictionary.* Retrieved 8 February 2007 from Dictionary.com. Available at: http://dictionary.reference.com/browse/profession.

REFERENCES

Adler, P. S. and Kwon S.-W. 2002. "Social Capital: Prospects for a New Concept". *The Academy of Management Review* 27:17–40.

Barr, L. L., Shaffer, K., Valley, K. L. and Hillman, B. J. 1993. "Mentoring. Applications for the Practice of Radiology". *Investigative Radiology* 28:71–5.

Bartlett, C. A. and Ghoshal, S. 2002. *Managing Across Borders. The Transnational Solution.* Boston, MA: Harvard Business School Press.

Baumard, P. 2002. "Tacit Knowledge in Professional Firms: The Teachings of Firms in Very Puzzling Situations". *Journal of Knowledge Management* 6:135–51.

Brewster, C. 1991. *The Management of Expatriates.* London: Kogan Page.

Cardona, P. and García-Lombardía, P. 2005. *How to Develop Leadership Competences.* Pamplona: EUNSA.

Cardona, P. and Wilkinson, H. 2009. *Creciendo como Líder.* Pamplona: EUNSA/IESE Business School.

Chang, L. and Birkett, B. 2004. "Managing Intellectual Capital in a Professional Service Firm: Exploring the Creativity–Productivity Paradox". *Management Accounting Research* 15:7–31.

Coff, R. W., Coff, D. C. and Eastvold, R. 2006 "The Knowledge-Leveraging Paradox: How to Achieve Scale without Making Knowledge Imitable". *Academy of Management Review* 31:452–65.

Collings, D. G., Scullion, H. and Morley, M. J. 2007. "Changing Patterns of Global Staffing in the Multinational Enterprise: Challenges to the Conventional Expatriate Assignment and Emerging Alternatives". *Journal of World Business* 42:198–213.

Empson, L. 2001. "Introduction: Knowledge Management in Professional Service Firms". *Human Relations* 54:811–17.

Empson, L. 2007. "Profession". In S. Clegg and J. Bailey, eds. *International Encyclopedia of Organization Studies.* Oxford: Sage.

Gardner, H. 2009."Feeling the Heat: The Effects of Performance Pressure on Teams' Knowledge Use and Performance". HBS Working paper 09-126:1–41.

Gintis, H. and Khurana, R. 2008. "Corporate Honesty and Business Education: A Behavioral Model". In P. J. Zak, ed. *Moral Markets: The Critical Role of Values in the Economy.* Princeton, NJ: Princeton University Press: 300–28.

Greenwood, R., Suddaby, R. and Hinings, C. R. B. 2002. "Theorizing Change: The Role of Professional Associations in the Transformation of Institutionalized Fields". *Academy of Management Journal* 45:58–80.

Groysberg, B., Lee, L.-E. and Nanda, A. 2008. "Can They Take It With Them? The Portability of Star Knowledge Workers' Performance". *Management Science* 54:1213–30.

Guthridge, M. and Komm, A. B. 2008. "Why Multinationals Struggle to Manage Talent". *The McKinsey Quarterly* May: 1–5.

Hitt, M. A., Bierman, L., Shimizu, K. and Kochhar, R. 2001. "Direct and Moderating Effects of Human Capital on Strategy and Performance in Professional Service Firms: A Resource-Based Perspective". *Academy of Management Journal* 44:13–28.

Itami, H. and Roehl, T. W. 1987. *Mobilizing Invisible Assets*. Cambridge, MA: Harvard University Press.

Khurana, R. 2007. *From Higher Aims to Hired Hands*. Princeton, NJ: Princeton University Press.

Khurana, R., Khanna, T. and Penrice, D. 2002. "Harvard Business School and the Making of a New Profession". HBS case 406-025: 1–22.

Khurana, R. and Nohria, N. 2008. "It's Time to Make Management a True Profession". *Harvard Business Review* 86():70–7.

Khurana, R., Nohria, N. and Penrice, D. 2005. "Management as a Profession". In J. W. Lorsch, L. Berlowitz and A. Zelleke, eds. *Restoring Trust in American Business*. Cambridge, MA: American Academy of Arts and Sciences: 43–60.

Khurana, R. and Snook, S. 2006. "Comments on Glenn Hubbard's 'Business, Knowledge, and Global Growth'". *Capitalism and Society* 1(3): 1–8.

Lazarova, M. and Cerdin, J. L. 2007. "Revisiting Repatriation Concerns: Organizational Support versus Career and Contextual Influences", *Journal of International Business Studies*, 38: 404–29.

Løwendahl, B. R., Revang, Ø. and Fosstenløkken, S. M. 2001. "Knowledge and Value Creation in Professional Service Firms: A framework for Analysis", *Human Relations*, 54: 911–31.

Maister, D. H. 1997. "Real Professionalism". In D. H. Maister, *True Professionalism*. New York: The Free Press: 15–22.

Marshall, T. H. 1939. "The Recent History of Professionalism in Relation to Social Structure and Social Policy". *The Canadian Journal of Economics and Political Science/Revue Canadienne d'Economique et de Science Politique* 5: 325–49.

Mason, J. H. 1992. "Innovation in Professional Services. Potential Productivity and Trade Improvement". *Technological Forecasting and Social Change* 42: 31–45.

Meadows, P. 1946. "Professional Behavior and Industrial Society". *The Journal of Business of the University of Chicago* 19:145–50.

Nahapiet, J. and Ghoshal, S. 1998. "Social Capital, Intellectual Capital, and the Organizational Advantage". *The Academy of Management Review* 23:242–66.

Nanda, A. 2002a. "The Essence of Professionalism: Managing Conflict of Interest". HBS Working paper 03-066:1–35.

Nanda, A. 2002b. "Who Is a Professional?". HBS Working paper 03-063:1–32.

Nanda, A. 2004. "Who Is a Professional?". HBS Technical note 9-904-047:1–9.

Nanda, A. 2005. "Managing Client Conflicts". HBS Technical note 9-904-059:1–13.

Parsons, T. 1939. "The Professions and Social Structure". *Social Forces* 17:457–67.

Snook, S. and Khurana, R. 2004. "Developing Leaders of Character: Lessons from West Point". In R. Gandossy and J. Sonnenfeld, eds. *Leadership and Governance from the Inside Out*. New York: Wiley: 213–33.

Valley, K. L., Moag, J. and Bazerman, M. H. 1998. "A Matter of Trust: Effects of Communication on the Efficiency and Distribution of Outcomes". *Journal of Economic Behavior & Organization* 34:211–38.

Valley, K. L., Thompson, L., Gibbons, R. and Bazerman, M. H. 2002. "How Communication Improves Efficiency in Bargaining Games". *Games and Economic Behavior* 38:127–55.

Index

Key: **bold** = extended discussion or term highlighted in the text; f = figure; n = note; t = table.

Ceci, S. J.   232, 235
Center for Creative Leadership   29(n7), 222
CEO Magazine   95(n39)
CEOs (chief executive officers)   ix, x, 3, 8, 32, 49, 89, 172(n4)
  character attributes   252
  educational quality   224–5, 236
  leadership development by creating trust   **252–5**
  leadership development by example   **250–2**, 261
  leadership by example   254
  perspectives (what companies expect from leadership development)   **xi–xii, 239–91**
  promotion of diversity   **255–9**
  responsibility for leadership development   **247–50**, 261
  role   18
  should facilitate work and family integration   **259–60**
  task to develop transcendental leadership   **261–2**
  tasks and responsibilities   249–50, 263
  tenure "getting shorter"   18–19
Chan Chao Peh   95(n35)
change   45, **46–53**, 55, 56, **61**, 241, 244, 252
character   228, 283, 286, 291
charisma   261, **282**
cheating   226, 229, 235, 236
Cheung, S. N. S.   134(n5), 137
Chief Talent Officers   218
children   150, 259
China   47, 50, 115, 160, 186, 197, 197f, 198, 258
China Europe International Business School (CEIBS)   xi, 109, 111

Chinchilla, N.   vii, xii, 241, 244, 245, 263
Choong, P.   226, 235
Christenson, A.   xii, 252, 262n
churches   137(n31), 160
civic leadership   **80–3**, 95(n35–7)
civil society   17
Clark, K.   218
client orientation   **276**
clients   254, 255, 262, 272, 279
climate of trust   **130**
coaching   35–**6**, 38, 42, 61, 223, 249, **272**, 281
  benefits   36
  in-house   36
  trickle-down effect   35
  see also "corporations/internal universities"
Coase, R. H.   119, 120, 132, 133(n2), 137
Coca-Cola   39
codes of conduct   40, **74–5**, 93(n18–20), 268, 287–8
  see also ethics
collaboration   62
  team leadership through ~   **77–9**, 94(n25–32)
  virtuous cycle   **54**
  see also teamwork
collaborative leadership   258
  dark side   56, 61
  incompatible objectives and value systems   57
  nature/characteristics   **45–6**
  new collaborative leader   **53–6**
  new perspectives in leadership development   x–xi, **44–63**
  preparation of young people   56
  teaching young people   **59–62**
  see also Future of Leadership Development

United Kingdom   50, 235
United States   x, xi, 4, 5–6, 7, 10, 12,
    27, 28, 46, 47, 50, 66, 76–7, 82, 90,
    97–100, 104–5, 108, 110, 114, 150,
    177, 179–89, 194, 202, 210, 211(n6)
  business school "density"   197f
  business–society gap (re
    globalization)   198–9, 200f
  degree dilution   84, 95(n41)
  demography   196–7
  demography: student applications for
    MBA courses   **85–6**
  editorial dominance of journals (home
    bias)   **191**
  leadership development   218
  social change   98
  student and faculty diversity   **182–4**
  surveys of business schools
    (1959)   67–8
universities   vii–viii, ix, 26, 65, 77, 89,
    100, 111, 119, 218, 227, 234, 287
  fund-raisers   247
  parents to business schools   9
  see also business schools
University of Cambridge: Judge Business
    School   44, 60, 61, 62, 63
University of Chicago
  Graduate School of Business   5, 100
  LEAD program   222
university hospital, "best model
    for business school" (Drucker)
    112
University of Navarra, see IESE Business
    School
University of Pennsylvania: Wharton
    School (1881–)   4, 98
University of Southern
    California   92(n10)
US News and World Report   228

utility functions   127, 150, 155
utility maximization   13, 146

Valero, A.   115
value chain
  fragmentation   **47–8**
  power equilibrium   48
value-added   58, 167, **209t**, 272
  by business schools   **113–15**
  leadership development courses   220,
    234(n1)
value-creation   49, 54, 96(n47)
  cross-country differences "powerful
    sources"   204
value-maximization   152, 153, 154, 157,
    160–1, 166, 174
  see also profit-maximization
values   15, 16, 22, 24, 57, **80–3**, 102, 103,
    105, 107–8, **115**, 216t, 219, 221, 226,
    229, 233, 234, **250–1**, 252, 261, 269,
    282, 283–4, 286, 287
  professional   **74–5**, 93(n18–20)
  reflection on consequences of
    actions   250–1
  see also codes of conduct
varieties of capitalism literature   209t
Vasella, D.   110
Vázquez-Dodero, J. C.   28n
Velilla, M.   172
venture capital   114, 221
Vernon, R.   191, 205, 206, 214
vertical integration   47–8
Vietnam 197f
Vietor, R.   28n
virtual environment   39
  see also business environment/context
virtual learning   **37–8**, 42
  applications (INSEAD)   **38–40**,
    43(n6)